DENNIS 'HURRICANE' DAVID

Dennis 'Hurricane' David

Dennis David

(Group Captain W. D. David CBE, DFC and Bar, AFC)

GRUB STREET · LONDON

Published by Grub Street,
The Basement,
10 Chivalry Road,
London SW11 1HT

Edited by Amy Myers

British Library Cataloguing in Publication Data
David, Dennis
Dennis 'Hurricane' David: my autobiography
1. David, Dennis 2. Great Britain. Royal Air Force – History
3. Air pilots, Military – Great Britain – Biography
I. Title
358.4'0092

ISBN 1 902304 46 2

Typeset by Pearl Graphics, Hemel Hempstead

Printed and bound in Great Britain by
Biddles Ltd, Guildford and King's Lynn

For M
with all my love, D

Contents

Preface		vi
Some of the Personalities in the book		vii
Prologue	Out of Ammo	1
Chapter One	Welsh Roots	3
Chapter Two	Per Ardua ad Astra	11
Chapter Three	The Battle of France	18
Chapter Four	The Battle of Britain	30
Chapter Five	The Battle is Won	44
Chapter Six	The Western Desert	55
Chapter Seven	'Where Elephants Meet'	59
Chapter Eight	The Capture of Akyab	63
Chapter Nine	'Japs Gone'	68
Chapter Ten	The Savage 'Black Buffaloes'	75
Chapter Eleven	Peaceful Berkshire	82
Chapter Twelve	Back to the Desert	87
Chapter Thirteen	Helping 'The Father of the RAF'	97
Chapter Fourteen	'Capitalist Vodka'	107
Chapter Fifteen	Trouble Brewing	125
Chapter Sixteen	'Send us Bandages'	140
Chapter Seventeen	Farewell to Hungary	158
Chapter Eighteen	Tangmere & NATO	167
Chapter Nineteen	A Sort of Retirement	179
Chapter Twenty	Gathering of the 'Eagles'	191
Chapter Twenty-One	Golden Anniversaries	199
List of Aircraft Flown		204
Service Career Details		205
Bibliography		208
Index		211

Author's Preface

For many years friends have asked me to write my memoirs, so here they are, with my thanks to all who encouraged me and to those who allowed me to use stories concerning them. My particular thanks to John Golley, Bill Gunston and Michael Pierce, without whose expertise and help this book would never have seen the light of day. I am also indebted to Ian Hamilton for his excellent computer work.

Another factor that decided me was that although many authors have contacted me and taken a lot of trouble to get their stories accurate, which I much appreciate, I have also been credited with remarks I never made, and events described very differently from what I recall, by authors who have never bothered to check with me. This book is about occasions when I was there, and people I have met. Some were passing acquaintances, others have become valued friends.

I have had the greatest difficulty in bringing back to mind my wartime experiences, as I can truly say that I have spent nearly sixty years trying to forget them. Anyone who has seen any similar horrors in past conflicts up to the present time of Rwanda, Bosnia and East Timor will understand. I survived by a lot of luck and some experience, but I never gloried in pressing the firing button and the times prevented one from grieving for those of one's friends who died.

My championship of the Hurricane fighter aircraft, and my unceasing efforts to get it the recognition and praise for its formidable achievements during the war are well known. I have always felt its glamorous counterpart the Spitfire caught the public attention to the detriment of the Hurricane. The Hawker fighter has never been given due credit for its much greater number of victories in both the Battle of France and the Battle of Britain. Thus, over the years, I have acquired the nickname of Dennis 'Hurricane' David, hence the title of this book.

My editor asked where the ladies and the romance were in this book. I told him that I have loved them all, God bless them, but there were too many to include, especially as we had to cut the manuscript already! In any case after a long life, I am old-fashioned in believing that one's private life is just that. This is a memoir of my working days.

A few years ago I met a little White Russian princess at a luncheon party, who had survived the Bolshevik Revolution after World War I because she was a talented ballerina. I feel life could not be summed up more succinctly than by a casual remark she made: 'You live, you die, so what?'

Some of the Personalities in the Book

King Abdullah of Jordan
Chancellor Konrad Adenauer
Yuri Andropov
Herman Arens
Douglas Bader
The Earl of Bandon
General F. A. M. 'Boy' Browning
General Sir Philip Christison
Noël Coward
Christine De Lisle
Lord Dowding
Hughie Edwards VC
King Farouk of Egypt
Sir Leslie and Lady Penelope Fry
General Adolf Galland
President Charles de Gaulle
Sir John Gielgud
HM King George VI
D. W. Griffith
The Gurkha Regiments
Arpad Habsburg,
Hungarian ruler in exile
A.P. Herbert
Trevor Howard
Hungarian Presidents Rakosi,
Gero, Nagy and Kadar
Lord Elwyn Jones
MacKinlay and Irene Kantor
President John F. Kennedy and
Vice-President Lyndon B. Johnson
President Nikita S Khrushchev
Cecil Lewis
Oliver Locker-Lampson
Lady MacRobert
Colonel David McFarland USAF
A. G. 'Sailor' Malan
Alistair McLean
Yehudi Menuhin
Mindszenty, Cardinal
Earl and Countess Mountbatten
of Burma
The Duke of Norfolk,
Earl Marshal of England
Lord Olivier
Air Chief Marshal
Sir Keith Park
Fred Perry
Christopher Plummer
HM Queen Elizabeth II
and Prince Philip
HM Queen Elizabeth the
Queen Mother
The Duke and Duchess
of Richmond
Roger Plumpton Wilson,
Lord Bishop of Chichester
Sheila Scott
Ian Smith
General Johannes 'Macky'
Steinhoff
Admiral and
Mrs. James Stockdale
Dora and Lester Strother
Colonel Paul W. Tibbetts
Lord and Lady Trenchard
Leo Thorsness
Elsie and Doris Waters
General Charles E.
'Chuck' Yeager

and many others

PROLOGUE

OUT OF AMMO

For 10 May 1940 I have an entry in my first flying log book in capitals: WAR REALLY STARTS. It is written in ink different from the actual events of the day, so it was obviously inserted at a later date, and with the benefit of hindsight. The pace of our activities in France was quickening by the hour, and that day was certainly a full one. I brought down a Heinkel 111 behind the Siegfried Line. In another engagement I brought down a Dornier 17 on the Maginot Line, and pursued another. I fired several bursts, but he made off into Germany and as I had run out of ammunition, I could not confirm him. An hour later, on the third sortie of the day, we attacked a formation of four Heinkels and managed to get two of them.

In those early days the Luftwaffe bomber crews were so supremely confident after their successes in the Spanish War and in Poland that they flew unescorted by fighters on most of their raids. We were not to be able to attack them in this way for very much longer.

The hectic day continued. We pushed our planes after each encounter to get back to base as soon as possible, in order to get them refuelled, rearmed and any repairs carried out speedily, so that they would be ready for the next call. In all I flew six sorties, and spent nearly seven hours in the air.

The following morning, in response to an Army call, our sadly diminished squadron flew to defend one of their tented hospitals. Six of us on this occasion found ourselves in a scrap with 40 Junkers 87 Stukas. I settled into what had become my instant and instinctive chase and attack routine. I lowered my seat, to make myself as small a target as possible, switched the gun button to 'fire', and switched the reflector sight on. This sight showed the position of the target, which increased in size as I came closer. Lastly, I increased my engine revs to ensure even greater manoeuvrability. We shot down 14, and turned the raid away. I brought down a Ju 87 and damaged another. Whilst following him I saw a bigger target, a Dornier 17; after a close encounter, this aircraft caught fire and crashed. I could not hang about to confirm any more, being mindful of my fuel gauge and also that I had expended all my ammunition. Initially I had felt rather satisfied that we had achieved a small but worthwhile victory, but soon after I turned for home I saw a fresh wave of 150 enemy bombers starting out on another raid, and my frustration at our lack of numbers to combat them was intense.

A short while later I noticed a curious fact, which any fighter pilot would confirm. In the midst of a dog-fight, at one moment the whole sky seems alive with aircraft; then suddenly there is nothing but emptiness everywhere, and one is left wondering how they could possibly have disappeared so completely.

After a while I noticed a lone Hurricane flying below me in the same direction as I was. It had obviously been in another scrap, as I could see the strips of fabric over his gun muzzles had been fired away, showing he had been using his guns. To my horror, I saw out of the corner of my eye a Messerschmitt Bf 109 lining up behind him, preparing to shoot him down. The Hurricane pilot was obviously blissfully unaware of his imminent danger, and I tried to use my R/T to warn him, but to no avail. It all happened so quickly that it was really a reflex action on my part: I turned my Hurricane and dived at speed toward the enemy fighter to divert his attention and come between him and his target.

Even as I closed on him, I remember telling myself what a stupid fool I was taking my Hurricane into such a situation with no ammo left. Fortunately my sudden appearance was a nasty shock to the German, who turned away and beat a hasty retreat, little knowing he was flying away from two quite defenceless Hurricanes. By then the Hurricane pilot had realised his danger. It was Squadron Leader 'Doggie' Oliver, the CO of 85 Squadron, our sister unit based at Seclin, just south of Lille. I formated with him for a while, and then had to turn off to return to my base, Lille Marcq just to the north. That night was certainly one of my happier memories of those stressful days, for 'Doggie' and I met in Lille for a celebratory drink. He confirmed what I suspected, that he, too, was out of ammunition, and he thanked me for saving his life.

CHAPTER ONE

WELSH ROOTS

In 1966, after nearly 30 years, I reached the end of my time in the RAF. At such a time one looks back and wonders 'what was it all for?' I had made so many good friends in my early days, only to lose them so quickly as the Battle of France and the Battle of Britain in particular took their heavy toll. Through it all, the RAF had been the mainspring of my life. It had given me an education I would never have been able to afford, and I had travelled the world, meeting people and seeing places that would not have been possible under any other circumstances. Suddenly the support and reassuring metaphorical umbrella that shield Service personnel from the realities of the world outside had gone, and it is amazing how vulnerable one can feel.

Because of a family rift in my childhood, I had not been back to my father's family home in Tongwynlais near Cardiff since I was about seven. For all my globe-trotting, however, Wales has somehow always exerted a pull, and I have the happiest early memories of times spent with my beloved 'Gran'. So after retirement I felt I would like to return to my Welsh roots, and possibly even pick up a few family threads. With what was undoubtedly going to be a very different new life lying ahead of me, this seemed a very good time to do it.

I feared the new motorway out of Cardiff might have swallowed up the little village, but to my delight I came upon a sign pointing to Tongwynlais as the motorway swept on. I drove down into the village, and there was the church, and the little houses, seemingly untouched by time. Surely that was the tiny shoe shop my grandfather owned? Now it seemed to be selling haberdashery, and other odds and ends useful to village life.

I parked the car and entered the shop. A tiny lady, with her grey hair drawn discreetly back into a bun, came forward and asked if she could help me. I enquired if anyone by the name of David had lived there. She pulled herself up to her full height, which meant that she could just about look at me comfortably over the top of the high and very solid mahogany counter, and said, 'I am Mrs Robert David' in a lilting sing-song Welsh voice.

'Auntie Beat!', I exclaimed, 'I'm Dennis'.

A look of total disbelief spread over her face, and then her eyes filled with tears, as she said 'Oh, Dennis! How you've grown!' It had been well over 40 years since I had seen her, when I was about seven years old.

The memories came flooding back, but I missed the smell of leather which had always permeated that little shop in my grandfather's day. I used to spend hours there watching him make shoes and miners' boots. Tongwynlais had been a mining village, and my lifelong respect and regard for coalminers were born of those days. It was a typical village community of that era. When a new baby was born, my grandfather would say, 'Ah! Another pair of boots for the future'.

On bitter winter days, with snow on the ground, I used to see children running around with just little singlets and no trousers, for many families could not afford them. The fathers could not pay for their boots outright, but would pay so many pence from their pay packet each week. On summer evenings, all the windows in the little street would be open, a Welsh voice would start to sing, and gradually the harmonies would be taken up by every household in the street. Welsh singing still brings a lump to my throat.

My grandmother, as I've only discovered in recent years, was not in fact Welsh at all, but born in Somerset. She was 'Gran' to the whole village, however. Everyone loved her, and she was a matriarchal figure. It speaks volumes for her that she was not only completely accepted as 'village-bred' but was also so well respected. She was never idle. With four big sons and two daughters to bring up, she could not spare a moment. She was only about 5ft 2in (157 cm) herself, and used to say that when she could no longer do any work she would die. This is just what happened, for when she was too frail to see to her chores, she simply died.

She loved her family and her tiny home dearly. Every nook and cranny gleamed, the brass polished, the kitchen flagstones and the doorstep scrubbed. I have inherited the Welsh longcase clock, dating from 1736, which used to stand in the kitchen. It is just over 6ft tall (183 cm), and I remember as a small boy standing by my grandfather, fascinated as I watched him wind it every day by simply pulling up the chain which had a 9 lb (4.1 kg) weight on it. Some years back I took it to an expert for an overhaul, and remarked on the rust on the chain. He touched it almost reverently, and told me it must never be cleaned, because it proved it was genuine.

'I'm sure your old kitchen had a flagstone floor, did it not?', he asked. He then explained that, as these old kitchen clocks have no enclosed base, the chain would inevitably have got splashed when the floor was washed. Hence the rust!

Being linked to the very house in this way made the clock seem even more personal, for I have so many happy memories of that kitchen and the smell of fresh baking. Gran's Welsh cakes were sheer perfection.

There was a great stir in the village when the Davids had the first flushing lavatory installed. It was in a special outhouse in the little back garden, and I remember the villagers calling round and, with due deference, asking if they might go out and see it, and perhaps be allowed to flush it. Some literally took a step back in amazement at this phenomenon, and it was generally agreed 'Ah yes, this is the future.'

Standing in that familiar little home once more, being warmly embraced by Auntie Beat and by one of my cousins who now lived with her, I found it hard to believe it was so many years since I had been there. I asked how it was that the village had not been swallowed up by the motorway? Auntie Beat informed me with a triumphant smile that they had made it too expensive for the authorities.

Auntie Beat was the last of the older generation. I bless the fact that I was able to see quite a lot of her before she died some years later. I do not usually care for the music at funerals, as I feel the occasion is too emotional for it to succeed purely as music. However, for Auntie Beat, the little church was packed, and with the first chord on the organ, the whole village seemed to harmonise just as I had remembered on those summer evenings. I didn't want the service to end. Afterwards there was a gathering of the clans, for word had gone round the valleys that 'Dennis the pilot' was coming, and relatives met up who had not seen each other for years. The sherry flowed, and one and all agreed that Auntie Beat had had a good send-off.

Most of the family were musical, even gifted, and my father, the eldest son, had been especially so. He played the piano by ear with a natural talent I've envied all my life, composed haunting melodies, and had a fine voice. My grandfather on my maternal side had been an organist of some ability, and used to play the organ in London's Albert Hall. These are the two instruments I have always longed to play. As a small boy I nearly drove the whole family mad while I practised endlessly the easiest hymn tune I could find, with no black notes, 'How welcome was the call', but to no avail. I never aspired to the organ, as I found I had no aptitude even for the piano.

My father had gone to London, where he became an estate agent. He and my mother, the eldest of two brothers and two sisters, met during World War I. She was a model, very *avant garde* for those days, and they made a handsome pair. It caused more than a little interest when young Billy brought his new young bride home from London on one of his visits. My father was away at the war for some time, and left my mother pregnant with me. When her time came in 1918, she took herself off to hospital and produced a 9 lb (4.1 kg) baby, me. Of course, she had to give up working, and with a baby to feed and clothe there was not much money left for extras. She never could afford a pram, so had to carry me everywhere until I was old enough to toddle along at least part of the time beside her. My father was inordinately proud of me. I was the first David grandchild, so mother had really achieved something for Wales, too! Now, I am the last of the male Davids.

Father had not been home from the war very long when his friend Oliver Locker-Lampson, my godfather, asked him to accompany him to try and help the White Russians who were fleeing from the Bolsheviks after the Revolution. Locker-Lampson was a very colourful character, a born leader, and a champion against oppression. He created a unit consisting of armoured cars, and he designed his own navy-style uniform! The unit performed heroically, and saved a number of lives.

Locker-Lampson was a great champion of oppressed peoples. At one time he had been asked if he would kill the mad monk Rasputin. Wisely, although I believe he could have named his own price, he declined. When Hitler came to power he rescued and gave shelter to Einstein. Every day Einstein would go to work on his theories in their garden shed during the six weeks he stayed with them prior to sailing for America. I was proud of my godfather, and he was very good to my mother and me.

From 1922-1945 Locker-Lampson was MP for Handsworth, Birmingham, and when I was a young pilot in the 1940s he took me out to a hilarious lunch at the House of Commons with his friend, the author A.P. Herbert. Since Herbert was in the Thames River Emergency Service and a chief petty officer of the Naval Auxiliary Patrol, we spent all our time calling each other 'Sir' and trying to persuade each other not to. They were both handsome men, and I couldn't help noticing the glamorous young secretaries they brought with them!

I can see now that much of what my father saw in Russia must have haunted him for the rest of his life. In those days, there was no such thing as counselling after traumatic experiences. We did hear of one happier episode in which he carried a young Russian woman to safety. In gratitude she gave him a beautiful white silk scarf, which he treasured. Later he was awarded one of the highest Russian decorations for bravery. Strange that almost 40 years later I was to be involved with helping people escape from the terror in Hungary.

When my father eventually returned to family life, there is no doubt the experiences he had been through had changed him. There was the same warmth and charm which had endeared him to all, and he did his work well but, as an old friend said to me many years later, 'It was an illness, and he drank with the wrong people.' He was always the first to help anyone, and no one could have been more generous. However, generosity can be expensive, and bills an irritation; those he did not like, he tore up.

I admired my father very much, but children are more perceptive than we give them credit for, and there were increasing rows as my mother realistically argued that bills did not get paid by being torn up. My father's reply was to go out to drink with his friends, to forget the unpleasant reminders. I had a constantly recurring nightmare of a wall falling on me as I tried desperately and ineffectually to hold it up.

When I was eight and while we were at Surbiton, my mother at last felt she could no longer cope with the situation, and she and father split up, which was a great wrench for me. Her own father, who was also a great character and almost a double for Edward VII, came to her aid, by helping her to buy an old Victorian house in London's south-west suburbs at a ridiculously small figure, together with some of its furniture.

I left my small public school at Deal, in Kent, which I had loved, but where I had learned virtually nothing except how to excel at most sports. The great attraction of Deal had been the sports. My mother used to say, 'If Dennis can't write it, at least he can put his name down and run in it!'

Instead, I was sent to Surbiton County School, where I was fortunate to have a wonderful headmaster, Mr A. E. A. Willis. For the first time in my life I found there was some point to learning and in working hard to obtain a good position in class. My competitive spirit came to the fore, because, as in sport, I hated to be beaten.

Mother and I were launched in our new life. We moved into the kitchen and scullery of the big old house we had taken on, and let every room in it. She went back to full-time fashion modelling, and also worked as a demonstrator. Many a night I would find her soaking her feet in a basin of hot water, almost asleep in her chair after a long hard day.

She showed her strength of character in the manner in which she tackled father's pressing debts. She pawned her silver dressing-table set and cigarette box, to pay the most urgent bills, and asked the butcher and the grocer to let her pay off so much a week. They agreed, and gradually every last penny was paid off to the creditors, and she was able to redeem her silver.

Because of the financial problems caused by my father's drinking, my mother and I had felt it wiser and more tactful for his family if we did not stay in touch with them, although this decision was a sad one. Some years later, after re-establishing contact, I explained how we had felt, and my father's sister put it into its true perspective, by saying in her wonderful Welsh voice, 'Well, there's daft!'.

Over the years, from the time my mother and father had first come to Surbiton, they had made some very good friends. It is significant to me that they all proved the worth of their friendship by the manner in which they stood by her through all the difficult times. Nor did we ever hear a harsh word of judgement about my father; rather there would be a kindly sympathetic smile about 'dear Billy' and his 'sickness'. Gradually, our finances took on a more healthy aspect. We were able to take over one or two more rooms, and I actually had a room of my own, which was unbelievable luxury. It was a small attic room in what had originally been the servants' quarters, and had no electric light, so I would take my candle up with me every night.

A great and happy influence in my life at the time was another family, the Stockings, who lived in a large house in the square across the street. Of two brothers and three sisters, the second son John became my firm and trusted friend. I was always made to feel part of the family, joining in many of their many activities, and we grew up together.

Outside school and study, sport and outdoor activities filled our leisure time. At weekends John and I would go off with our dogs, taking a packed lunch. We would walk anything up to 15 miles (24 km) during the day. Across the Thames, in Home Park, the countryside leading to Hampton Court Palace was beautiful. Then there were the Oxshott Woods, which still look lovely today amidst all the urban development. In the summer, after school, and later when I first worked in London, I would get home about 7 p.m., rush through supper, and then I might cycle up to our local tennis club to play two hours' tennis until dark. Or I might go for a swim round Taggs Island, or Ravens Eyot, for the Thames was at the bottom of our road. There were no pollution problems in the river in those days.

Tennis has always been one of my favourite sports. I had quite an aptitude for it, and so was welcome to make up matches, both at the club and with friends. Although membership of a club was cheap then, all my spare money went on tennis, and even the cost of replacing a broken string for my racket was a serious matter.

One afternoon I was playing tennis with some friends on the St Andrew Square court in Surbiton. Fred Perry, the English tennis champion, was visiting friends locally, and stopped to watch. He had recently won Wimbledon, and was admired by us all. He spent the rest of the afternoon talking to us, handing out tips and encouragement. He played a set with me, and was generous enough to let me take a game off him. He will never know how much his interest and encouragement meant to us. Somehow, I fancy he had the wisdom to realise that that game he let me win, and the gracious way in which he congratulated me, fired my ambition, and I sought to improve my game and learn from anyone willing to coach me. Any promise I showed was never realised, however, for World War II intervened, and by 1945, I was too old to take up serious tennis. Nevertheless in 1948 I did play at Wimbledon in the RAF Championships. Even if it was not the All-England Championship, it was still part of a dream come true.

In 1953, while a student at the Flying College, Manby, I was playing captain of the successful Lincolnshire squash team. I was also playing captain for the United Services squash team in the Middle East. The highlight of my squash career was a match with the world champion Hashim Khan, who, like Fred Perry, let me win one game.

When I was 14$\frac{1}{2}$, I persuaded my mother and my headmaster to let me leave school. He made the one condition that I continue my studies at night school, and that if I did that and obtained my passes, he would always be there should I need a reference in the future.

My uncle was the managing director of a wholesale clothing and footwear business, John Lovey's in London's Farringdon Street, and I was delighted when he said that he would take me on and train me from the bottom up in all departments. My wage was a princely 12s 6d (62$\frac{1}{2}$p) a week. I caught the workmen's train from Surbiton, which meant travelling from seven in the morning, at a special fare of 2s 6d (12$\frac{1}{2}$p) per week. Being so early, I was able to walk from Waterloo terminus to John Lovey's, a mile and a half away, and thus save on further fares. I was able to pay my mother 2s 6d towards my keep, and my lunch for the six working days cost another 2s 6d, and so I had the rest over to spend on clothes, or on my tennis and squash. A new string for my racket cost me 1s 3d (just over 6p), a costly outlay, but I felt myself a young man of independent means now, and no longer such a drain on my mother.

My first day at work was a rude awakening! All thoughts of any privileges as the young nephew of the managing director were immediately dispelled. I was given a tough khaki overall, and helped with unloading the vans. At the end of the day I was expected to sweep out the yard and any stairs and rooms that needed it, sprinkling the area with disinfectant to keep the dust and germs down.

I worked with all the regular carters who delivered to the warehouse in drays drawn by two enormous carthorses. How beautiful those horses were, with their gleaming coats and huge feathered feet. They looked so majestic, and for all their great strength were very gentle. I sometimes went with the carters to the East India docks to collect loads. They and the dockers were big tough men, and must have been amused by the efforts of this green youngster. They never let on, though, and with the utmost patience they taught me all the tricks of lifting and carrying the awkward loads, weighing up to two hundredweight (224 lb, 100 kg). They would drink heavily, but had hearts of gold. I will never forget Big Tom. He was a giant of a man, and seemed the same dimension from whichever way one viewed him. He was a carter for the old London and North Eastern Railway, and he in particular built my confidence, and never once made me feel an ignorant boy. What he taught me has been useful all my life.

Another task was called 'lifting', which was either carrying the goods up the warehouse stairs, or by lift (elevator) which was operated by hand, protected by a stout glove, by pulling on a rope. No electricity at that time to lighten one's work! Gradually I was moved on to learn other aspects of the trade, and enjoyed it all, finding it most interesting. By the time I was 16 I was a salesman in the ladies' shoe department, which was quite a change from the miners' boots I had watched grandfather making.

Throughout all this time I kept on with my night-school work, and managed to obtain good passes. I was fortunate to be tutored in science, maths and English by a retired schoolmaster, who vetted my studies, and I continued with them until I joined the RAF.

CHAPTER TWO

PER ARDUA AD ASTRA

When I was 17, my uncle had a serious talk with me. It is hard for today's younger generations to understand that, in the 1930s, we almost expected there to be a war about every 20 years. Uncle had seen service in the trenches in World War I, and along with many others was watching the rise of Hitler and the Nazi Party with apprehension. As I grew up I was beginning to feel that I should be joining one of the services as an Auxiliary, doing part-time training. My inclinations turned towards the Honourable Artillery Company, where my friend John Stockings already was. They still had cavalry, and it seemed wonderful to be paid to work with horses. Unfortunately, just at this time they switched over to tanks, which had no appeal for me at all.

I recalled that in 1925, when I was seven, as a special holiday treat at Margate, Kent, my mother and I went up in an Avro 504 of the Cornwall Aviation Company. Though I was surprised at the din, this must have sowed a seed inside me. Now I discovered that, if I joined the RAF Volunteer Reserve, they would teach me to fly at no cost! One merely had to put in so many hours each weekend, and have the necessary scholastic qualifications. However, I felt that I had hit a big stumbling block in having left school so young, so I went to see Mr Willis, my former headmaster, to take him up on his offer of help.

He kindly vetted all the work that I had done at the night school, and gave me a personal report as to my abilities, which I took along to the RAF. Thanks to him, they agreed to accept me for training.

First I had to do a lot of theoretical study, to show I could grasp the technical side. Having accomplished this, in May 1937 I was allowed to start learning to fly at No. 5 Elementary and Reserve Flying School in Hanworth, Middlesex. This was a tiny grass field, with a clump of trees in the centre and surrounded by houses, which made the approach quite tricky. I had to line up with a tree seen between two houses. Today it is hard to believe that this little field rejoiced in the name of London Air Park. We flew civil-registered Blackburn B.2

biplane trainers, very like a Tiger Moth but with the pupil and instructor seated side-by-side.

I soon realised that piloting had a magic all its own, and knew it would in time become a total commitment for me. It is still hard for me to find the words to describe my sheer delight and sense of freedom as the little biplane, seeming to strain every nerve, accelerated across the grass and suddenly became airborne. The stick came back and the nose pointed joyfully skywards, and we soared into the air, experiencing the nearest thing to flying like a bird that one could imagine.

The delight of those early days was the wonderful feeling of freedom and independence that it gave me. Just over two miles to the north was Heston Airport, and three miles to the north-west was the Fairey Company's grass field called Heathrow (today the chief London airport), but we had no radio and no air-traffic control. Once free of the ground and away from the airfield we were on our own. I quickly found an affinity with flying, and over the years it has become a major part of my life, but those early days were special.

I can see now that it was inevitable that I was to become a fighter pilot, fighting my own battles. I have enormous respect for the bomber crews, who had to work as a team and became as close-knit as a family, and yet from the start I was a loner. It was just me and my aeroplane, hoping that neither of us would let the other down. I worked hard, learning all I could, but I have always realised that success stemmed from the inborn ability I was lucky to be able to draw on.

Only recently, when I was giving a talk to some youngsters at a school, my first question, from an eager nine-year-old, was 'Do you still want to fly?' On my immediate response, 'Oh, yes', came the next question 'Why?' How can one explain to anyone who has not experienced it, the magical and relentless hold it has on one?

The RAFVR liked pupils to take instruction every day if possible, in order to keep up the continuity, but I could only manage two nights a week and alternate weekends. I approached my first lessons with some trepidation, but also with a great sense of excited anticipation. My flying instructor was Flight Lieutenant Gibbon, who was a part-time serviceman, having finished a short-service commission. The relationship between pupil and flying instructor is a special one, and I shall never forget what I owe him. I was equally fortunate with my ground instructor, who had the unlikely name of Flight Lieutenant Rivers Old-Meadow. He had the born teacher's knack of explaining just why we were learning particular aspects of mathematics, and how they were applicable to flying. This made it all much easier, and logical to assimilate and remember.

One day, quite unexpectedly, Flight Lieutenant Gibbon got out of his seat, saying, 'Right, you are ready for your first solo. Off you go.' My emotions were a mixture of enormous exhilaration and equally great apprehension. However, the take-off went smoothly, and I soon relaxed to the pleasure of the sensation of flying. This was to be short-lived, however, for all too soon I had to face the challenge of coming back to land. Far more of an undertaking than taking off! I concentrated with every fibre of my being, and to my great relief made quite a reasonable landing. Gibbon came over and said he was very pleased, and now I was to take off and do it all over again. I had just heaved a sigh of relief that I had actually flown solo, and was safely back on *terra firma*, and now I was being sent off straight away to repeat the exercise! Calling up all my powers of concentration once more, and once again trying to remember everything I had been so thoroughly taught, I took off and flew round and landed again, once more successfully.

Of course, my instructor had been quite right. It was the only way to gain confidence, especially as it was to be several days before I was able to attend again and do another solo. Once more all the butterflies were there, as I had to face the task again on my own after a few days' break, instead of being able to keep up a continuous progress from the previous day's lesson. All went without a hitch, and that was a big milestone passed. I knew then that I could fly, and above all that I loved doing so.

As I proceeded with my flying instruction, I began to give serious consideration to a full-time career in the RAF. I discussed this with my uncle, who had been hoping that I would find a future in his firm. He said that, much as he regretted it, he felt that the best thing for me to do would probably be to go ahead with my plan to make a career in the RAF. He would support me in this in any way he could. I went back once more to Mr Willis, who like my uncle felt that it would not be long before there was a war, and the sooner I was established in a Service career the better it would be.

I went ahead with my application for a short-service commission, and underwent the various examinations before I could be accepted. This included a stiff medical, which to this day is one of the toughest anywhere, but I passed with no problems. Over the years I have seen a lot of heartbreak with promising youngsters who at the last moment have fallen at this hurdle, perhaps through colour-blindness or some other seemingly minor but vital aspect of their physical make-up.

I was accepted and signed on, and the first part of my training continued with the flying at Hanworth. From there we went to Uxbridge for officer training. Our instruction there included drill, and how to give orders and receive them. We were drilled by corporals, who, although polite, were very demanding. I can still hear their ringing tones of 'Now then, *gentlemen*!' They taught us to drill squads of men, and supervised our physical training as well. Uxbridge covered administrative subjects, and every aspect of learning how to be an 'officer and a gentleman', even down to the correct procedure for official dining in the mess.

Whilst there we were sent up to London to be measured for our uniforms, having been given our uniform allowance of about £60. We needed a greatcoat, two uniforms, and a full mess kit, plus shirts, socks, two pairs of shoes, caps and other items. It was all worked out to a nicety. We could choose our own tailors, and they came to fit us, carefully supervised by senior officers. We had to have all our uniforms complete by the time we were due to be sent to No. 5 Flying Training School at Sealand, near Chester. About 30 of us were sent on there for training on more advanced service-type aircraft.

We were all young and keen, and above all shared an over-riding passion for flying. That was what we wanted to do above all else, and the more we notched up our flying hours the more we loved it. There was a marvellous feeling of camaraderie, and I was privileged to share so much of my youth with men like these. The RAF was indeed my university, and I enjoyed my early days with it as every young student does, relishing the challenges and fun of these never-to-be-forgotten times.

Amongst my fellow students at Sealand I was delighted to find a wonderful group of New Zealanders, including Jack Strang, who had been on the selection list for the All-Blacks, and who became a particular buddy of mine. Once again it was a chance to enjoy friendships already made, and forge new ones.

At Sealand we flew much more powerful aircraft, notably the famous biplanes made by the Hawker company: the two-seat Audax and Hart, and the exciting Fury single-seat fighter. We gradually learned all types of air combat, including firing on towed aerial targets with live ammunition. We had to live in mess, and dress for dinner every night. This usually meant two nights a week in full mess kit, three nights dinner jacket, one night a lounge suit, and on Saturdays usually a dark blazer and flannels, with of course a tie. We attended church parade every Sunday morning. It was a very strict routine, and there was not much spare time, but it was a marvellous grounding for every aspect of our future lives, and we enjoyed it immensely.

After three months at Sealand, and successful completion of the course, it was an enormous relief to find I had achieved a Distinguished Pass. I knew then that all those hours of night-school study, which at times had seemed tedious, had paid off, and every minute had been worthwhile. I think it is the most momentous moment in any young pilot's career in the RAF when he can wear his wings for the first time. There was no formal occasion for this great turning point, but now we knew we were the senior term of officers under training, with a new course of juniors coming in. I think we all stuck our chests out just a little those first few days, hoping no one would miss seeing that precious new emblem which meant so much to us. How confident and happy we all looked in those first photographs!

I completed my training at Sealand in 1938, and then awaited a fighter squadron vacancy. In the meantime I passed some valuable time at Ford in Sussex, where I flew Royal Navy navigators in Blackburn Sharks and Supermarine Walrus amphibians, so that they could gain air experience. On the other side of the airfield Alan Cobham, famous for his flying circuses which gave so many youngsters like myself their first taste of flight, was carrying out trials for in-flight refuelling. I met him and told him of my flight with him as a child in the early 1920s. I thought him a most generous man, prepared to spend time talking with a young aviator. It is good to see his lifetime of work in aviation led to the award of a knighthood.

One morning I opened the *Daily Mirror* and, with more interest than usual, I read the headline, 'Hurricane from RAF Debden dives into the ground at 400 miles per hour at night'. The following day the posting came through for me to go to Debden in Essex to join 87 Hurricane Squadron! Having received travel vouchers from the adjutant at Ford, I said goodbye to my many friends there and made my way by train to Saffron Walden, where I was picked up by RAF transport from Debden.

No. 87 Squadron was flying the Gloster Gladiator biplane, but was being re-equipped with Hurricanes. Suddenly I was faced with a fighting monoplane, with a Rolls-Royce Merlin engine of over 1,000 horsepower, the Hurricane. After studying the fuel system, I went solo. Normally one would have dual-control instruction on a Fairey Battle, which also had a Merlin engine and was the standard monoplane advanced trainer at that time. However, 87's Battle was unserviceable, so the squadron commander asked me if I had flown an aeroplane with flaps before. I mentioned that I had flown the Walrus at Ford.

He jokingly said, 'This is a bit different, but you might as well have a go!'

The first circuit – one take-off and landing – was approved by my flight commander, and I was told not to retract the wheels. This big experience went off without incident. Of course the whole station watched the new boy with interest. A new pilot's greatest fear is to make a bad landing in front of his peers, and this terror has haunted pilots even after surviving an air battle.

I heaved a sigh of relief, switched off the engine and got out, only to be met by the flight commander, who said I could now go straight off on a sector reconnaissance for half an hour with wheels up. That half hour was the start of a love affair with the Hurricane which has lasted to this day. I recently attended an airshow at Biggin Hill, where I was interviewed by a young girl from a local newspaper. She got it in one: her write-up began, 'Dennis 'Hurricane' David'!

The first Hurricanes could be dangerous, in that the engine could cut on take-off. Usually the engine picked up again, but not always. It was a niggling worry, and was due to the exhaust system not coping with the escaping gases. It was quickly remedied by a new design of the exhaust, which also gave a little extra power.

Four months before the official order came through, the Hawker Aircraft directors had gone ahead on their own initiative with full production, such was their faith in the Hurricane, and the feeling a war that was going to need every one they could produce was not far off. They were only too conscious, however, that their decision could ruin the company, but as it turned out, their courage meant that, when war did come, we already had several hundred more Hurricanes than would otherwise have been available.

One wonders why it is that Britain always seems to get saved against all odds. It happened at the time of the Armada, then again in Nelson's time, and later in our modern times at Dunkirk. I cannot help but feel that we must have a special Guardian Angel watching over us.

I have waged a long campaign to get the Hurricane given its due as the major victor in the Battle of Britain. Although today it is far less famous than the Spitfire, in fact Hurricanes shot down more enemy aircraft in the battle than all the Spitfires, anti-aircraft guns and other aircraft combined. Of course, it was not so pretty as its partner, and certainly the name Spitfire conjured up a magic image. I flew them both in battle, and since the war have been interested to hear from several Luftwaffe pilots that any German who was shot down and survived, or had his aircraft damaged, always preferred to tell the story of how he had encountered a Spitfire, never a Hurricane. Somehow they thought that that would have been *infradig*! They also told me that many a tired fighter pilot dropping off to sleep in their mess after a long day could be galvanised into instant action by the cry '*Achtung Schpitfeuer!*' The bomber pilots have a different reaction: they have told me that the Hurricane was the aircraft they dreaded.

The Spitfire was a wonderful aircraft to fly, with superb manoeuvrability and speed. It was the thoroughbred racehorse, compared to the pure-bred hunter Hurricane. One looks at the fabric of the Hurricane today and one marvels at its seeming fragility and lightness, but it was amazingly tough, and saw us through our worst hours in the Battles of France and Britain. The ground crews could repair damage in a matter of minutes, as they could patch the holes with fabric, stuck on with dope (cellulose paint). The Spitfire was an all-metal aircraft which required a metal panel to be inserted and riveted, and this of course took much longer. My loyalties are divided, however, as I have flown and loved them both. They both deserve their place of honour in history.

Once at Debden, I felt established as an officer, and having opened my first account at Lloyds Bank I became the proud possessor of a cheque book. In those days we looked upon bank managers as respected friends, and they took a paternal interest in our affairs. So I decided it was time I bought my own car, so far having had only part-shares in motorbikes and cars with friends.

I went to see Mr Benn, who was the manager of the Services Department in the head office in Pall Mall, London. He was known as 'Uncle Benn', which explains everything. I told him I wanted to buy a car, and, now I had my new cheque book, could I write a cheque in order to do so? He very kindly explained that in order to do this I had to have collateral, and as the car would cost about £50 I would have to wait until I had accumulated rather more than that before I could put my name to one of those magic pages in my virgin cheque book! I was disappointed, but understood the reasoning behind it. In the event I managed to purchase an old Hillman Husky for £10 cash. I kept it at Debden until I left for France in September 1939, when I sold it to a fellow officer for £10.

The days passed quickly at Debden, full of activities of one sort or another. We all played a lot of sport, but above all we snatched every opportunity we could to get in as many flying hours as we could manage. Life was geared to a seven-day week. However, the war clouds seemed to be gathering ominously, and we became more twitchy. Our prime minister, Neville Chamberlain, returned from Munich in September 1938, with his famous piece of paper, and proclaimed 'peace for our time', but somehow none of us believed him.

CHAPTER THREE

THE BATTLE OF FRANCE

In early 1939 we were put on 'a state of readiness', which meant gradually longer and longer hours awaiting an emergency, and in the last months before war was declared we were sleeping in the hangar, to be ready and near our aircraft. There were many false alarms. Chamberlain is often decried and derided, but, whatever the political rights and wrongs of his policy of appeasement towards Hitler's territorial claims, he bought us a vital year before the declaration of hostilities. At the start of that year, though we were 'at readiness', we sat in our aircraft with no guns or ammunition! At last in the summer we received our Browning 0.303-in machine guns, eight for each aircraft.

War was declared on 3 September. The news that at long last we were actually committed came almost as a relief, as we had felt for so long it was inevitable. We were given a few days' short leave, and then proceeded with our aircraft to Boos, near Rouen in northern France, to become part of the British Expeditionary Force. We had always known that our role in war was to provide cover for the British Forces, and ground support. In reality this was laughingly unrealistic, with only four squadrons of Hurricanes in all, two based in the south and ourselves and another squadron in the north near Lille. There were initially 12 operational aircraft per squadron to cover hundreds of miles of frontier between France and neighbouring Germany. The British Advanced Air Striking Force, comprising Blenheims and Battles, almost defenceless, was to the south. The Luftwaffe outnumbered us by at least ten to one.

We arrived at Boos, and were appalled at the lack of technical support. We had to refuel our Hurricanes using four-gallon cans poured through chamois leather in funnels. The chamois absorbed any water there might be in the cans, and so the job took a very long time. Whilst at Boos we lived in the Hôtel de la Poste in Rouen. I remembered that it was in this city that Joan of Arc was burnt at the stake, and visited the actual place, which is marked with a plaque. A few days later we were sent to Merville, a village near the city of Lille.

Despite everything we were still young and high-spirited, and we quickly found that we could fly under the bridge over the river Lys by the town. This was frowned upon, but of course it did not deter us from regularly repeating the practice. I must say the French entered into the spirit of the exercise, but became a little concerned as their hanging trolleys were suspended beneath the bridge while they were painting and repairing it. I vividly remember watching them haul themselves up at speed out of danger as they sensed our approach. I felt the French were subdued: perhaps it was their behaviour, or perhaps it was an atmosphere I felt very tangibly at the time. I also noticed an almost complete absence of French officers, which was disquieting.

The French were placing inordinate trust in the impregnability of their Maginot Line fortifications along their border. This took care of most of the army officers, but I was then told that the Armée de l'Air, the French Air Force, was concentrated around Paris and the south. I rarely saw any sight of it. The north they had apparently left to us.

It was the end of September when we arrived in Merville, where we stayed at the estaminet while we waited for our accommodation and base to be established at Lille Seclin. When it was ready, we found a great improvement on our previous conditions, with proper hangars and technical support.

From Merville we used to fly to Le Touquet to patrol the Channel, where the boats were ferrying the troops from Dover to Boulogne. We had heard rumours that the Luftwaffe was going to attack these ferries. This patrol was a popular duty because it meant a lot of flying, and we quickly got to know the area well. I vividly remember looking at the White Cliffs of Dover, and thinking how inviting they were, as I turned back to France. We normally carried out this duty with two aircraft at a time, and we were allotted about an hour over the boats, which were never left unescorted.

So we drifted into the so-called 'Phoney War' period as autumn turned into winter – and a bitterly cold winter it turned out to be. We had been surprised when we arrived at Lille Seclin to find that the huts where we were to sleep were on wooden piles about 18 in (46 cm) off the ground. This was disastrous as the bitter cold could assault us from all sides and from top and bottom. Our only heating was a small solid-fuel iron stove in the middle of the hut, around which we all huddled. I went to bed wearing my Irvin fur-lined jacket, thick socks and fur-lined gauntlet gloves. Everything we could find we piled on top of the beds, including our heavy greatcoats, and still we could not get warm. Ice formed on the inside of the windows, and once when one of my friends poured water, which we had kept liquid by the stove, into his glass to take some Eno's salts, the water froze the moment it was in the glass.

We had two first-class flight commanders. Voase Jeff was a nephew of J. Arthur Rank, the film mogul and flour magnate; the other was Cyrus Colmore. Their great gift was that they were teaching us all the time, for we were little more than boys, and they showed us leadership in the everyday life we shared with them, as well as how to lead in the air. It proved invaluable training, for when the air battles really began we were in a position to take over leadership when casualties took their toll. For all the sadness and discomforts of those days, my overriding memory is of the total unselfishness of everyone and of the wonderful bond we forged. It was indeed a privilege to share one's youth with such comrades. We were always able to laugh together, which helped so much to overcome the difficulties. Is it my imagination, or do young people laugh less these days?

We always had a flight (three aircraft) at 30-minutes availability, and a flight from our sister squadron, 85, was at one-hour availability. This entailed being on call throughout the daylight hours. On special occasions, such as VIP visits, we would have pilots in their aircraft waiting at two-minute readiness, which would sometimes mean that we would sit in our aircraft for several hours, maintaining R/T contact with Flying Control which handled all aircraft in the area. I used to write all my mail at these times, and my mother received a lot of letters in those days.

On 6 December 1939, a day even more bitterly cold than usual, I was section leader of the three aircraft designated as stand-by section when we were visited by King George VI. His Majesty was supposed to drive past my section to a reception parade. Imagine my consternation when I saw the King's car stop, and he got out and made his way over to my aircraft, followed by his brothers the royal Dukes of Windsor (his elder brother who had abdicated) and Gloucester. They were accompanied by Lord Gort, who had been a general in World War I, and who was now commander-in-chief of all British forces in France. He was accompanied by yet another general, the legendary Ironside. There were others in the party, but that was more than enough for me.

I got through to Control at once on my R/T, and told them of the King's change of plan (we later got to know that this was typical of him, he enjoyed impromptu royal disruptions such as this). The reply from Control was not tremendously helpful; I was told, 'He can't have!'

I assured them he was walking towards my aircraft at that moment. Control said, 'Do the best you can,' and left it to me. I had been at readiness for about four hours since dawn, and did not feel fittingly turned out to meet my monarch. I told my No. 2 at readiness to take over the section, wrestled with undoing my parachute and holding harness, and scrambled out of my Hurricane, to find the King waiting by the propeller with his hand outstretched to shake mine, and all his entourage gathered round him.

Never before or since have I been surrounded by so many royals. The King never stuttered (as it was said usually happened), but I certainly did! He was well-informed as to the current situation. My impression was that he and Lord Gort were very close, and both questioned me searchingly about how we felt about the Luftwaffe, and in particular their strength. I told him we had reports of their superior numbers, but I assured His Majesty that our morale was high, and we were in no way dismayed by these reports and would do our best in all circumstances. He seemed pleased to be with us, and to be seeing things for himself. He came over as a good leader, and a man of determined character. His visit meant a lot to us, and he in fact spent a long time at our station.

He was already held in great esteem and affection by the British nation, having overcome a difficult start to his reign. In addition to this, he had, by sheer perseverance, largely overcome his speech impediment. As Duke of York, amongst other duties, he had been the RAF 'royal', and indeed had served at Cranwell as adjutant. He was also a brilliant tennis player of Wimbledon standard, and had represented the RAF on many occasions. A story about him was that when he was adjutant he found it difficult to say the S of seven, so anyone who would normally have received a seven-day confined-to-barracks for some misdemeanour could expect to receive 14 days if they had the bad luck to come before him.

Because of his special association with the RAF he honoured the Battle of Britain Fighter Association, formed after the War, by agreeing to be its patron, and he took a very active interest in it. After his death his widow, Queen Elizabeth the Queen Mother, graciously took over this role. She never undertakes any role without taking a personal interest, and when the Battle of Britain Museum at Hendon was opened in November 1978 she performed the ceremony. This occasion was to be attended only by senior officials and those concerned with the administration of the museum. However, it was typical of her that she perused the guest list a day or two before the occasion, and then asked, 'And who of the 'boys' am I going to meet?' She was informed that no one else had been invited, and I understand that for once she made her wishes known forcefully.

Battle of Britain veterans were frantically telephoned if they were anywhere where they could get to London in time for the ceremony. I lived nearby, and so was able to tell a hot and bothered young man on the other end of the phone that I would be delighted to attend. The sigh of relief was audible, and a surprising number of us managed to get there. As always it was a delight and a privilege to be greeted by the Queen Mother, who always manages to make even a line-up a personal occasion, and we all took a mischievous pleasure in the knowledge that our attendance was almost by royal command. The Queen Mother also made a generous donation of her late husband's RAF uniform, which has become a treasured exhibit in the museum.

After the King's visit in France, we established personal contact with the British Army. Some of my friends were in the Black Watch with the BEF (British Expeditionary Force), whom I have always held in the highest regard. In May 1940 these men fought like tigers when the Germans pushed their way through France in overwhelming numbers. Bren-gun carriers and similar inadequate equipment were no match for the German tanks. Their casualties were horrendous, and few of my friends survived.

The rest of what has become known as the Phoney War, which ended so abruptly in the spring, was taken up with training, and liaison with other forces. We visited the Blenheim squadron at Toul-Rosières for affiliation exercises. The Blenheims had previously been liaising with Gladiators, and I well remember their consternation when practising dogfights with us, and suddenly realising that our speed and manoeuvrability were so much greater. A few practice sorties against the Hurricanes dispelled their optimism. The enemy were of at least the same calibre, and in some cases even faster, and the RAF bomber crews had been given a false impression of their impregnability.

Despite this disquieting new knowledge the morale of the Blenheim crews remained magnificent, and they grimly continued to set about their allotted tasks to the best of their ability. The Fairey Battles, however, were another story. In spite of the incredible heroism of their crews, these aircraft were decimated. In later years I have met some of the German pilots who flew at this time, and all agreed for them it was a 'turkey shoot'. Whoever was responsible for allowing such slow and vulnerable aircraft to be part of a striking force, against an enemy whose superiority was already known, deserves to be censured.

The bitter cold of that winter will never be forgotten. At Rosières there were no hangars for our Hurricanes, and starting them up could take a nightmarish three hours. Even with the skill of our ground crews, who had followed by road, maintaining our aircraft was a formidable problem, and our liaison with this comforting back-up became even closer. Each aircraft, its ground crew and pilot worked as one. There was a special affection, not only amongst the men concerned, but for the Hurricane itself, which seemed to take on a personality of its own. This feeling of a bond with an inanimate machine was very real.

Our greatest concern in the Phoney War was how to combat the cold. The Blenheim crews were outstanding, and made us all feel welcome in their mess. They had no illusions about the difficulties encountered in starting engines. Theirs were air-cooled Bristol Mercury radial engines of 840 hp, which in freezing weather could have their oil diluted with petrol to make starting easier. Ours were Rolls-Royce Merlins, an engine of well over 1,000 hp with 12 liquid-cooled cylinders. The ground crews of the Blenheim and Hurricane squadrons co-operated in every way possible. In that sub-zero winter they spent ages straining to wind back the huge wooden propellers of our Hurricanes in order to make the oil less viscous. For starting, we had 'trolley-accs', heavy accumulators on wheels, but at 20-below they seemed to run down in no time. The luckless 'erks' (the ground crew) then had to start the big Merlin using handcranks on each side. At night we tried to cover the engines with a tarpaulin and place a little Aladdin oil heater underneath, but next morning the oil would still seem almost solid, and the cranking by gloved hands numb with cold seemed never-ending.

When our affiliation exercises were complete we returned to our parent unit at Lille Seclin. Through all this time, leave boats and Channel ferries were covered by our fighter patrols. The days at long last started to lengthen, and the terrible winter grudgingly gave way to warmer weather.

On 10 May, the eventful day I recalled in the Prologue, we were on detachment at Senon, north-east of Verdun, from where we acted as escort for RAF Lysanders on reconnaissance over the Maginot and Siegfried Lines. The first warning we had that the Germans were suddenly becoming active was two Dornier 17s strafing our airfield. Luckily no one was hit, and our aircraft survived. Though it was a half-hearted attack, it was a tremendous shock to all of us. It was probably also a surprise for the Germans to find us there. I had just been cleared to fly a sector reconnaissance with Garry Nowell, and we were actually on our way to our aircraft at the time of the attack.

Garry and I were immediately ordered to try to intercept two raiders in the vicinity. I took off with Garry following at full throttle, and then was told to come back. The reporting system was so out of date that the bombers could have been the two we had seen earlier.

Returning to the airfield I was surprised to see some trees I had not noticed before. Suddenly, to my horror, I realised these were not trees but bomb bursts, and that the airfield was under attack. Instead of landing I opened the throttle and chased the bombers, followed by Garry; I shot one down, damaged a second, and Garry got a third. We returned to base highly elated, as were our ground crews.

Thus started a long day, and I flew another five sorties before returning to Seclin late that evening. We felt the Phoney War was suddenly over, and that the Germans had started their offensive. They had gone round the northern end of the Maginot Line, as well as penetrating it with 'Fifth Column' troops disguised as French officers. The awful realisation that the Maginot Line was not impregnable at all had a demoralising effect on the soldiers whose left flank was now wide open.

Things now began to happen fast. We quickly learned to adopt new aerial tactics as used by the Germans, notably never to fly in tight formation, but to concentrate on weaving in pairs. Many Germans were very experienced, as they had fought in the Spanish Civil War; as our tactics were based on 1918, we had no such advantage.

We learned to get very close to be sure of making a kill. After two days I obtained permission to resight my guns, drawing them in to the nearest single point without damaging the propeller tips. The eight guns of my Hurricane were thus trained on a fixed spot at 167 yds (153 m) and not at 250 yds (229 m) on a spray sighting as had been mandatory hitherto.

The ammunition on a Hurricane would be fully expended in 14 seconds if the thumb was kept on the button. Hence we tended to fire in bursts of about two seconds only. With its rigid wings the Hurricane was a first-class gun platform, and this, combined with the extra numbers we had in the early days thanks to the foresight of Hawker Aircraft, accounted for its overall impressive total of victories. I gained all my 21 victories in Hurricanes.

The next ten days were hectic, with constant operations against the enemy. We were never overawed by them, but they certainly outnumbered us. One day we ran into 40-plus Ju 87 Stukas dive-bombing a British Army field hospital. We shot down 14 of them, and the raid turned away after this treatment. However, on the way back to my station I saw about 150 more Ju 87s en route to another target. Having no more ammunition, I could but wonder at their resources before returning to base. Alas, not all six of us returned.

On 12 May I engaged a big Heinkel 111 over Lille. I attacked from the stern and saw it catch fire. He was obviously crippled, and, dropping his wheels, he proceeded to make a forced landing. My windshield was covered in oil, and I thought his rear gunner had hit my engine; it continued running, however, so I stayed with the enemy bomber until he crashed in a field by Herlies, a few miles north-west of Lille. I saw the pilot get out, and as I flew over he waved and saluted. I had hardly flown past him when I felt a powerful 'thump'. On looking back I saw that the Heinkel's bombs had exploded, and the pilot was no more. This saddened me, for in that brief moment of mutual acknowledgement we had not been enemies but fellow aviators. I returned home in a sombre mood, worried about the oil on my windshield. To my great relief I got down safely. My ground crew inspected the Hurricane for damage, as they too were worried about the oil. You can imagine our delight when they found that the oil was from the Heinkel, but I was shaken at finding out how close I must have got to the enemy.

This inspection took place during my absence, as I had gone to the site of the crashed bomber. I arrived at Herlies to be met by the town mayor, and the first French Army officer I had seen for a long time. He spoke no English, so I had to do my best to converse with him in French. It turned out that he was a bomb-disposal officer. Upon being told that this was my fifth victory, he embraced me, kissed me on both cheeks and declared, 'Vous êtes un ace!' Five victories is the definition of an ace, though on this occasion it was pronounced 'arse' – you could say a fundamental error, and not the first time I have been called this! The mayor also showered congratulations on me. On my return to base my ground crew were delighted to tell me all was well with my Hurricane, and I took off on another sortie that same afternoon.

Many a time I hugged my faithful old Hurricane when we had both managed to make it back to base after a particularly tough encounter with the enemy had left her peppered with bullet holes. How many of these bullets missed me I will never know, but by tracing the trajectory from the holes in the cockpit it was easy to see that some had been less than half an inch from my head. How wise I had been to lower my seat! A short time later I had the encounter with a 109 when I was 'out of ammo' as already described.

These episodes are typical of what was going on continuously until 20 May. Whatever we did in the air, and no matter how many German aircraft we destroyed, it seemed to make no difference; the German forces kept advancing and seemed invincible. But all the time we were learning from them, for they were the experts. The German *Legion Kondor* had already fought in the Spanish Civil War in 1936-1939, and in Poland, and were now experienced and formidable adversaries. I have always maintained that the Battle of France was our rehearsal for the Battle of Britain. Indeed, I recently discussed this with one of the German aces. He told me that his CO had said to him, 'These Brits are different, they are shooting us down,' but our numbers were too small and our losses too great. Every day it seemed another friend did not return, and there were little bundles of personal kit to be sent home. We grew up fast. I stopped making any close friends, and that says it all.

It is strange, but somehow one never thinks of it like that at the time. Similarly, one tries not to think of the lives one is ending when lining up an enemy target in one's sights. The night I saved 'Doggie' Oliver's life, I could not help feeling it was somehow ironic that I had obviously killed people when I shot down the German bombers, and yet had so instantly reacted to save one life. I hoped that our combined efforts earlier in the day had saved some of those in the Army hospital, too. I thought of a good friend of mine whom I had just lost, Chris Mackworth. He had given his life selflessly, pitching it against overwhelming odds in another German raid on a canvas hospital. Whether or not these targets were recognised for what they were, we shall never know. The result was the same, however, and Kit was dead. His father wrote to me soon afterwards to tell me that he had heard from one of the doctors at the hospital. They had buried Chris, but had no means of marking his grave other than by writing his name on a piece of paper which they put in a beer bottle on top of it.

One day when my aircraft was unserviceable, I went up the road and talked to some of the refugees who were walking from Belgium towards France. Belgium had been under fierce attack since 10 May, and despite valiant resistance was to surrender on 28 May. The refugees were pushing prams and small handcarts, with a few horse-drawn carts, and there were even fewer cars. Women were carrying their babies, while toddlers staggered along holding their mother's hand or dress. I borrowed an old motorbike from an army unit, and found a scene of desolation which it is impossible to describe. Old men, women and children, grandparents and babes in arms, not to mention dogs and horses, were strewn over the roadside, mostly dead, but a few with just a flicker of life remaining. All had been torn to pieces by the bullets from strafing German aircraft, whose aim was to prevent the road being used by the British Army, which was hoping to reinforce the British units already fighting the enemy further east.

The whole episode utterly sickened me. How could defenceless fleeing citizens be slaughtered like this? Little did I know that years later such outrageous scenes were to become an all too familiar sight on our TV screens, showing similar atrocities happening again and again all over the world.

My Celtic blood boiled, and I felt a white-hot anger. I hastened back to my Hurricane, and hoped I would be spared to shoot down a few of those who could be part of a policy which produced such one-sided slaughter. I rejoined my unit in a more determined mood than ever to destroy the enemy. My ground crew seemed to sense this change in me, and we all turned with renewed dedication to our tasks.

Some fighters came over from England to bolster our numbers by day, but although they had to return by nightfall, they proved invaluable. As an experienced combat pilot by then, I found myself leading a varied assortment of Hurricanes; formations were put together as and how they might be. Maps were in short supply, and our R/T left much to be desired, but the lads were magnificent in their aggressive and supporting roles.

Within days the Germans had the impetus of victory, and were on the crest of a wave rolling forward on all fronts. A seemingly endless supply of Ju 87s softened up targets ahead of their advancing tanks and troops. This rapid Panzer-type movement was masterminded by some of their best generals, including Rommel, and it took the Allies by surprise.

Our BEF, which had been unable to advance into neutral Belgium until the Germans had struck on the 10th, was by this time having to fight a defensive and desperate rearguard action every inch of the way. Lost battles get a poor press, and rearguard actions are the worst. Many Victoria Crosses were earned in that retreat, but the citations were never written, as the commanding officers who would have written them died alongside their men. Anyone who had a relative who was part of the BEF in France can be very proud.

We could hardly believe the rapidity of the fall of Holland and Belgium, and it seemed that northern France was about to go the same way. Soon we had orders to retreat back to Merville. While these retreats were speeding up, my friend Jimmy Joyce had a bullet in his leg, which should have meant a straightforward extraction. He kept on being moved on, however, from one field hospital to another, as the Germans pressed on our heels, and by the time he at last reached an established service hospital in the rear, gangrene had set in. He lost his leg, and the RAF lost a pilot for some time.

Garry Nowell, whom I mentioned previously, crash-landed his Hurricane after being badly shot up. Apart from other wounds, his foot and leg were seriously damaged. He, too, developed gangrene, and was awaiting amputation, which he was understandably and desperately keen to avoid. In hospital back in England, to his horror he saw the wound crawling with maggots while it was being dressed. The medical staff told him he was fortunate, for the maggots would feed on the putrid flesh, and would probably save his foot. This was the case, although his foot is troublesome to this day. Throughout over 20 months in hospital his wife daily spent every hour she could with him, and her devotion kept him alive.

All the time I was in France I never flew from any but grass airfields, which, though well maintained, had limited facilities, for the French had thought that we would look after the area north of Paris. The French Air Force Dewoitine, Curtiss and Morane-Saulnier fighters fought very well; they shot down hundreds of German aircraft, and we can be thankful that these additional numbers did not face us later on. All too often this contribution to the overall war effort has been overlooked, and the dedication and heroism of the French pilots deserve greater recognition and honour, for the heavy losses they incurred.

However, many of the French seemed to have no will left. Memories were still vivid of the First World War, and the collapse of the Maginot Line after their belief in its total invincibility had them reeling. They appeared to have no alternative or back-up plan of defence. Nevertheless, amongst the loyal French there was a passionate desire to defend their country and fight the *Boche* invader.

I had just landed my Hurricane at Merville after the retreat from Lille, when a French *sous-officier* came up to me at the head of a column of men, who were all wearing light-blue World War I uniforms. They were towing an antiquated 75-mm gun by hand, which dated from even earlier, as did its ammunition. They were a reserve unit, and the middle-aged *sous-officier* told me all they wanted to do was kill *les Boches*. How could they do this?

I asked him why he had singled me out, and where his officers were; he replied that I had been pointed out as an Englishman who spoke some French, and that he had not seen any officers. Luckily I knew there was a British Army unit nearby, and told him they could go there. At least they would be fed.

After ten days of non-stop fighting in the air we were completely worn out. Accommodation was nil in the village, and we young pilots were thankful to have clean straw to sleep on in a pig-sty. It was to be my last night in France, as next morning, on an early reconnaissance, I was shot up and crashed on landing. My CO and closest friend Johnny Dewar, who thankfully was still alive although his arm was in a sling after a crash as a result of enemy action, ordered me back to the UK. I was so exhausted, all I can remember is that the aircraft – it might have been an old Handley Page 42 of the newly created BOAC, with Red Cross markings – was flown by someone I knew well, Captain Bill Cummings. I also remember how small and green the fields of Kent looked.

I remember little about my arrival in England, except that it was at Hendon. Somehow I made my way to my home in Surbiton. My mother was not a little surprised by my unannounced arrival, took one look at me, and sent me to bed, where I slept without moving for 36 hours. She became quite concerned, and actually called the doctor, who said I was obviously completely exhausted, and should just be left to sleep.

CHAPTER FOUR

THE BATTLE OF BRITAIN

I eventually surfaced from my deep sleep, with no idea of the passage of time, but feeling refreshed. Much to my mother's consternation, my first action was to get in touch with the Air Ministry, our part of which was situated at Adastral House at the southern end of Kingsway in London. This has now become St Catherine's House, and holds the official records of UK births, marriages and deaths, although a plaque on the wall outside commemorates its former name. Whenever I see it, it always brings back memories of the central part it played in my life.

When I reported there I was told that 87 Squadron would be reforming at Church Fenton, near Leeds. They said leave could be granted by the squadron, but that the prime objective was to establish a coherent unit again. I had arrived back on 20 May, had my long sleep, and reached Church Fenton by train on the 26th.

Johnny Dewar and I flew down to Dover right away to welcome the Dunkirk heroes. Operation Dynamo, the evacuation of the beaches, began on the evening of the 26th, and there had been reports of anti-RAF feeling, in that not enough had been done to stop the Germans strafing the beaches while the evacuation was taking place. From the survivors, however, all we heard was, 'Give'em hell whenever you can.' They knew that we had been doing our best, without respite. These men had no equipment, and readily understood our similar predicament, for none of us had been adequately prepared for this war. The bravery and fortitude of these exhausted men as they came ashore left me misty-eyed. We watched some of the Guards, although practically asleep on their feet, form up, pull themselves to attention and *march* off the dockside. I felt very proud to be British, and the thought in my mind was that we could never be defeated.

The Navy was magnificent, ferrying every man they possibly could rescue back to England. They braved attack from the German gun batteries, which by this time were in range of the Channel, as well as strafing and bombing from the air. Throughout it all they never ceased to tend the exhausted men, many of whom were seriously wounded, with no places available on a hospital ship.

Working with them were the famous 'Little Ships', the hundreds of privately-owned little boats with which families had had fun on the rivers, or with just a solitary owner who had enjoyed a weekend sail. Every shape and size responded to the call for help in saving the beleaguered men, endlessly crossing and recrossing the Channel to Dunkirk. Many were invaluable as they could go into shallow water and take a few men at a time out to the larger vessels. The soldiers waited stoically, hour upon hour standing in the miraculously calm sea, helpless targets for the Luftwaffe, all the time praying that there might be room on the next vessel to reach them.

A grateful nation later acknowledged its debt to the 'Little Ships', and every boat that participated was given a commemorative plaque. Several little boats that sailed from Surbiton-on-Thames survive to this day. It still brings a lump to my throat whenever I walk where these boats are moored, and I catch a glimpse of one of those plaques proudly displayed on the foredeck.

One interesting fact that came to light at this time was that doctors who treated the wounded, and especially those suffering from burns, found that they had benefited from being in the salt water. Until then the healing qualities of salt water had not been fully appreciated. The long ordeal of the wounded standing in the sea cleansed their wounds, in many cases causing healing much faster than would normally have been expected.

Throughout the evacuation the RAF had naturally done all it could to defend the almost helpless men and ships, but we were woefully outnumbered in men and machines. The ultimate achievement was that some 338,000 men were lifted from the beaches, whereas the most optimistic estimate of the planners had been about 30,000. It seemed that the whole nation held its breath whilst nothing short of a miracle took place. How is it that we British seem on so many occasions to snatch victory from defeat?

Twenty-five years later, the film *The Battle of Britain* showed Al Deere, one of our New Zealand pilots in the RAF, about to take off to escape to England. Seeing a French friend of his watching his departure with despair on his face, Al reacted typically. He threw out his parachute saying, 'Come on, we will make it together somehow!' The Frenchman scrambled into the Hurricane and Al sat upon the Frenchman's lap which made for a very difficult take-off. But they did make it, and the incident as depicted in the film is a true one. In fact, several pairs flew back in single-seaters, ready to face the next onslaught of the Germans in the Battle of Britain.

My groundcrew remained in France for a short time after I left, to destroy any equipment that had to be abandoned. What fuel could not be used was blown up, or used to burn anything that might be useful to the enemy. Every serviceable aircraft was flown out, of course, but mine, alas, was past that.

Many years later I heard stories of how the downward-hinged cockpit door of my last Hurricane, in which I had managed to make my final landing at Merville, had been brought back to England by one of my groundcrew, George Mowat. He had removed it before the aircraft had to be destroyed. I kept trying to discover its whereabouts, as I heard of it turning up in various museums. At last I traced it to the Air Historical Branch in Whitehall, where it had been placed for safe-keeping. I made an appointment to visit the office, and could scarcely believe my eyes when it was brought out and the serial number on it, L1630, proved that it was indeed mine. Of course, the Branch could not part with what was officially Government property, but it was signed over to me for safe-keeping when I explained that I wanted it to go on display in the Shoreham Aircraft Museum in Kent. This museum has excellent security, and they liked the fact that all its profits go to RAF charities, especially to help the 'Guinea Pigs' (the badly burnt pilots).

This door proved to be of great interest, and younger generations find it hard to believe how fragile our aircraft were. To us at the time, though, they seemed a haven of safety! I like to feel that my beloved old Hurricane is still in some way alive and of use.

In recent years I have been able to make contact by letter with George. He told me he been flown back to England, where Lord Trenchard (founder of the RAF) was greeting the homecoming aircraft, and congratulated George on bringing back the door. Much to his disappointment George was not allowed to keep it, and the Military Police had relieved him of his burden, as it was Government property.

Despite the notion of 'Government property', both aircrews and groundcrews felt fiercely possessive of 'their' aircraft. The relationship between the fitters, riggers and armourers and 'their' pilots was unique, and worked both ways. I only discovered much later with what great concern and anxiety they would be awaiting their pilot's return. Often their concern would be turned to sorrow, and for a time there would be a quietness which was almost tangible, as everyone went about his work, each with his own thoughts and memories of a very personal relationship.

Fifty-eight years on I have just met up with George again, and he told me very quietly how true this was. He also told me that as they destroyed the final remains of our aircraft, and the last serviceable ones flew out, the German tanks were already at the edge of the airfield. He gave me a poem he had written about 87 Squadron: I include it here with pride exactly as he wrote it.

The Fighting 87s

The Fighting 87 plunged into wartime first
With Hurricane and pilots brave, prepared to do or die,
And many did, the roll is great, now 'Airmen of the Sky'.
To Foreign soil in fine and stormy weather
Pilots and crew all pulling together.
True top Old England and Freedom's Honour,
Giving the Enemy no easy ride,
Filling the skies, with dedication and pride.
The Merville Mill, the Lille hangars spring to mind,
Dossing down on palliasses, and whatever you could find.
Back Home across the Channel, preparing for England's Blitzkrieg attack,
Posted here and there to drive the foe right back,
Pursuing Flying Bombs and cover for our towns.
And in our final Fighter's Fight our 'Battle of Britain'
Many sacrifices but each one giving of his best.
The turn of Tide, the Bombers did the rest.
When peaceful days upon them fell, away to Italy and Germany to end.
Well done 87. Your name will never die,
We salute all living comrades, and those 'Up in the Sky'.
Your name shall never end and memories passed from friend to friend.
When I depart and maybe go to Heaven,
I hope to join the ranks of good old 87.

G.A.M. 20/5/97

This poem and a letter I received at Christmas 1989 from my rigger describes, I think more eloquently than I ever could, how we felt in those days. I met Francis Pecket some while back at an 87 Squadron reunion, and we have kept in touch ever since. He wrote:

Now the festive season of Christmas is nearly with us, time rolls on. As this time approaches I cannot forget the years, also Christmases past, especially the ones which I had in the RAF while in B-Flight with 87 Squadron at Debden.

The one which will forever remain in my memory is 1937.

> Most of the squadron personnel, including pilots and groundcrews, proceeded on leave, usually for twelve days or more, or whatever was due to them, leaving a skeleton staff of volunteers from the squadron to remain. Usually these were Scotsmen or Geordies, who preferred to be away for the New Year.
>
> Most of the officers came up to the hangar in civilian clothes, usually the day prior to the day of the squadron stand-down, to wish their groundcrews the compliments of the season.
>
> I can still visualise Voase Jeff in a smart double-breasted heavy overcoat, grey suit, brown suede shoes, and immaculately dressed, and his black hair parted at the side, carefully brushed, walking across the hangar out of the small side entrance door to the hangar.
>
> Alas this was to be the last year of an uneasy peace, as the following year 1938 was to be the year of the Czechoslovakian crisis, when, as you will remember, Dennis, a percentage of pilots and groundcrews had to be available at all times. This put the spanner in the works, so to say.
>
> Then of course Christmas 1939 we were in France on the Belgian border, at Lille Seclin, in the frost and snow, the most adverse conditions. The following year 1940 I had left the squadron and was in Malta.

He ends his letter:

> In the meantime take great care of yourselves. God keep you safe in His keeping.
>
> Most Kind Regards,
> From one 87 Sqn B-Flight Veteran to Another,
> Yours,
> Francis.

I owe both Francis and George so much, for they taught me such a lot. They have both gone on to do well in their lives and, typically, have both been concerned in helping with worthwhile charity work. Voase Jeff was always a special pilot to Francis, and it was tragic that he was killed early in the Battle of Britain.

After the war, when I was back in London, I was asked to participate in a BBC programme called *What's My Line*? You signed on in front of a panel of TV stars, who then questioned you to try and discover what you did for a living. In my case one of the panel was Kenneth Horne. He had been in the RAF and we had often met in the RAF

Club, but he never let on that he recognised me. After the panel had found out what one's line was (or not, as the case might be), there was a little general conversation about it. I told them what a marvellous support our groundcrews had been to us all, and what a magnificent job they had done in keeping our aircraft serviceable. I was stopped on my way out of the studios by a BBC official, who told me that ever since my remarks the telephone had scarcely stopped ringing with callers thanking me for what I had said.

Our groundcrews took enormous pride in keeping 'our' aircraft in peak condition, and it must have been very discouraging to have us return with them riddled with bullet holes and, as one of them put it, 'all our good work messed up'. Yet, perversely, they were proud of our battle scars. The greater the damage sustained, the greater the pride with which it was shown off to other groundcrews.

Towards the end of the Battle of France, Air Marshal Dowding, who was in charge of the fighter defence of the UK, had been put under extreme pressure by the French and British politicians alike to send more RAF fighters over to France. With great foresight, he realised that with the very limited numbers at his disposal he must conserve what he had to defend the British Isles, otherwise the war would be lost.

The Luftwaffe greatly outnumbered us, and Dowding had written to the air minister telling him this in no uncertain terms, and these comments were forwarded to the prime minister. The result had inevitably to be that no more fighters could be spared for France if the British Isles were to be saved. As well as the shortage of aircraft, Dowding was deeply conscious of the great losses of the limited number of experienced pilots he had already suffered in France, for these pilots were virtually irreplaceable at the time.

He was a great leader, with a deep affection for his young pilots, which was returned by all those who served under him. Great leadership is always a two-way intangible communication, and it is not always popular with the political hierarchy at a time of crisis. We felt implicit trust in Dowding, and gave him unswerving loyalty. Only those held in affection are known by their nicknames, and his was 'Stuffy'.

Years later, when I was a participant in a seminar in the USA on the Battle of Britain, a talk with a German ace highlighted the difference between the leadership of the two air forces. Dowding always understood our problems, and we knew he did. In contrast, the Luftwaffe ace said, 'When we were winning Goering was popular with us, because he praised us a lot, but when things went badly he called us cowards, and then we did not like him so much, and he was not so popular.' To my mind, nothing could show the difference between our leaders more clearly.

During a different seminar another German ace told me of an occasion when he had to report at the end of the day to his commanding officer, who was Goering. He was ushered into his personal apartments, and he could not believe his eyes. Goering was clad in a long brocade robe, his hair swathed in a hair net held by a large ruby clasp in the middle of his forehead. The mind boggles that such a man could be leading a country in wartime. My German friend said he did not know where to look.

In the crucial Battle of Britain Dowding was lucky to have a brilliant leader under him, Keith Park. He was a New Zealander, and a World War I fighter ace. He was in charge of the fighter defence of the south-east of England, designated as 11 Group. Park was 6 ft 3 in, good-looking and altogether a charismatic personality, very different from Dowding who was quiet and reserved. Park was a magnificent and loyal support to him. He was a brilliant tactician, and we were all happy to follow his ruling, although at first it did not seem as if we were beating the enemy. We had been told our prime target was to aim at the leaders of the bomber formations on their way to their target. Park knew that this was difficult, because of course the escorting fighters did all they could to stop us. Park always tried to maintain personal contact with his pilots, and, flying his own Hurricane, would visit the stations under his command. These occasions were always a great morale boost, and we knew he cut a lot of red tape by taking any of our specific requests direct to higher authority. We were lucky to have him, and the British will always owe him a great debt.

In a matter of weeks we reformed 87 Squadron, bringing the numbers back up to 12 aircraft, with four reserve. All the time we were deeply conscious of the urgency of the situation, and of the acute shortage of experienced pilots. We were still tired from our efforts and lack of sleep in France, and I will never forget the kindness and warm hospitality we were shown at Church Fenton by the wonderful people of Yorkshire. We did not want gin and tonics, we longed for the home comforts of tea in the kitchen. Instinctively they seemed to understand this, and made us feel at home and part of the family.

Much to my surprise, I received notification that I had been awarded the DFC on 31 May and a Bar to it on 5 June, and that I was to attend an investiture to be held by the King at Buckingham Palace. To my delight Johnny Dewar was called to attend the same investiture, to receive his DSO and DFC. We felt very proud, as they were some of the earliest RAF awards of the war, and altogether it proved to be a very memorable and happy occasion. It was wonderful that my mother was able to share it with me.

Johnny and I flew down to London and stayed overnight. Mother and I were driven up to London from Surbiton by an old friend who had flown in the Royal Naval Air Service (RNAS) in World War I, Captain Hallett-Carpenter. He had pioneered landing on an aircraft carrier. In those days the aircraft had to be held down by hand, indeed by as many as possible to prevent it from slipping off the deck after it had landed. I met up with Johnny and other RAF recipients of decorations, and we were especially pleased to find that we were sharing the investiture with some of the heroes of Dunkirk.

It was amusing to watch the nervousness and discomfort of all these wonderful men while waiting to meet the King. After unflinchingly facing incredible dangers, they seemed far more disconcerted by this occasion. Somehow many of them had had the foresight to arm themselves with hip flasks, and these were generously passed round for a quick 'snort', to brace ourselves. To have had this day with them made it a unique memory, and His Majesty also seemed to share our pleasure.

Johnny and I spent an all-too-short couple of days in London, and he came to lunch with mother. She fell under his spell, as did everyone who knew him. Altogether it was a much-needed break from the stress we had been under. We returned to Church Fenton refreshed and in good spirits. We did our best with the fresh pilots to get them as much flying practice as we could before the air battles which we knew lay before us, because we were aware that, although our boys had more than enough courage and dedication, they were as yet no match for the experienced German pilots.

Typically, one day two new pilots reported to me for duty. They were both about 18 years old, and each had less than ten hours on Hurricanes. I felt I must try and help such keen youngsters as much as possible, and give them all the chance I could to become more experienced before facing the enemy. I was already conscious that, at the great age of 22, I was immeasurably senior to boys like this. Looking back to those fateful days in France I knew I owed my life very largely to the fact that I had had about 300 hours on my Hurricane before I had to face the enemy at all. In those early days my newly sewn-on DFC and Bar ribbon helped a lot to inspire confidence, and I flew with the boys as much as I could, training them in formation flying and aerial combat. They had to learn to throw their Hurricanes around the sky as they would in a dogfight. In the time available this was an almost impossible task, but we did our best.

Whilst training these newcomers one of them hit my elevator with his wingtip, and I suddenly found myself aiming straight up at the sky!

I eventually landed, with great difficulty, and ruefully surveyed the damage. The young pilot who had hit me came running over full of apologies, as he had anxiously watched my problems as I came in to land. I told him no further action would be taken. He was cautioned, and I knew he had learnt a hard lesson. As always, the groundcrew got on with repairing the elevator, and the plane was flying again the next day. It illustrated yet again the Hurricane's resilience and toughness, despite the deceptively fragile appearance of this fabric-covered aircraft.

I was able to express my gratitude in person to the workers at Hawker Aircraft's factory in Kingston, which built parts of the aircraft, as my mother was a friend of Mr and Mrs Frank Sherras; he was Hawker's contracts manager, much respected for his financial expertise. He asked me if, some time when I was visiting my mother, I could go along in my uniform with him on a morale-boosting visit. It gave me the greatest pleasure to do this, and the visit proved a great success.

Whilst this re-equipping was going on, in the relative safety of Yorkshire, we were sent south as soon as we were deemed ready once again for operations. We re-formed at Exeter, under our old commander in France, a World War I fighting ace, Wing Commander Jack Borêt. Apart from the joy of meeting him again, we had the additional satisfaction of Johnny Dewar being promoted to Wing Commander Flying at Exeter.

Very soon after settling in at Exeter the Battle of Britain began, as we had expected. From the start we were fighting vastly superior numbers of fighters, escorting phalanxes of bombers. We also had to contend with the rear gunners of these bombers, who seemed better controlled than those we had encountered over France. Despite this, we continued to attack the leading aircraft whenever possible, and with some success.

The Germans had changed their tactics, and their bombers were now always escorted by fighters, which meant that we had to get a bomber quickly before the Messerschmitt Bf 109s were on our tails. It was very different from France, where their bombers seemed to be unescorted and easier prey.

As confirmed by some of the German pilots I met 40 years later, it was this attritional form of attack that paid dividends. On my asking one of them,'Why did you stop coming over?', his reply was, 'You had shot down too many of our leaders.' I saw this once again as a complete vindication of Dowding's leadership, and of Keith Park's tactics. Subsequently I have received exactly the same response from other German aces. This was the first time that we in Britain had learnt from combatants who took part in the raids how our attacks had affected them, and had thus made a major contribution to overall victory.

Possibly our national characteristics also had a bearing. As a race, the Germans are immaculately disciplined, and will go through hell and high water to follow orders from their leader, but they do have to have this leadership. German courage is unsurpassed; so is the British, yet the British courage is very different. In our island race perhaps every man is an individual island in his own right, for certainly every man is prepared to be a leader if circumstances demand. Basically we are a lazy race, and are at our best only when pushed to the limit. When we first stood alone after the capitulation of Europe, Churchill had it right when he said that history would record that 'this was their finest hour'.

The number of sorties we flew each day in the Battle of Britain varied greatly. Some days we flew a lot, and others were spent sitting around at readiness. The photos are familiar, pilots with a dog at their feet sitting in the sunshine, a very relaxed-looking scene. A few minutes later those same young men could be in the air fighting for their lives, and some of the dogs would wait in vain for the return of their masters. To this day the sound of a telephone can make me jump. The battle seemed to go on endlessly, as did the glorious summer weather. How we prayed for clouds in the sky to give us cover, but they never seemed to come.

Meanwhile, the ordinary people of southern England watched the sky being filled by our woven vapour trails. Little did we know they were writing history in the skies. Many people told me in later years that their most vivid and abiding memory of the time is the criss-cross of white trails on the blue heavens as these 'knights of the skies' fought to preserve our freedom.

Through September 1940 the Luftwaffe's raids increased in both frequency and intensity, and then the proportion of bombers coming over at night grew even more rapidly. Between the world wars the RAF had paid little serious attention to the problem of intercepting bombers on dark nights, and what soon became known as the 'Blitz' presented us with grave problems.

To meet public demand, Churchill had to ask Dowding to switch some of our more experienced day forces to the role of night fighter. I was one of the pilots chosen to seek the enemy at night over Bristol and Cardiff. It proved to be a complete waste of time, as it was impossible to find the enemy by visual contact. Ground Control did better, but until we had the Beaufighters with radar it was a hopeless task. On more than one occasion I hit the enemy slipstreams but still could see nothing, an eerie feeling. For instance, our closing speed of 500 mph (800 km/h) says it all, and we desperately awaited aircraft with airborne radar.

My childhood memories were vividly revived by the knowledge I was flying over Cardiff, my beloved grandmother's home. On the spur of the moment one day I wrote her a short letter, saying we knew they were all having a very tough time, but that she must try not to worry too much, as I and some of my friends were flying over her at night, doing our best to look after Cardiff and to win the battle. I had not seen her since I was a child, but had always loved her dearly. Some years later a cousin of mine told me how Grandma had treasured that letter, and had told one and all in the village, 'Isn't it wonderful to think of little Dennis flying around up there looking after us?'. Almost as if I had my own pair of wings! It apparently gave her immense comfort for the rest of the war, when in fact I was in the Western Desert or Burma. One never knows how such a spontaneous little letter like that can come to mean so much. I shall always regret that by the time I was in contact with the family again, she had died, so I never saw her again.

Night flying was hazardous, to say the least, and many of our experienced pilots were killed. Because of the countrywide 'black-out', not a single light was visible, so we had no sense of any horizon, and no guiding lights for our take-off. We had to rely on instruments alone, which in those days were nothing like as sophisticated as those of today. Having got airborne, we then had to find our patrol lines at night. This was done with the aid of three tiny 'glim' lamps set down on a predestined location, usually on a hill. Once we had found this, we then had to fly on a set compass course for a specified number of minutes, until we found another set of glim lamps; we then took another heading until we reached our patrol line. After about 30 minutes we had to find our way back. It was incredibly hazardous, and one of the most frustrating tasks I have ever undertaken.

Weymouth was always a prime target because of the Navy oil tanks. I remember following Johnny Dewar with my two faithful 18-year-olds, by this time considered to be fairly experienced pilots, into a large armada of Heinkels bent on bombing those tanks. There were six of us in all, while the remainder of the squadron tried to keep the Bf 109s away from us. We were assured that some Spitfires would be sent in to help deal with the enemy fighters. I could not do much for my youngsters, except put them in line-astern behind me, and tell them to pick their own targets.

I was greatly relieved to find one of my young pilots, who had obviously been in the thick of it, safe on my return to base. On the way back we had heard from the other on his R/T that he had had his left hand shot off, but that he hoped he could manage to make it. We heard no more, and with great sadness realised that this gallant boy would have no hope of surviving such a wound, with no means of staunching the bleeding. I had accounted for one of the enemy bombers; I saw it catch fire and crash, but this was no recompense for our loss. Many of our young pilots were killed in their first fight, but each one played his part in winning the final victory. No man can give more than his life in devotion to a cause.

An incident with a happier ending took place on the afternoon of 11 August. I was returning to base with not much ammunition or fuel to spare when I saw a pilot bail out of a stricken Hurricane at about 20,000 feet, which had been in the same dogfight with me shortly before. To my horror, I saw a Messerschmitt closing in and firing on the pilot as he hung in his parachute harness. I chased after the German and fired a one-second burst; he peeled off very quickly. Then a second 109 appeared, and he also was lining up to have a go at the helpless pilot. I turned on the German and managed to chase him away also. When I was quite sure he had departed I returned and circled round my friend, whom I had recognised as John Cock, an Australian from our squadron. To my relief I could see that he was not badly wounded. I watched until I saw him come down in the sea, where he managed to free himself from his parachute, and divest himself of his clothes in order to swim ashore to Chesil Beach. Being an Australian he was a good swimmer, and this was fortunate for he had a badly injured left arm, which had part of his TR.9 R/T embedded in it. I was delighted to see him make the shore, get out of the water wearing only a pair of light blue underpants, and wave to me with his uninjured arm.

When, 50 years after the Battle of Britain, the prestigious book *So Few* was produced, in which 25 surviving pilots were asked to write an account of their most vivid memory of that time, I chose to tell this story. Of course it is especially good to feel one has been able to save the life of a friend. With a sense of relief I turned for home, but this was instantly replaced by a new anxiety when I looked at my fuel, which by now was very low. I made it back with about a thimbleful to spare.

There is an interesting sequel to this story. Many people have made a study of where crashed aircraft from those days are buried, and in 1983 one such group felt sure they had found the location of John Cock's Hurricane. They found out John's address in Australia, and wrote to him to say that they were hoping to salvage what remained of the aircraft, as they were pretty sure it was his. If he could come to England, they would postpone the start of their operations until he could be there. John could not resist this, and arranged a trip over with his wife.

The young salvage team helped to organise a small reunion of members of 87 Squadron, some of whom had not met since the war. More details of the original incident now came to light. First I learned that I now had another confirmed 'kill' to add to my previous total of 20. John had watched what was going on as he drifted down in his parachute, and said that the first German I had seen off had crashed. This I had never been able to confirm as I was fully occupied seeing off number two.

The salvage experts told us that it appeared that John's Hurricane had come down in a flat spin, and had landed in the soft mud bank between the sea and a tidal lagoon. They confirmed that it was not buried very deep. We were all amazed when talking to John to hear him say that at no time did he ever have any thought that he might be killed, but that he had been interested in watching the shroud lines of his parachute 'pinging' as they were severed by the German's machine-gun fire, and wondered how many it would need to remain intact to keep him supported! He obviously meant it, when he said he never had any doubt that he would survive the war. Not many of us had felt so optimistic.

The boys doing the salvaging looked after us veterans marvellously, providing us with extra wraps and rubber boots where necessary when we went out on an old barge to where the wreckage was lying in only a few feet of water. It was so shallow the boys could dive in just wet suits and snorkels. The light metal was battered like a crumpled toy, but parts of the wooden propeller came out preserved by the silt. The nuts on the oil-feed pipes unscrewed as if they had just been done up, and out flowed oil which had not seen the light of day for over 40 years. Then they recovered a panel with the serial number on it, confirming it was John's, which was an emotional moment.

Just before John left to return to Australia a small dinner party was arranged at which the boys presented him with the gunsight from his Hurricane beautifully mounted on a plinth of English oak. I think everyone's eyes were misty; John had to take his glasses off and wipe them before he could make his speech of thanks.

It was so good to pick up that friendship with John again. Soon after his return to Australia he sent me a little paper-knife he had carved from a piece of his propeller they had given him. He said he had made one for both of us. He incised his Hurricane's code letters LK-V, and the dates 11.8.40 and 3.5.83, on the handle, and it is one of my most treasured possessions. Sadly, he died of cancer a few years ago.

It is a pity that so many of the younger generation who have grown up since the war do not know about the great debt we owe to the loyalty and bravery of the members from what was then the British

Empire, both Dominions and Colonies, before it became known as the Commonwealth. They gave their service and their lives for the cause of freedom, and to support the mother country in her hour of need. Their enormous contribution to the ultimate victory is too often forgotten. I have always regretted the manner in which they were to all intents and purposes just cast aside, when we joined the Common Market, now the EC. It makes me feel uncomfortable when my friends from the Commonwealth have to enter this country via the 'foreign country' channel at Customs.

Among them, I have already mentioned Keith Park from New Zealand, and John Cock from Australia. There was also 'Sailor' Malan from South Africa, and Ian Smith, who later became prime minister of Rhodesia. General Smuts, the prime minister of South Africa, was counted a personal friend by King George VI, and it was he who rushed troops to protect the Kenyan border with Abyssinia (now Ethiopa) when Italy entered the war. The Italians had conquered Abyssinia in the 1930s.

The bravery of the Australians and the New Zealanders in Crete, the Western Desert and in Italy is legendary. In fact, it was the Australians who cleared the Western Desert minefields before the big advance, using just their bayonets! It is essential that we never forget the heroism and sacrifice of the members of the Commonwealth in our hour of need. They believed in us then, and our current generation must carry that torch forward.

The Germans called 15 August 1940 *Adlertag* (Eagle Day). It was the day when Goering threw the whole might of the Luftwaffe at us, but we managed to withstand the onslaught. Then, on the night of 24/25 August, a German bomber became separated from the main force and mistakenly jettisoned its bombs over London. This gave Churchill the excuse to bomb Berlin, something that the German people had been told would never happen. Hitler was furious, and decided there and then to forget his prohibition on bombing London and to concentrate on bombing our cities instead of our airfields, in order to try to break the morale of the civilian population. This change of tactics in fact lost him the battle. We were at a critically low point in both men and fighter aircraft, and our bases had been badly damaged. This respite enabled us to start building up our numbers once more, and generally recoup.

CHAPTER FIVE

THE BATTLE IS WON

Operation *Seelöwe* (Sealion) was the name the Germans gave to their plan for the invasion of England. For months we had watched the build-up of barges and landing craft at the French and Belgian Channel ports, realising only too well what this meant.

From about 15 September 1940 I was interested to notice that, far from these numbers increasing, they were decreasing. This date is taken as being the date when Sealion was officially cancelled, and has since been kept as Battle of Britain Day, our official anniversary of victory in the Battle of Britain.

German pilots later told me that about this time some of their number developed what came to be known as 'Channel Sickness' as they dreaded the thought of yet another raid escorting the bombers across the English Channel. Remarkably, Adolf Galland, one of their most famous aces, refused to allow his fighters to carry radio, in order to lighten the aircraft to permit it to gain greater height and prolong the time the fuel would last. This edict was very unpopular with many of the pilots, but he was adamant. His pilots were also told that they must stay with the bombers, even if their red fuel warning light came on. I was flabbergasted to learn that on one raid 19 out of 21 Bf 109s crashed in the Channel through obeying this crazy order. The pilots were never found, and losses of this nature were never publicised.

At about 4.30 am on 15 September I was at readiness in my dispersal hut, near my Hurricane, when the order came to scramble. By this time we were allowed to sleep in the beds in the dispersal hut. We never fully undressed, but it was realised that we had to get sleep and rest when we could. When the order came to scramble I pulled on my flying kit over my pyjamas, as my groundcrew were starting the aircraft, and we were airborne in less than five minutes.

My favourite controller, Dudley Mumford (who became a well-known antique dealer in the West Country after the war), vectored me on to a single incoming bomber, with his familiar call-up, 'Crocodile Blue Leader, I have some trade for you.' It was a Heinkel 111, carrying out an early-morning meteorological reconnaissance. I was lucky to get behind it before it could escape into the clouds, and gave it a long and accurate burst from close astern. As often happened if one hit the hydraulics, the wheels fell down, and then my No. 2 fired at it. The aircraft later crashed into the sea. I reported to Dudley what I had done, and said that it was the first time I had shot down an aircraft in my pyjamas. Little did I appreciate that that Heinkel was to be the first of at least 60 Luftwaffe aircraft shot down on 15 September.

Shortly after this I was posted to 213 Squadron at Tangmere, near Chichester, on the Sussex Coast. I was to see more of Tangmere than any other RAF station, eventually, to my delight, commanding it towards the end of my career. Tangmere is steeped in RAF history; indeed, it was famous for its connection with the Royal Flying Corps in World War I. Those pilots who knew it would say, 'One can always get in to Tangmere when the weather is dicey.' Chichester, and all the nearby villages, always took great pride in Tangmere, and not least, the civilian police were marvellous. They realised how important it was for us to be able to let off steam on the rare occasions when we could leave the station and get together in a pub. Instead of reproving us, they would drive us back to our own dispersal hut!

At Tangmere in September 1940 I met Jack Borêt again, who had been promoted to group captain, and was station commander, which made us feel we were in good hands. I was OC B-Flight of 213 Squadron, and another friend, Billy Drake, was OC A-Flight. Tangmere had just been badly dive-bombed by Ju 87s. Not only had it caused considerable damage, but many WAAFs (members of the Women's Auxiliary Air Force) were killed, as the raid coincided with a change of watches in the operations room. Despite shock and great sadness at the loss of their friends, the girls maintained high morale throughout, and showed great devotion to their duty.

Soon after my arrival I heard that Johnny Dewar's body had been found, riddled with bullets; he had been murdered while descending in his parachute. A man of his calibre, leadership and character can never be replaced, and all who had the privilege of knowing him felt this. Indeed, 40 years later I met a man who owned a hotel in Durban, South Africa, and Johnny's name came up. He could scarcely believe that I had known him, and told me that Johnny had been his head boy at his public school, and even then he made an outstanding impression on all who knew him. The manner of his death made me a more remote character, yet even more dedicated to destroying the enemy. He was the last close friend of my young days, and after losing so many in France, I had withdrawn from making any more.

We flew a lot from Tangmere, which was strategically placed within easy reach of London, Brooklands (which made Hurricanes), Southampton (where Spitfires were assembled), and the naval base at Portsmouth.

On 19 October, I and my No. 2, another experienced pilot, were asked if we would investigate an intruder which had been picked up on radar. He appeared to be thinking he could duck safely under the clouds, and return unchallenged to his base in France. We had been plagued by many such nuisance raids, and as Peter Townsend said in one of his last interviews on TV over 50 years later, 'It made us especially angry because they always seemed to come over at lunch time.'

Though the cloud base was at less than 100 feet we made the coast safely, and flew east as directed by Control. We intercepted the German, a Ju 88. He jettisoned his bombs in the sea, and I engaged him from the rear, trying to get my usual close range to make sure of my target. After my first long burst the rear gunner stopped firing, and I then pulled to one side to let my No. 2 have a go. He did, and more damage was done, smoke pouring from the 88's engines. We flew alongside, and saw the German pilot slumped over his controls. I could not believe the aircraft could still fly after such punishment. I left it dipping towards the sea, black smoke belching from both engines, but felt that, as the coast of France was looming, we had better return to Tangmere.

Upon landing I rang up Control, and told them what had happened. Control was elated, having already heard from the French Resistance through their contact in London, and their words were, 'Send us back more like this one!' I was amazed to learn that we were in such immediate contact with the Resistance.

All the crew but the pilot were dead, and he was badly wounded, and the aircraft was a complete write-off. I have been told since that news of this episode got around the Luftwaffe at that time, and had a bad effect on morale. Anyway, it was, for a long time, the end of such intruder raids.

In November I was posted to 152 Squadron at RAF Warmwell, in Dorset, to command my first Spitfire flight. Much as I missed my Hurricane, I was enthralled by all the Spitfire had to offer. It was a beautiful aeroplane. About this time a new vhf (very high frequency) radio was introduced, and this made all the difference to our communications with each other. Of course, cockpit pressurisation was unheard of, but we did use oxygen sparingly from 10,000 feet upwards. I found this seemed to help keep my brain and reactions alert.

Reg Davies, the flight lieutenant in charge of our engineers, was aptly known as 'the wizard'. A slightly older man, he had been one of the engineers who had worked on the winning Schneider Trophy team of racing seaplanes. As they won it three times running (1927, 1929 and 1931), England kept the trophy. I knew how fortunate the squadron was to have him.

Reg took a fatherly interest in us youngsters. In the absence of the CO one day, I had to run my first squadron orderly room. This is similar to a court in handing out punishment to miscreants, and in this case it was someone Reg had put on a charge. He prompted me that I must put my hat on before I took my seat behind the desk, and then called for the evil-doer to be marched in. Many years later, he recalled, 'They were all so young,' he said with an indulgent smile, 'The poor little sod didn't even know he had to put his hat on.'

As pilots, 152 were also inexperienced. Inevitably, there were mistakes and mishaps, which apart from danger to their lives, could mean damage to desperately needed aircraft. Many a time someone had to rush out and fire a red star from a Very pistol as a Spit was seen to be coming in to land with his wheels up. There were so many important points for new pilots to remember. One young pilot did land his Spitfire wheels-up, damaging it seriously. Much later, 'the wizard' told me he happened to have a 'spare' (!) Spitfire for immediate use, whilst he covered up the mistake with some rapid repair work.

One day the renowned artist Cuthbert Orde came to stay in our mess. He was compiling a book *Pilots of Fighter Command*, with his portraits and a short write-up which he also provided. It has become a classic. A World War I fighter pilot, he was a charming gentleman, and I felt very honoured to be one of the pilots chosen for his book.

When at Church Fenton earlier in the year I had been fortunate to have my portrait drawn by Sir William Rothenstein, a grandfatherly man to my own generation. He was famous, and had been a student of Rodin. The sculptor had obviously had a great influence on his pupil, for his portraits of the pilots were very powerful. I was fascinated that he took so much time drawing my hands, when he seemed to have completed the features comparatively quickly. When I asked about this, he was full of eloquent explanation, how important he considered hands to be, and how difficult they were to portray convincingly. He said they showed so much of the character of the model. My picture shows the sadness on such a young face, and the eyes still seem to reflect the horrors I had so recently witnessed in France, and was so different from the photos of the confident new pilot proudly showing off his wings. He generously gave us the opportunity to purchase the originals at a modest fee, but this was still beyond the reach of most of us. However, the originals were exhibited in the Imperial War Museum, and my mother was thrilled to go along and see me 'hung' there.

Towards the end of 1940 we began to feel that we at last had the measure of the Germans, and were beginning even to get on top. This may have been only a personal feeling, but there was something intangible in the general atmosphere. In retrospect, there are several occasions pointing to the turning point in the battle, but the greatest to my mind was the switch of the German bombing raids from our airfields to the towns, by which they mistakenly thought they could break the morale of the British people. It seemed it was largely pique on the part of Hitler and Goering, for no other explanation can be given. Suddenly the skies seemed empty, and gradually we realised that the great battle was over.

As a rest from operations I was sent from 152 Squadron to an operational training unit, where our fighting experience could be passed on to new pilots. OTUs were in the safer areas, and I was sent to No. 55 OTU at Usworth, just south of Newcastle. It is now the site of a Nissan car factory.

In all I spent two years in these units, and helped train pilots of many nationalities, including Norwegian, Polish, French, Dutch and Belgian. Many of them were already experienced from fighting before their countries were overrun, but they needed to be integrated into the RAF. We also had Canadians, as well as Americans (not officially in the war until the end of 1941) who had joined the Royal Canadian Air Force.

It was a most interesting and rewarding time. The calibre of the men concerned was exceptional, and their keenness to learn was matched only by their personal bravery. Many had overcome great personal dangers simply to get to England. Those from the Continent had made it by many circuitous routes, usually arriving with nothing but a few coins in their pockets. Many of the Norwegians had sailed across the North Sea in boats little larger than dinghies, proving their Viking ancestry was not forgotten.

Linguistic difficulties were overcome with good humour. We were all united in a common cause, and burned with a determination to regain freedom for those whose countries had been over-run.

After a few months at Usworth, I was promoted to squadron leader and appointed CFI (Chief Flying Instructor) of No 59 OTU. This was located at Crosby-on-Eden, near Carlisle and close to the great wall built by order of the Roman Emperor Hadrian. Here, some of the pilots were Free French, and on a momentous day we were visited by General Charles de Gaulle, their charismatic leader. I had to be host at the lunch for him, and he quickly realised the limitations of my French. To my surprise he gallantly did his best with his equally fractured English, and we managed to communicate with much humour, which was contrary to all I had been told of this very correct and unbending man. His great height and patrician appearance combined to give him an air of aloofness, but this, together with the sadness of his countenance when in repose, was instantly transformed by the sudden warmth of his smile.

The enthusiastic welcome given him by his fellow-countrymen, and their obvious loyalty to his cause and leadership, must have fortified him at a time when he was grief-stricken for his beloved France. He questioned me searchingly about the French pilots, and when I told him I was proud of them all, he seemed delighted. I felt he was happy to be in their company, and that they lifted his spirits. The visit was certainly a highlight for them, and I found I gained a deep respect for this uncompromising, disciplined man of high principle. Here most certainly was a leader. Whatever his failings, he passionately loved 'la belle France' as he called her, and was years later able to lead a grand parade up the Champs Elysées of liberated Paris.

I was fortunate indeed to have amongst my Free French pilots Lieutenant Henri Lafont. He had reached England having escaped from France via Spain, eventually arriving with only 30 centimes (a few pence) in his pocket, and a determination to continue the fight against the Germans. He was an excellent pilot, and displayed qualities of exceptional leadership and administrative ability. His English was of a high standard, and he proved to be invaluable to me, not only as an instructor but also as an interpreter.

Little did I think at the time, however, that after the war he was to become 'Mr Paris Air Show'. He built this up himself from its earliest days when it consisted of a field and a couple of sheds into 35 acres with displays and stands for worldwide aviation commerce. It is now acknowledged to be one of the world's largest air shows.

Just before his retirement in 1991, he invited me over to Paris to see the Air Show, and also to attend the annual reunion of the French Resistance leaders. This was an unprecedented gesture, as even the French outside the Resistance are not invited, let alone foreigners. The ceremony was held in the Chancery of the Cross of Lorraine, which was the emblem of the Free French Forces. The occasion was honoured by the Presidential Guard, resplendent in their magnificent uniforms, an impressive sight as they stood stiffly to attention and saluted each arriving guest.

It all made a deep impression on me, and I felt privileged to meet some of those heroic men, now battling with the years as well as the infirmities which were the legacy of their times of torture. Many were accompanied by their wives, some of whom had been in the Resistance themselves. One of the heroes I met was Monsieur Perrier, whose ancestors had started marketing the famous mineral water. He had long been confined to a wheelchair, but kept up his strength by exercising with Indian clubs, and so it was he who had the idea of the shape of the well-known bottle!

Everyone was in great spirits, and one could see what a happy time of reunion it was for them. Friendships forged in such traumatic times are unique, and I could relate to them as I thought of my own special friends who had survived from our Battle of Britain. Whenever we get together there is always laughter, and so it was at this gallant gathering. The occasion was enjoyed and savoured to the utmost despite sticks and wheelchairs, with the added relish of French food and wine.

The Air Show was well covered by the French press, and Henri introduced me to a young French reporter, and told him that I had shot down 14 German planes in the Battle of France. He shook my hand warmly, and without disturbing the cigarette in his mouth said, '*Mes félicitations, monsieur!*', and scribbled rapidly in his pad.

During that memorable three-day visit, I was travelling on a bus at the end of their rush hour, to go to visit Henri and his wife for dinner. It was a special weekend as it marked the anniversary of the liberation of Paris from the Germans and, as always, a great Tricolour hung down in the centre of the Arc de Triomphe. Billowing in the gentle breeze, it was a glorious sight. I was having trouble producing my correct fare for the patient driver of the bus, and as I stood in the crowded aisle, looking out rather anxiously to make sure I did not go past the stop I required, a young man manoeuvered his way up to me, carrying a very long and heavy antique firearm. He excused himself, saying he knew the English did not like to be accosted, but he had heard me trying to find out what my fare was, and so knew I was English. Very politely he said that whenever he had the opportunity of speaking to a Britisher he just liked to say, 'Thank you for our liberté.' I felt completely overwhelmed, and did not know what to say.

He had no idea I had been in any of the Services, except by my age I had obviously been through the war; I was not even wearing a Service tie. He confirmed the stop which I would need, and left a stop earlier himself, with an effusive farewell. A meeting I shall never forget. So many people feel the French really do not care about the British, and indeed almost dislike us, and meeting someone like this of a generation born not so long ago makes one realise just how wrong generalisations can be.

Next morning Henri had arranged that we were to have lunch with some of my former pupils who had been with us at Crosby and whom I had not met since 1941. Never will I forget that moment as their car doors opened and out got all four. Could it really be 50 years on ? I think we were none of us dry-eyed as we embraced warmly, and each of us was engulfed by his own special memories of all those years ago.

If Henri had hoped he would impress '*mon commandant*', he succeeded beyond his wildest dreams. The Paris Air Show was superb in every respect. Our visit was just after the Gulf War, and we saw all the latest airpower proudly displayed. Particularly of interest was the strange rectangular box that contained the famous Patriot missile which had played such a vital part in the successful conclusion to that conflict.

The American F-117A 'Stealth' aircraft was also on display. How well-named it is. There was something sinister and eerie about it. It looked almost like some nocturnal bird of prey from another world, with its dense black colour, which showed in silhouette from whichever angle one viewed it. Henri told me that no one was allowed to touch it, as its radar-defying coating was still a closely-guarded secret.

In complete contrast, I personally could feel nothing but amazement that I could walk right up to the latest Russian fighter and examine it closely and have my picture taken beside it. What a contrast to when I was Air Attaché in Hungary during the 1956 Uprising, and would take great risks to try and get long-distance photographs of very ordinary Soviet service aircraft to send back to the Ministry of Defence.

Our tour of the vast airshow was like a royal procession, with a metaphorical red carpet rolled out wherever we turned up. Only to be expected, I suppose, when hosted by Henri, who held in his gift every franchise. We met up with my former pupils for lunch, together with two of their wives, and Henri's wife Françoise. Of the four, three were French and the fourth was Belgian. All had done extremely well.

To return to the days of those memories, within a few months I was promoted to wing commander and made responsible for all training back at 55 OTU. There was at least one other Hurricane and Spitfire OTU, and we were able to share our problems and their solutions. The South African 'Sailor' Malan was Chief Instructor at the Spitfire OTU at Heston. He was the top-scoring ace at the time, an inspiration to his students and very popular with his contemporaries. I got to know him well, and he was always most helpful, and delightful company.

Soon after my return to Usworth, it was decided, in view of the balloon barrage over Newcastle and also in the hope of better weather, that 55 OTU would move to Annan, near Dumfries in Scotland. Moreover, this also moved it further from the enemy.

A regular training exercise was dinghy drill. We took the whole course of students by bus to the swimming baths at Carlisle. One of the students, in full flying kit, including his helmet, would leap into the bath and get into a pilot's inflatable dinghy with all possible speed, cheered on by the other students. This accomplished, relaxation at a popular pub was necessary, and, when the convivial evening ended at closing time, the bus returned everyone to base.

Whilst I was with 59 OTU at Crosby I was asked if I would take on an older man as my CGI (Chief Ground Instructor). I naturally asked about him, and discovered that as a boy he had sailed round the world as a deck-hand. In World War I he had flown with the RFC, but he broke his back in a crash. He had later been an aide to Sir Charles (later Lord) Portal, Chief of the Air Staff. As Gerald Bowman, he was an established author, and had a daily column in the *Evening News* as G. B. Mann. He sounded a most interesting character, and I was eager to see how he got on.

A kindly, unassuming man turned up, who, I quickly found out, had great warmth of personality as well as great knowledge and ability. Being just that bit older made him the perfect 'uncle' figure for the youngsters. They could confide in him in a manner that would be impossible for them to do with me. He could reassure them, and share his wealth of knowledge with them, and I soon saw how beneficial this was to all concerned. The students had a deep regard and affection for him, and he certainly had a great rapport with them, loving their youth and enthusiasm. I knew I had struck gold; I had the ideal man for the job, and so I made sure he moved with me back to 55 OTU. We forged a friendship that lasted until his death some 35 years later.

Gradually I began to find out that, apart from a brilliant intellect, he was indeed multi-talented. One of his greatest gifts was the way in which he took an inquiring interest in any subject to which he was exposed. Part of his job was to take the pupils through all aspects of the cockpit, teaching them how everything worked. All too often, he had seen that lack of thorough knowledge had cost lives. Gradually he managed to gather bits and pieces of equipment and put them together to build up the first cockpit simulator, which enabled young pilots to spend hours familiarising themselves with the controls of their aircraft without any danger or cost.

Like so many people with inventive and rewarding ideas, 'Bow' as we affectionately called him, never got any recognition for this idea. Another invention his lively mind conjured up was the little cartoon character of the 'Gremlin'. This little fellow became almost real to all of us in the RAF. We came to blame things that aggravatingly went wrong on the activities of the mischievous and devilishly-clever Gremlins. I treasure to this day the original of the demobbed Gremlin cartoon he gave me. The invention of the Gremlin was later ascribed to someone else, but typically, Bow said it was not worth having a fight about.

OTU training was intensive and demanding. We older pilots, aged 22 or 23, were conscious of the fact that there was much to be learnt. Apart from their youth at 18 or 19, many pupils had less than ten hours' experience on a Hurricane. They had learnt to fly in the cloudless blue skies of Canada and the USA, and had no experience of our treacherous weather conditions, let alone of deadly combat. The main role of instructors was to instil into the young pilots confidence in their own ability to fly and also to fight with their Hurricanes, even in vile weather.

Knowing the system whereby pilots like myself would be supposedly sent for a 'rest' period, at the end of an operational duties posting, to instruct at OTUs, I did my best to select for my OTU as many as I could whom I knew personally, or knew something about, and there were many happy reunions. I thus collected a wonderful cross-section of talent and character at these OTUs.

Squadron Leader J.A.S. Storrar, known as 'Jas', pronounced 'Jazz', was in charge of air-gunnery training. This all-important subject could not have been in more competent hands. He had falsified his age at 16, and by 17 had destroyed his first enemy aircraft. A charismatic figure although so young, he inspired tremendous confidence. Like his father and grandfather before him, he went on to become a famous vet, specialising in farm animals, in particular cattle. Long before BSE was exposed, he predicted grave health risks from cheap cattle feed that was becoming popular.

Wing Commander 'Bush' Bandidt was a great Australian, who had been RAF putting-the-weight champion before the war. He was a pilot who had specialised in the technical branch, and he was our Wing Commander Engineering, with all technical matters under his wing. He maintained a very high serviceability of aircraft by his personal drive and leadership, and his prowess and easygoing manner made him very popular. His party trick was to aim, with incredible accuracy, at the open fire in the mess, through a gap in his two front teeth, a half-mouthful of whisky. The instant conflagration captured the amazed attention of the entire room, except for Bush himself, who would continue his conversation without batting an eyelid.

In complete contrast, Flight Lieutenant Bobby Oxspring was a very quiet man. A brilliant pilot, he was the fighter ace of Sheffield, and very proud they were of him. Flight Lieutenant 'Flash' Le Roux was a South African, and the nickname is self-explanatory! Devastatingly good-looking, he seemed irresistible to the fair sex. In contrast again,

Flight Lieutenant Norman Hancock, another quiet personality, was a perfectionist in all he undertook. To help give the students confidence, and to make our instruction more interesting, from time to time we would do a flying demonstration with our aircraft tied together with light cords.

The untiring hard work of all my instructors is something I shall always look back on with gratitude and admiration. Many of their pupils know they owe their lives to them. One of my English pupils was Richard Hough, who became a famous author. He got in touch with me when he was collaborating with Denis Richards in writing *The Battle of Britain*, the Jubilee History for the 50th anniversary in 1990, and told me he was an ex-pupil of mine at the OTU. It made me laugh when this elegant man remarked with a smile as he left, that it was like coming to see his headmaster! He had learnt to fly in California, and on his arrival at my OTU he suddenly realised all the dangers of foul weather, and mountains, and above all the total concentration required for combat flying, when it is imperative to know every aspect of the capabilities of one's aircraft in any circumstance. Richard and I kept in touch ever since until his recent death.

When my time at the OTUs came to an end in early 1943, I was posted to the Middle East. After a short spell in Palestine, as Israel was then called, I went on to command No. 89 Squadron, a Beaufighter night-fighter unit, at Tripoli in North Africa.

CHAPTER SIX

THE WESTERN DESERT

I was sent out to be Senior Air Staff Officer 209 Group MEAF (Middle East Air Force). I went by troopship to Freetown, which was the reinforcement route at that time in order to avoid enemy action. We then flew by air convoy across Africa to Cairo, then finally to HQ 209 Group at Haifa. Only a short time later, the appointment to No. 89 Squadron came up, and with Dave Rockall, a New Zealander, I flew from Haifa, Palestine, to Cairo, Egypt, and then on to Tripoli, flying a Martin Baltimore, a US-built bomber. 'Rocky' was thrilled, as he was joining a new anti-tank squadron at Tripoli, flying Hurricane IIDs with a giant 40-mm Vickers S gun under each wing. It was a 2,000-mile trip, so he was glad of the lift with me.

On landing at my new airfield of Castel Benito, I was met by my Australian senior flight commander, Francis McGhie, always known as 'Mac'. He surveyed my aircraft somewhat ruefully, and asked, 'Did you like this aircraft, Sir?' I told him I had, and he then told me the last one that had landed there had ground-looped (spun round like a top because of directional instability) and killed all on board. He could not believe that I had never flown one before. I decided then not to tell him that I had only flown the Beaufighter, a notably demanding aircraft, once before, and that for about 30 minutes, as here I was as his CO about to take over a Beaufighter night squadron. A typical wartime situation!

No. 89 Squadron was famous. It had no fewer than 30 aircraft, and already had 150 kills at night to its credit. It had been the pride and joy of George Stainforth, who won the Schneider Trophy outright for Great Britain. After his engines cut out through lack of fuel, George had attempted to stretch the glide on his Beau at night, and had paid for this error with his life, when the aircraft stalled and dropped like a stone. This was a rare mistake by a wonderful pilot, and I was lucky to inherit such a fine unit. We were then covering almost the entire Mediterranean and Malta at night, and also Tripoli and Tobruk, and even Lydda in Palestine. The Canal Zone was taken care of by another night-fighter squadron. Such a far-flung command took me a full week to visit all its detachments. We soon became known as 'David's Dark Dicing Desert Demons'.

I quickly put some hours in on the Beaufighter, which was bigger than anything I was used to. On short familiarisation trips it needed only a pilot, but I usually had someone keen to go along with me. I was impressed by its power and strength; its firepower was four 20-mm Hispano cannon and six 0.303-in machine guns. Its two Bristol Hercules sleeve-valve engines developed about 1,600 hp each, and the Beau cruised quite comfortably at 300 mph.

Desert conditions were quite new to me, and not surprisingly our greatest problem was shortage of water. The temperatures varied from intense heat during the daytime hours to bitter cold at night. I would have as many as seven army blankets on my bed! At the beginning of August 1943, after assuming command, I was ordered to move the squadron eastwards to Bu Amud, near Tobruk. A crashed Bf 109 was a well-known landmark for any pilot looking for the airfield in the featureless landscape. For instance, turn right at the 109 and you will come to the squadron maintenance area, or go due west from the crash and you will come to the personnel area.

As CO, I shared a tent with the deputy commander. All of us slept in tents with stretcher beds, and all shared the primitive conditions. It was the boast of each tent to have its own 'Desert Lily'. This vital edifice consisted of a hole dug about three feet into the ground, filled with stones, and with an inverted four-gallon petrol drum cut diagonally in half to provide a most important urinal. Each was adorned with a miniature windsock, which gave the would-be performer an idea of the wind direction. We were all inordinately proud of our Desert Lilies, and they were flushed with our precious washing water when we had finished with it. We each received less than a litre of brackish water per day. New Lily sites were repeatedly found, and the old ones filled in. Once I found my squadron pennant proudly flying in place of my windsock!

The station commander was an acquaintance from a Blenheim squadron from my prewar days at Debden. Someone else I met at this time was Ian Smith, from Southern Rhodesia, who flew a Spitfire in 123 Squadron. They had a pet monkey, which never got used to the sudden noise of low-flying aircraft. One flew over when it was sitting on Ian, and his uniform needed a lot of cleaning afterwards! Many years later, on a private visit to Rhodesia during that country's Unilateral Declaration of Independence (UDI), I met Ian Smith again. By then he was his country's prime minister, and the days at

Bu Amud seemed very distant.

We kept our aircraft at readiness round the clock, but carried out night intruder raids over Crete with the aim of enticing the Germans to come up and fight. For some reason we always referred to the desert as being 'out in the blue'. One day I went back to Cairo on leave, in a Beaufighter which was being sent back for replacement. I took some Army types from the 7th Armoured Division with me, who were allowed to come on the understanding that they would attend hospital in Cairo and then return to their unit. Somehow they got lost in a bar, but I did manage to get them back finally to their original unit hospital. The doctors and nurses were very understanding, and thought the detour might well have been good for them!

I had been with 89 for four months when we were suddenly ordered to assemble the whole squadron at Idku, near Alexandria. Our night-fighting responsibilities were taken over by another unit.

Many of my men had been out in the blue for a long time, and were due for a rest and return to the UK. Imagine my dismay when I received orders to take No. 89 to the Far East. This meant reducing our aircraft to 16, and obviously all thought of returning to the UK was gone. My men took the news philosophically, but it was a shock to us all. The posting authorities, however, did promise that tour-completion dates would be honoured, and this was adhered to meticulously.

There followed hectic days while we prepared for the long journey, and made sure each aircraft was worth the journey to the Far East in hours, which were many more than it takes to fly the distance today. This meant a major inspection of each aircraft. As well as the radar operator, each Beau would carry one technician so we could have our own technical experts alongside us.

An even more pressing problem was the collection of pets. Much loved by their respective owners, they were not all dogs. George was a king cobra, who we had been assured, had had his fangs removed, but I was never certain about this! His great love was milk, and he seemed generally friendly. The most difficult pet of all was a loris monkey. He appeared to be slow-moving, as he looked at you with those huge eyes, and then suddenly with the speed of lightning he would sink his teeth into your hand. There were a few birds, and I myself had a beautiful near-Alsatian called Alex. He loved his daily ration of bully beef. I can see him now, running up with seemingly a smile on his face, and wagging his curly tail, as I called him to his dinner with the words, 'Bully, Bully, Bully'. He loved flying, and would curl up and sleep in the well behind me above the four cannon. He liked the technician who flew with me, and together they slept their way across Mesopotamia and India as we headed towards Ceylon (now Sri Lanka), our first Far East base.

When we landed at Karachi for refuelling, we off-loaded our technicians and pets near the edge of the airfield before taxiing on to meet the officials. History does not relate how these ingenious technicians coped with the dogs, snakes and birds, not to speak of the loris. We picked them up again before leaving, and I thankfully left all these arrangements in the capable hands of Flight Sergeant Marshall. The whole operation was repeated as we flew the length of India.

An unexpected emergency occurred when one of my most experienced pilots, John Beazeley, CO of A-Flight, came up to me at one of the stops and said he was sorry but he had been feeling rotten, and now could not see well. He was bright yellow; he had jaundice. Thereafter he flew in my aircraft, and one of the relief pilots took over his aircraft. Thus after 21½ flying hours, over a journey which took a week, we got to Vavuniya in Ceylon. In Sinhalese Vavuniya means 'where elephants meet'. They did, too, just north of our camp, but gave us no trouble.

To our relief, the station commander welcomed both us and our pets. He seemed to understand how much they meant to us. He got John to hospital with the minimum delay, where he soon recovered. The station commander's surname was Louis, and his nickname 'the governor' seemed very suitable. He was an outstanding organiser.

CHAPTER SEVEN

'WHERE ELEPHANTS MEET'

After the desert, the plentiful supply of water and clean sheets of Ceylon seemed unheard-of luxury! Additionally, our diet in the desert had been very limited: tinned bully beef and hard biscuits were the norm. Often in the scorching heat the contents of the tins were completely melted, and just poured out when the tin was opened.

Although during our time there we became used to the intense sun and, having got very tanned, seemed to suffer no ill effects from it, today everyone is wiser not only to the immediate dangers of sunburn but also to damage that might manifest itself in the future. Even then we were very strict with the newcomers. Anyone ignoring precautions to avoid sunburn and sunstroke could be put on a charge.

Lack of fresh fruit and vegetables had caused a lot of skin problems. Most of us had what were called Desert Sores, which were quite deep, open and running, and difficult to heal. I carry the scars on my shins to this day, and they have left the skin there very vulnerable to any damage, including sunburn.

Thus Ceylon seemed to us like the Garden of Eden. The lush green everywhere took some getting used to, and the fresh fruit and vegetables provided us with the Vitamin C we had lacked for so long, soon banishing the Desert Sores. All was not paradise, however. Here we encountered malaria, and a daily dose of mepacrine turned us a strange yellow tinge, but this drug was considered more potent than quinine in controlling the disease.

We were welcomed with the most generous hospitality by all the local settlers. The tea and rubber plantations were the life-blood of the country, and residents had watched the seemingly unstoppable advance of the Japanese with a general feeling of apprehension. Ceylon had already suffered raids from Japanese carrier-borne aircraft, which had achieved good results against inadequate defences, particularly at night. Everyone was concerned at the ease with which Japanese aircraft had sunk the great capital ships *Prince of Wales* and *Repulse* in December 1941, and the aircraft carrier *Hermes* four months later.

The AOC (Air Officer Commanding) Ceylon had a lot on his plate. His main concern was naturally maritime defence. Colombo and Trincomalee were wonderful natural harbours, and from 1942 Trincomalee had housed the whole British Far Eastern Fleet. The AOC knew his weakness was night protection, and our arrival was most timely and welcome.

The day after our arrival we made our aircraft fully operational for night fighting, and started affiliation with Ceylon's ground control. To my great relief, this was of a high standard, particularly as they had had so little opportunity for real operational practice. I sent a detachment to Ratmalana and one to Madras, keeping the main part of my squadron at Vavuniya. We still had only the few technicians who had flown out with us. The rest of my squadron was still at sea, having sailed from Port Said in Egypt, and would take weeks to get to us. It naturally came in convoy, and was under the orders of the Royal Navy, who had to contend with the Japanese and German submarines which were active in the area.

Imagine our delight when, the day after they had set up for business, the detachment at Ratmalana destroyed a large Japanese Navy flying boat, a Kawanishi H6K, which had been going to bomb Colombo. The Japanese did not expect night-fighters of the calibre of the Beaufighter to be in the area. They never again attacked Ceylon at night, and the esteem in which the locals held our squadron was enhanced. We were the flavour of the month!

The body of the H6K's navigator was later washed up. Most unusually for a Japanese, he was well over six feet in height. He still had his body belt on, in which he carried his personal mementos, and, most important from the intelligence point of view, his return bus ticket from his home to his flying-boat base, confirming its location.

Three weeks after my arrival in Ceylon I went down to meet the rest of my squadron at the docks. The boys could not believe their ears when they were told they would be sleeping between sheets, and what is more, there was *butter*! Their response was, 'There's *what*?!'. It was a commodity they had almost forgotten. They were greeted with the good news of our early success, and this and their safe arrival was a good excuse for a celebration!

We were now able to concentrate on improving our general capability and working closely with Ceylon ground control. Trincomalee had become a prime target, and it was our night duty to provide cover from Vavuniya. Navy signals are renowned for their precision and brevity, and two also illustrated their humour. When Sir James Somerville, C-in-C of the Far Eastern Fleet, was awarded a KCB to match the knighthood he already held (KBE), a signal was sent by another Admiral, 'Twice a (k)night at your age is an accomplishment.' On another occasion the fleet started to sail out of harbour, and then for some reason was re-called by London. When we lesser mortals enquired as to the reason for this sudden change of plan, signals came back that 'The Admiral has forgotten his pyjamas.' The enduring sense of humour in the services kept morale high throughout, and indeed helped us to win the war.

We continued our patrols, but the Japanese now left us alone. For a while I was station commander at Minneriya, after handing over my night squadron in central Ceylon. Apart from two squadrons of Hurricane day fighters, we were the home base for Royal Navy aircraft when they came ashore. The offensive wing of Fairey Barracuda attack bombers was headed by a major in the Royal Marines, Ronnie Hay, who led 810 and 847 Squadrons against targets in Sumatra, such as the oil tanks at Palembang. He asked me as his CO for permission to marry an attractive Wren (WRNS, Women's Royal Naval Service); Barbara was part of the Trincomalee staff dealing with signals. I was delighted to give Ronnie and his bride permission to marry, and it was an even greater pleasure to meet them both at London's Guildhall some 45 years later. During the Korean War Ronnie had transferred to the Royal Navy, and he retired as a commander. Another Wren serving at Trincomalee was Monica Dickens, who inherited her great writing skills from her ancestor Charles.

Dear old 89 was still at Vavuniya, where I had handed over command to 'Mac' McGhie, who had come with us from North Africa. Soon after I arrived at Minneriya, Mac flew in and said the squadron had a present for me which they wanted to represent every man on the unit, and they would like me to fly down to Vavuniya to receive it. There, Mac produced an illuminated parchment scroll over 30 inches long which every man had signed, and they had then had it framed. He also gave me a silver cigarette box, cigarette case and lighter, to which all the boys had subscribed. I was completely lost for words, and simply did not know how to thank them. I said as much to Mac, who replied, 'They want you to remember them.' As if I could ever forget them! Those gifts occupy a treasured spot in both my heart and my home.

Many in our all-important MT (Motor Transport) section had been London bus drivers, and their ingenuity at finding equipment, even in the North African desert, was unsurpassed. One day after the war I was walking down the Strand in London in my pin-stripe MoD (Ministry of Defence) suit complete with bowler hat, when a London bus stopped abruptly, and the driver leapt out and hugged me. To the amazement of the passengers and the passers-by, all he could say at first was 'It's my old CO!' All who witnessed this happy reunion realised it was a very special meeting. There were general smiles of approval, and tolerant understanding. All too soon it was over, and the bus was back on its way.

Another memorable meeting took place some years after this, when I attended an 89 Squadron reunion in England, and was told that McGhie was now living in the UK. When I entered the mess I asked if McGhie had arrived, and was told he was in the bar. I reckoned that figured, his hangovers had been legendary, but they never seemed to affect his competence. The door opened and Mac strode towards me and enveloped me in a bear hug, saying, 'Dennis, it's good to see you. God, you were a hard bastard . . . but I loved you!' We saw a lot of each other until he died.

To return to Minneriya, on 15 May 1944 Lord Louis Mountbatten, then Supreme Allied Commander South East Asia, came to visit us. He had film-star good looks, and great charisma. His staff told us that he would require an ammunition box to stand on when he called the troops around him, and I was flabbergasted when he spoke to the Indian troops in Urdu. He was renowned for his attention to details like this, and fortunately our own arrangements for him went off smoothly.

At the end of June, 847 Squadron was absorbed into No. 810, and late the following month the combined squadron flew off to HMS *Illustrious*. From her they carried out precision attacks, particularly against oil bases in Sumatra. One of the pilots was John Willie Buchan, a direct descendant of one of my all-time favourite authors.

An unexpected visitor to Minneriya was the famous actor Noël Coward. We had been getting a poor standard of entertainment for the troops before he turned up unannounced. He was a personal friend of Lord Louis, and felt he wanted to 'do his bit'. His concert was of a totally different standard; indeed at first it was a little too sophisticated. He soon tuned down to his audience's taste, and was much appreciated. I had admired his work, especially the blockbuster film *In Which We Serve*. Over dinner he described how 'Dicky' had steered his destroyer, the *Kelly*, with the deck heeling over at 45 degrees after a torpedo hit, and how this inspired him to make the film. While he was telling the story I realised that 'Dicky' was of course Lord Louis.

He gave me a poem he had written in his beautiful handwriting. Called 'Lie in the Dark and Listen', it was a moving tribute to the RAF which became famous. His patriotism made a profound impression on me. As he was taking his departure, I gave him an ebony ruler and said, 'Hit Basil Dean over the head with it for sending out such poor entertainment.' He asked pertinent questions, laughed, and said he would relish doing so.

CHAPTER EIGHT

THE CAPTURE OF AKYAB

In October 1944, while I was at Kankesanturai, Ceylon, I was promoted to group captain. Shortly after this my posting as air liaison officer to the 15th Indian Corps came through, and I was to join General Philip Christison, the C-in-C, on the Arakan front in Burma. At the end of October I flew a Liberator up to Calcutta, on my way to HQ 15th Indian Corps at Shalimar Camp, near Cox's Bazaar, taking a crew of nine with me, together with my kit and the faithful Alex.

My old squadron, No. 89, had been sent to provide Calcutta with defence at night. Alex and I were pleased to spend a couple of days with them, and I was especially glad to see how well Mac was dealing with his command. They laid on one of their famous, or infamous, parties to celebrate my promotion to such a dizzy height at the age of 26, and the boys seemed duly impressed with my new hat, with its prominent 'scrambled egg' (gold braid) round the brim. While I was having a few drinks with Mac in his room, we noticed that most of the squadron had moved outside. I might have expected it: they had formed a ring round my hat on the ground, and were peeing into it and laughing uproariously.

I was able to obtain a new hat before reporting to my new AOC in Chittagong, Air Commodore Lord Bandon. Paddy Bandon (the Abandoned Earl, a nickname he gave himself, and which seemed eminently suitable) was a charismatic character, with a wonderful sense of humour. He took a special delight in things going awry on pompous official occasions, which endeared him to us.

Having paid my respects to Paddy, I then went to see General Christison. Almost on meeting him I felt a great liking for the man, and there seemed to be a happy rapport between us. This was a good omen, as I was the first RAF member to be on his staff in the post of air liaison officer. The Celts thus seemed well represented: a Scot as general in charge of the overall set-up, an Irish earl OC the Air Force, and I flew the flag for Wales in a close-support role. We also had an English admiral, Admiral Martin, who seemed to fit the company well, his nickname being 'Blood and Guts'.

The general too had a nickname, 'Christie'. His father and grandfather had acted as guinea pigs with Simpson when he was experimenting with the anaesthetic properties of chloroform and ether. When his father sailed with an expedition in 1852 for the 2nd Burmese War, Simpson told him of a man making chloroform in Calcutta. Christie's father obtained a bottle from him, and in 1853 there were battles at Pegu and Doabeu where an ensign of the Ninetieth Foot was brought to his dressing station with a musket ball lying against his femur. Using a knife given to him by Simpson (and now in the museum at Surgeon's Hall, Edinburgh) he removed the ball under chloroform, the first recorded use of it in British military history. The ensign later rose to become Field Marshal Viscount Wolsey.

Like Dowding, Christie's prime concern was to save the lives of his men when he could. With his inherited interest in medicine he was conscious of the fact that scrub typhus and similar jungle illnesses seriously affected the fighting strength of his forces. It was largely due to his initiative that the cure for scrub typhus was found, in the serum extracted from the lung of the American cotton rat. Christie had realised that one wounded or sick man could mean ten men having to carry him, for we never left anyone for the Japanese to take prisoner and torture.

The Stinson L-5 Sentinel was an excellent short take-off light aeroplane for casualty evacuation, for the rear seat could be reassembled for a man lying down. Experienced pilots went with the Army into the jungle to supervise the preparation of small airstrips suitable for an L-5. Thus, each 100 sick men so removed to the rear meant 1,000 men released for fighting. Moreover, many lives were saved by the quicker and easier journey. I flew on many of these missions, and can verify that it was a very satisfying undertaking all round. The L-5 also meant that I was able to fly Christie to visit his troops in the jungle as necessary.

Lady Christison was with her husband at Quetta (today in Pakistan) when he was commandant of the Staff College, and she was a senior official in the WASBIs (Women's Auxiliary Service, Burma and India). She was a wonderful support to Christie, particularly after their brilliant only son had been killed by a single bullet in a Japanese ambush on 7 March 1942. I flew her and Christie to Imphal where he received his KCB from Lord Wavell, who deputised for the King.

Lady Mountbatten also came to visit us. She was chief of the WASBIs, and was tireless in her efforts to help in any way she could. The WASBIs were mainly concerned with looking after the troops' welfare. Paddy wrote a letter home saying he had just flown a new WASBI from Cox's Bazaar up to Chittagong, and the censor told him very firmly that he should know he must never mention the name of any aircraft concerned in operations, much less a new one!

The 15th Indian Corps was to carry out an offensive along the southern strip, ultimately to recapture Rangoon. At the same time the 14th Army, under General Sir William 'Uncle Bill' Slim, was to carry out the major thrust through central Burma to Rangoon. The jungle itself had to be seen to be believed. Its dense cover meant that opposing forces could suddenly come face to face (known as 'bumping'), and such encounters entailed fierce hand-to-hand fighting. The Japanese were a first-class fighting force, but our Indian Army troops were more than a match for them. I grew to admire these loyal and courageous men.

Christie soon set up a Combined Services Headquarters at Shalimar. He was always a great advocate of combined services operations, and many new ploys were used in this campaign, which never appeared in any textbook. For instance, he told me about his earlier unconventional tactic carrying Sapper-type boats through the Buthedong tunnels, enabling our troops to attack the Japanese from an unexpected direction. The attack was successful, and the Japanese withdrew north towards Akyab.

Akyab was a strategic seaport containing the only safe harbour in that part of the world, and its invasion was planned meticulously for weeks in late 1944. The Navy, with the battleship *Queen Elizabeth*, with eight 15-in (38-cm) guns, as well as four cruisers and six destroyers, was to bombard strategic points. The Army had field guns ready to fire from Foul Point a few miles away, and a division of troops ready to invade with their assorted landing craft. The RAF had 500 bombers waiting with targets designated. It was to be one of the biggest amphibious operations in that area so far.

For some time I had noticed that there were no Japanese aircraft around. I carried out a low-level reconnaissance in an L-5, and saw nothing, and even Akyab airfield seemed deserted. I flew back to Cox's Bazaar to pick up an RAF photographer, and returned, asking him to photograph all we saw. Suddenly, I noticed a white flag being waved from a large field on the western tip of the island, and circled it. As the only armament we had between us was my 0.45 revolver strapped round my waist, I was being very careful. Then an Army artillery spotting aircraft appeared, and feeling I was no longer alone I decided to land, and the Army aircraft did likewise. All this time the photographer was taking pictures.

The man waving the white flag was the village headman, who spoke some English. He told me all the Japs had left, and I forbore to tell him that Akyab was in imminent danger of being pulverised. The only casualties would have been the villagers and their cattle. The Army pilot, who was outstandingly capable, had no passenger with him, and I persuaded the headman to fly back with him. He was somewhat apprehensive about this, but we all returned to General Christison's HQ. Luckily, Judge Bradley, who had been the peacetime judge of the island, was visiting us; he had been planning to return after the capture, and he knew the headman.

We were then faced with the problem of calling off the massive bombardment – just the sort of disruption to plans that delighted Paddy. The General sent a signal to Kandy in Ceylon, to which Lord Louis replied that he would call off the whole operation if General Christison could rely on Group Captain David's report. If facts proved to be incorrect, the General must take the blame. He showed me the signal, and asked me how I felt about it. I told him I was sure all would be well, so the huge operation was cancelled right at the eleventh hour.

Christie then turned to me and asked if I would fly him in so that he could welcome the troops ashore on 3 January 1945. I managed to land him on the beach on the hard-packed sand by the water's edge. No one could be happier than Christie, Paddy and myself, but other senior officers felt more than a passing frustration at their long-laid plans being thus aborted, together with their visions of the personal glory which would have attended such a victorious undertaking. I realised that it did my promotion prospects no good at all!

The landing force shared in our delight. The big fleet of landing craft edged up on the beach, the ramps came down, and the 'invasion force' came ashore to be welcomed by their commander with smiles and handshakes, and a very happy headman, who had been flown back for the occasion. The relieved villagers were all smiles in the background.

I remember thinking at the time of all the lives that had been saved, plus an incalculable amount of money. Later I was to learn that Christie had wanted to give me a Military Cross, but that Paddy as my CO had told him I would not want it. It would in fact have been one of my most valued decorations, for it would have been not only from Christie, but from the Indian Army, for whom I had the greatest regard and admiration.

Unknown to me, the photographer, realising what a scoop he had, had arranged to have his pictures and story sent back to the Air Ministry in London. It was released to one of the newsreels, as it was considered a cheering story, and especially one from the campaign being waged by what came to be called the 'Forgotten Army' in

Burma. It so happened that my mother went to the cinema in Surbiton, and suddenly there was the whole story. She was so excited she stood up and called out, 'That's my son!' Until then she had no idea where I was, other than somewhere in the Far East. The manager of the cinema told her she could come and watch every performance she wanted to with his congratulations and compliments. He did good business, for mother lost no time in telling her friends, and they all went along to see the film for themselves. Of course, TV broadcasts had been discontinued on the outbreak of war, so cinema newsreels were the only way the public could see what was happening.

About 35 years later I was having lunch with a friend of many years, a charming Hungarian lady. She knew nothing of my time in Burma, but had asked an old friend of hers, a Colonel Frederick Sudbury, whom she thought I would be interested in meeting because of his wartime career. He was now a Lloyd's underwriter, but it turned out that he had been a member of the 15th Indian Corps, and had landed with the troops on Akyab. He told me he felt there should have been something to commemorate the landing, and had at the time designed a postage stamp. It had a green background to symbolise the green field, with a little brown moth on it to denote my little aeroplane landing there, and in the corner a white flag.

Some 50 years after the capture of Akyab I met a young girl who mentioned she had been born in the Far East. On my enquiring just where, she replied, 'Oh, on a little island you will never have heard of called Akyab.' I told her the story, showing her the pictures and press cuttings of the event, and she was speechless. We got copies of them for her, and she said she could not wait to show them to her mother and father. We were both quite overcome by the chance of it all. She said, 'It is wonderful, somehow it is like being born again. If it had not been for you I might never have been born at all.'

CHAPTER NINE

'JAPS GONE'

We set up our joint Air/Land HQ in tents adjacent to the airfield south of Akyab, and much planning was accomplished between the three services for future actions. Throughout their retreat through the Arakan region the Japanese fought like tigers, and they always left one or two rearguards who went on firing until the last man was killed. Myebon was one such rearguard action, and our Royal Marines took over responsibility for this attack. Admiral 'Patsy' Poland, RN, ironed out many wrinkles in the tactics. Myebon was very difficult to attack as it was on a hill, and could be assaulted only from below. Many hundreds of marines were killed, but the recapture of Myebon meant that the attack on Ramree island could succeed. Here again the remaining Japanese had left, apart from the rearguard who fought to the last. The capture of Ramree on 21 January 1945 opened the way for an advance towards Rangoon, for an eventual link-up with the victorious 14th Army coming through central Burma. At last we felt the tide of the war in the Far East was turning in our favour.

The capture of Rangoon was to be a big affair. Admiral Lord Louis joined us, as well as his Chief of Staff, General 'Boy' Browning, who three months earlier had commanded the airborne assault on Arnhem. He had been in no way responsible for the disastrous planning and faulty intelligence of that venture, and should be given far more credit for the way in which he extricated as many of his men as he could. He was naturally involved in the assault on Rangoon, as it was to be an airborne operation.

When the final stages were being worked out, I flew Browning, who told me that the main troops taking part were to be Gurkhas, and that the Dakotas for the assault were to be supplied by the USAAF, as the RAF did not have enough to mount this operation. I was delighted to hear that the Gurkhas were to be involved as they are a remarkable people, and I had always admired their courage and loyalty.

Some years later I was fortunate to make a close friend of a Gurkha officer, who explained that in their homeland of Nepal, the sun reaches only one side of the high mountains where they spend most of their lives. His father was Gurkha, and his mother, from the UK, was the first white woman doctor in that part of Nepal.

Chuck, as he was known, was fiercely proud of his lineage; he was a fighting man through and through, yet with a great love of and knowledge of animals. His family had reared abandoned young animals, and cared for injured ones. These were usually returned to the wild, but in a harsh winter would invariably turn up for food and shelter. A bear they had raised as a cub developed a cataract when it was getting old, which Chuck's father managed to remove, and from then on the bear rarely strayed far from the family.

Chuck grew up with a young elephant. He went overseas and joined a Gurkha regiment. Years later he flew back to Nepal on leave. His friends met him, and told him his elephant seemed to know he was returning, and was very restless. Would he please come to see it right away? As soon as the elephant saw him it produced a brick, and insisted that Chuck must accompany it to the water, where it waited while he stripped off, so he could go into the water and scrub it with the brick as he always used to do. This tough warrior would become misty-eyed as he recalled such incidents.

He had a magnificent physique, and was also a judo expert, teaching some of our London police self-defence and unarmed combat. When he was 70, on leaving his local cinema one night, he saw three youths attacking an elderly man about to get into his car, and Chuck immediately took on the three thugs, quickly rendering them helpless. A policeman nearby arrived to find Chuck not even out of breath, and three young louts wondering what had hit them. The policeman had great difficulty keeping a straight face as he recognised his instructor.

When the case came to court, the prosecution made much of the bravery of a pensioner going to the aid of another in trouble, and warned Chuck when he came to give his evidence not to enter the witness box two steps at a time. Chuck said he took great delight in walking very slowly, and leaning heavily on the handrail. Yet, despite his high intelligence, medical knowledge and exceptional stamina, Chuck literally smoked himself to a standstill. He contracted emphysema, and it was dreadful to see him reduced to dependence on an oxygen cylinder by his chair where he sat helpless. He bore it courageously, but did once ask me, 'Dennis, why could I not have had a clean death like a bullet in battle?'

For many years he had told me that true Gurkhas hand on their kukri, their lethal curved knife, only to another warrior. His had been with him all his adult life, and was kept by his bed, but suddenly, during a visit one day, he asked me to fetch it. With a great effort he stood up and, partly drawing it from its sheath, formally handed it to me as it lay across his half-raised left arm, and said, 'May this blade bring you good fortune.' I solemnly accepted the kukri, and Chuck slumped back in his chair, and reached for the oxygen mask. He died two days later.

The Japanese were terrified of the Gurkhas. In recent years I have felt ashamed at the way their loyalty has been ignored by our country. I once asked Chuck what would happen if our Queen was in trouble, and he replied that, if necessary, every Gurkha would walk from Nepal to defend her. This remark was made after there had been considerable reduction in the Gurkha regiments, but he was adamant that they would still feel total loyalty to our monarch. Knowing their prodigious feats of endurance, I could well believe that they would indeed walk that far. I, and some of my friends who feel the same, try to show our appreciation of these wonderful people by supporting the Gurkha Welfare Trust, which sends funds where they are needed most.

By using Cox's Bazaar, Akyab and Ramree for the launch of the airborne assault, which coincided with invasion by sea and land, Rangoon was recaptured on 3 May 1945, and there was little fighting. The 14th Army had come through from the north, and Burma was free. Two days later I flew into the airfield at Rangoon, and there met Major-General George E. Stratemeyer, of the USAAF, who was overall C-in-C of the area. We were both on fact-finding missions. For some time we had seen a large notice painted on the roof of a prisoner of war camp, saying 'Japs Gone'. This fact was verified, and the prisoners were reached and released.

The streets of Rangoon were full of Japanese scrip paper money, the banks having been looted, and all this money was worthless. The civilian population seemed to be keeping out of sight, except for those searching for food.

Rangoon is a beautiful city and has many large pagodas, some on stilt legs, as are so many of their buildings. Fortunately it had not suffered too much damage, for there had been little fighting there, but there had been a lot of deprivation during the Japanese occupation. I was glad I had suffered the very unpleasant plague inoculation before going there, for rats were everywhere, but soon we were recalled to India, to prepare for 'Operation Zipper', the invasion of Malaya.

In May 1945 the war in Europe came to an end, but as we were still busily engaged in warfare with the Japanese the fact passed almost unnoticed. We certainly felt that our war was far from being over.

We had a large RAF Headquarters at Yellahanka, near Bangalore, India, at which the only accommodation available was in round bell tents. These were on the surface, instead of having the floor dug about a metre down, which we had had with our square army tents, where the extra height had meant that we could stand upright anywhere inside. Our lighting was by gas fuel pumped under pressure.

On 16 August the war was officially brought to an abrupt end, entirely because of the two atomic bombs dropped on Japan. Despite this, towards the end of August Operation Zipper, the planned landing in Malaya, went ahead, if only to establish that the Japanese had ceased hostilities. I was given command of the Combined Services reconnaissance party. We started from Madras to join the main convoy of ships, and during the several days the voyage took I was able to get to know my excellent team. Our landings were to take place at Morib beaches, which we were informed were gently shelving. In fact, as we left our landing craft we went straight in up to our necks in the sea, and there was certainly no shelving beach. We lost all our kit, and watched in dismay as it either sank or floated off down the Malacca Straits, before anything could be done to recover it.

We scrambled ashore as best we could, and the sappers with us set up a strip at nearby Kalang for our aircraft to land. We informed our command ship, where Paddy, Christie and Admiral 'Blood and Guts' awaited news. The decision was made that 'Zipper' should proceed as planned. The full landing was achieved in an orderly fashion, and there was no fighting.

The Japanese troops in the area had been ordered by their superiors to assemble in the rear, and we had no trouble from them. It was fortunate that events had worked out as they did, for the landing as originally planned was an absolute shambles, and, had hostilities continued and the Japanese been defending the position, I dread to think of the carnage that would have followed. Another hazard we had been told nothing about was that there were many deadly sea snakes in those waters, and we were lucky not to have encountered any. The only saving grace was that the sea that day was calm and warm.

I found Malaya to be a beautiful country, and the inhabitants had such old-world courtesy that I was charmed. Their generous hospitality had to be experienced to be believed. They hated the Japanese, who had treated them harshly as inferior beings. In fact, they are highly intelligent, with a deep sense of tradition, and very artistic.

Once we had established the beachhead and prepared the airstrip, I said goodbye to the reconnaissance party, and proceeded to check the local airfields. Paddy asked me to do this as soon as possible, as the Allies would be using large transport aircraft sooner than expected. I was able to get my hands on an L-5 which had been crated and carried with us, and with an Army colonel I flew to Kuala Lumpur. I remember thinking how incongruous it was as we were flagged in by a Japanese ground crew.

About this time I had a joyful reunion with Alex, who had been flown in by an old friend. Alex always seemed go to war in style, which I did not begrudge him for he was such a marvellous companion. As usual, he soon made friends with the female canine fraternity, and his enthusiastic efforts must have started a new breed of near-Alsatians with curly tails. His exploits periodically appeared in the squadron orders of the day.

The airfield at KL proved to be most satisfactory, and played a large part in our getting things back to normal. While at the airfield I asked a local Indian Army translator, who had been sent by the colonel, to take me to the hospital where the sick Allied troops had been held prisoner. No words can describe the filth and squalor the Japanese medical authorities had forced upon the troops. There were no beds, and all they had were verminous rags on the floor. One Indian *niak* (corporal) looked up from where he was lying, and I saw a flicker of life fleetingly in his eyes before he died, but he seemed to recognise that the hospital had been recaptured in his last moments. In another part of the hospital I was proud to find the sick Gurkhas all standing to attention, even though many were in the advanced stages of beriberi.

Medical aid was on its way, but I left with a heavy heart because for many there it would come too late. The colonel with me was as appalled and as angry as I was. We had both seen the Japanese general and his staff nearby, but I did not trust myself to speak to this man, who wanted to surrender his sword, which I would not have dreamt of accepting.

Having verified that everything was in train for the arrival of the Allied aircraft, I was recalled to Singapore in mid-September to rejoin Paddy. We set up RAF Group Headquarters again, and absorbed all new units as they arrived by land, sea, and air.

The Army had taken over responsibility for Allied prisoners. I cannot praise the Army enough, for it was a task requiring much understanding and compassion, and could be undertaken only by people of great strength of character, who could cope with the horrors they found. I visited the infamous Changi prison, where the Japs had placed most of the Allied prisoners. Many of them were just too ill for any emotion other than hatred for their past tormentors, or relief at their release.

The Japanese Army looked upon the Allied troops as cowards, for at Singapore some 300,000 of them had been ordered to surrender to 30,000 of the invading Japanese. The Japanese never understood this, and logistically it posed them a great problem; they despised this mass surrender, which was a factor that contributed to the almost insane cruelty which they nearly all meted out at every opportunity during the ensuing years. Not all Japanese were so mindlessly cruel, and there were cases when common decency and humanity prevailed, but these cases were very much in the minority.

Once Lord Louis, Keith Park and the general in charge had established their HQ in Singapore, we were moved to KL to control our group. Paddy Bandon had completed his tour and was replaced by a fine veteran of World War I, Air Vice-Marshal John Breakey. I was his Chief of Staff, and quickly established a good working relationship with him. John was an exceptionally fine golfer, and I was not surprised to find that we were sharing a house right by the golf course. Fortunately John was fond of Alex, who once again soon had everything organised to his liking.

Occasionally, however, officialdom did not require Alex's presence, which he could never understand. Such an occasion was the Joint Services Church Parade service at KL church. I had locked him up in the house, which was some way from the church. I was sitting in the front row, next to John and all the high-ranking service chiefs, when I heard unmistakable footsteps going pit-a-pat down the aisle. Alex arrived triumphantly at my side, wagging his curly tail, but with an enquiring look on his face, as if to ask, 'Why was I left behind?' I was enormously relieved by John's reaction, when he whispered how clever he thought Alex was, and how had he traced me there, as we had all travelled by car? I had to lead Alex down the aisle, to the consternation of preacher and congregation, and leave him with our driver outside. Secretly, I was very proud of Alex, and it cemented my friendship with John.

One memorable occasion we all three shared was when we were travelling in an open Jeep. On turning a corner we suddenly came upon a large king cobra coiled up in the middle of the road, with his head held erect and his hood out. With John's rapid approval I immediately turned the Jeep round, and we beat a hasty retreat. The king cobra never moved, and watched us triumphantly as we found another route.

Another time I was driving a Jeep when, rounding a bend, I found the huge head of a tiger looking out of the bushes right beside the road. I had not previously realised how much bigger they are than a lion. I felt that the best way out was to put my foot down and get away as fast as I could. We slept in *bashas*, which had walls of woven palm fronds, and we would often hear a tiger snuffling round outside. They are known to have a taste for dog, and the scent of a tiger was the one thing that really frightened Alex. Big though he was, he would crawl under my bed at night, although there was only a few inches' clearance. In the morning we would find pug marks outside the size of soup plates.

Christie was C-in-C in Java with part of the old 15th Indian Corps, and he asked Keith Park if I could join him. A few days after hearing Christie wanted me in Java, I received the posting note, and Group Captain Hughie Idwal Edwards, VC, was sent in as my replacement. I had never met him before, but a rapport was quickly established between us. I was torn, not wanting to leave Johnny Breakey, whom I had so enjoyed serving, and wished I had more than a few days to hand over to Hughie. Later he became Governor-General of Australia.

My greatest sadness was having to post my faithful Alex back to 89 Squadron, as grim fighting was still taking place in Java despite the official end of the war. Alex was always officially on the strength of 89 Squadron. He had risen to the rank of sergeant, and his posting papers were always made out in that rank, but unfortunately he was several times demoted to corporal for being absent without leave whilst courting. I knew he would be warmly welcomed back in the squadron, and one of my particular friends there was going to look after him.

I flew to Batavia, the capital of the Dutch East Indies in November 1945. Christie was in overall command, at Koningsplein, where I reported to him before taking up my new post as Senior Air Staff Officer, RAF, Netherlands East Indies.

CHAPTER TEN

THE SAVAGE 'BLACK BUFFALOES'

One day in 1986 I received a letter forwarded on to me by the Ministry of Defence, which in itself told me that the sender had gone to a lot of trouble to locate me. I opened it with some curiosity, and on reading the first few lines I was transported back 40 years to a day in Java. I will return to this letter later.

Some of the toughest days of my service career were those spent in Java. My post meant that I was in charge of all air operations, in conjunction with the British and Indian services in Java and neighbouring islands, and apart from clearing up pockets of Japanese resistance, we found ourselves involved in a totally different and unexpected type of warfare. Although known as a day and night fighter pilot, my speciality was air support to the land offensive. I think, too, I was a lucky talisman for the Army, and they seemed to feel this during the Arakan offensive in Burma.

In Java I found the situation to be far worse than I ever imagined. My initial brief was to help in the capture of Japanese war criminals. These had helped to inspire a terrorist national feeling in Java, with the aim of preventing the return of Dutch rule. The worst Javanese terrorists called themselves the Black Buffaloes. We found a very difficult situation on our arrival, and it seemed impossible to get across to either the British or Dutch Governments its critical nature, and the ghastly atrocities that were constantly being perpetrated. Eventually we had to take matters into our own hands. Throughout, the British and Indian troops, and in particular the RAF Regiment, were magnificent, and as always, the RAF groundcrews were untiring in their day-and-night efforts.

It was a hideous time trying to clean up after the Japanese occupation. The atrocities against the civilian population had been horrendous, and were in fact still occurring. Dutch women and children were still languishing in prison camps, and many were still being brutally abused. The women, as ever, were fair game for rape and other sexual assault, and little blonde children were often found killed, usually left in ditches with their eyes gouged out. Although the war was officially over, this meant nothing to some of the Javanese terrorists whom we still had to locate and deal with, and they were meting out violence indiscriminately. I had bullets miss me by millimetres even in my own office.

However, some humanity still shone out from what seemed like an enveloping pall of evil. One of our greatest assets was a Japanese major and his company. They were even used to help us free some of the Dutch women and children from the Javanese who were terrorising the Japanese camps. He and his troops performed many deeds of bravery for us, and Christie said, if only he had been one of our officers, he would have recommended him for a DSO.

While I was there I shared accommodation with several other officers in a large house which had previously belonged to someone in an important position. I kept my car in a concrete shelter adjoining the house so I could get straight into it, without going outside. Two armed guards stood either side of the entrance, with machine-guns at the ready. I would drive out with two or more guards from the RAF Regiment in the back of the car, with machine-guns pointing out either side, ready for any trouble.

A famous brigadier of the British Army, Alistair MacLean, and I had the idea it would be fun to give the poor little children in the camps a party for his birthday. We organised buses to bring them to and from the house, and had a large birthday cake and some extra goodies baked by the RAF chef and his staff, who all thought it was a great idea. Alistair, an expert piper, and an authority on Scottish dancing, dressed up in his kilt and came along with his bagpipes. He played up and down the stairs, and the children were amazed. Even after Alistair had finished they gazed wide-eyed at the stairs. Suddenly it dawned on us: they had never seen stairs in their lives! We said they could go up and down them as much as they liked, and they formed a silent well-disciplined line for each one to have a turn. Inhibitions began to fade, and the highlight of the whole party was being able to run up and down and play on the stairs! The beautiful cake was much appreciated, too, but they were so used to their meagre rations that each very politely asked if they could take most of their slice back to their mothers in camp.

Our operations were almost unknown in the outside world. One of our Dakotas crash-landed near a village called Bekasi, with the RAF crew and a full load of Indian troops. They were on their way to support our garrison at the eastern end of Java. The Black Buffaloes captured them and literally cut them all into little pieces in the village square, while onlookers from the village watched and cheered. Christie determined to teach these evil people a lesson, and an armoured column of British and Indian troops captured Bekasi to administer justice. I had Thunderbolts and Mosquitos ready to strafe the Black Buffaloes if any tried to flee, and this action had a salutary effect on future terrorism.

Shortly after this Christie was posted home. I came to hear that the UK had received only garbled reports of the Bekasi incident, and there were likely to be ugly headlines on his return branding him as the 'Butcher of Bekasi'. Luckily a few British journalists had actually seen the ghastly remains of the Dakota passengers; some were physically sick, including Noel Monks, of the *Daily Mail*, who said that in all his long career he had never witnessed anything so brutal. I got hold of Noel and told him exactly why we had mounted such an immediate and punitive response, and the salutary effect such an action had had. He listened intently, and questioned me at length. Eventually, having seen the results of Black Buffalo savagery with his own eyes, he put his hand on my shoulder and said, 'Don't worry, Dennis, I will see the boys get the true story. Just leave it to me.' I did, and my trust was well placed. On many occasions I have had to go to the press and say, 'This is how it is, please print the true story.' I have never been disappointed.

One day, a very tall Dutchman arrived at my office, and asked if he might speak with whoever was in charge of flying operations. So it was that I first met Herman Arens, from whom in 1986 I received a letter via the Ministry of Defence. He had gone to a lot of trouble to locate me, and on reading the first few lines I was transported back forty years to Java.

Herman told me that day in my office that he and his fellow Dutch pilots were desperate, as daily they saw more and more women and children still being brutally treated, and often murdered. He had been awarded a DFC for Allied Pathfinder missions from Darwin, Australia, and had landed in Batavia on 13 September 1945, as the first of the Dutch forces. Since then he had organised mercy missions throughout Java with Japanese aircraft under the aegis of RAPWI (Rehabilitation of Allied Prisoners and Women Internees). With losses due to attacks by insurrection elements, he now needed more aircraft, but although he had tried other channels, few top officials of the Dutch government had arrived. With the terrible conditions, risks had to be taken, especially since some of the Japanese recognised a marvellous chance to meddle, secretly handing powerful weapons over to the insurrection.

The rising Javanese were led by Sukarno, who had been interned by the Dutch government before the war, because of his illegal activities. Now he wanted to be the spokesman for all the Indonesians, throughout the huge archipelago, rather than for Java itself. The Dutch government in London, the British government and the Australian government all had their own priorities, and showed little interest in the atrocities in Java.

I thought for a moment, sharing Herman's feelings of frustration and impotence in this tragic situation. Then I told him that we had several captured Japanese bombers. If we painted them white, with red crosses, would he and his friends be able to manage the logistics of the operation from there? Joyfully, he said that would be no problem.

We both knew the risk we were taking, for the responsibility would be ours should anything go disastrously wrong. Worst of all would be for one of the aircraft to crash with great loss of life, but we both felt it had to be done. His courage and determination to undertake yet more dangerous mercy missions endeared him to me for life.

In 1986, with his letter in front of me, I pulled myself back from these vivid memories, and proceeded to read it in a quiet suburb in London. It seemed that Herman was in England, on a short visit from the USA where he now lived. He had recently retired and had been endeavouring to contact me, hoping we might meet up. Such a letter required immediate action and led to a speedy reunion. My house was small, and this big man entered, his arms full of gifts, and he seemed to fill the whole room with warm goodwill.

He told me the fascinating sequel to the story in which I had shared. He had taken lists of names from the women queueing up for the flights to freedom. At the end of the day, at about five o'clock, he said he was sorry but he had his quota for the first flights, although they could be assured that he would be back and they would all be taken care of. A beautiful woman was next in line, and immediately asked if he was staying at an hotel there that night? Somewhat surprised, he said that he was, whereupon she said, 'Then, you will give me the key to that room tonight, and I will stay there, and you will stay in the camp! If you had stayed in a Japanese camp for three years, you would not stay in one for five minutes more if you could help it.' In due course Herman married this very special lady! I had the great pleasure of meeting Ans with him when I went to Washington a few years after seeing him in London.

When Herman returned from his first flight into Batavia on 13 September he had collected many scraps of paper, some no larger than a postage stamp, on which the internees had written their first survival notice to their families. These precious scraps were the only bits of paper the internees could find, and were put into envelopes to be sent to the addresses throughout the world. Much later Herman was told that these messages had become valued collectors' items.

After his demobilisation, and totally exhausted, Herman became an American citizen. He acquired a law degree, and was appointed as a law clerk to the US Supreme Court, and finally as an executive to the president and editor of the National Geographic Society.

His wife Ans, after their daughter had grown up and qualified as a doctor of medicine, bought a small precision-engineering business. One of her customers was NASA, and she was told that a small part her firm had made was now on the moon. She said it gives her a special feeling whenever she looks at our satellite, knowing that something from her little plant is actually up there.

A few years before Herman came to see me in England, he had some throat trouble, and he went to see a specialist in Washington. The specialist asked, 'Were you in Java, and then Singapore in 1945?' When he was told 'yes', the specialist told him, 'You were the first person to bring me news that my wife was still alive.' One of those tiny fragments of paper, at least, did have a happy ending, and Herman received no bill for the treatment of his throat.

In February 1946 I completed my three-year tour overseas. First I flew from Java to Singapore. After three months away from there, I detected great changes. It was cleaner, everything was running more smoothly, and there was a feeling of people getting their lives back to a state of normality after the nightmare of the past four years. I had dinner with Sir Keith Park and his wife. It was a wonderful evening, but sadly it was the last time we were ever to meet.

In those days most repatriation took place by sea, and my ship was SS *Monarch of Bermuda*. Two friends, Elsie and Doris Waters, were also on the passenger list. I had met them in Burma when they were entertaining the troops, having come out at their own expense. From many years before the war they had been known to every Briton as Gert and Daisy, two Cockney characters, who did many radio programmes depicting all the trials the ordinary folk in the UK were facing daily. They wrote their own words and music, delivered with a ready wit, and in the war did a tremendous amount to boost morale, and not only on the 'home front'. In Burma they visited the sick and wounded, and would sit on the beds and write letters for those unable to do so for themselves. As well as giving their concerts, they took countless names and addresses of families back home, whom they contacted to give personal news of loved ones they had seen in the Far East. Neither cost the taxpayer a penny, though little was known of this by the general public. I stayed in touch with them for many years until they both passed away.

Another passenger was a princess of Siam with her young son 'Dom Brom', whom she was taking for treatment at London's Great Ormond Street Children's Hospital. She was tiny, gracious, and one of the most beautiful women I have ever seen, and also blessed with a delightful sense of humour. Of course, she had a tough bodyguard, but eventually in the course of the long voyage he grew to trust us.

I had been told when I boarded the ship that, as senior RAF officer present I would be responsible for over 100 RAF mutineers, who were aboard under open arrest. I quickly made contact with these men to ascertain their story of the so-called mutiny. It was not as depicted. They had been told to congregate in a darkened room, where they had been harangued by the leaders of the 'mutiny'. They told me that they had been threatened, and told not to leave the room, and so later, when ordered to leave the room, they refused to go. They were ordinary reasonable men, and now realised that they had been misled.

It all seemed childish, and I found the whole matter hard to comprehend. I enlisted the help of Elsie and Doris, knowing how good they were at communicating with people, and the upshot was that, after a lot of talking, we were able to leave a lot of smiling faces. I told them I had been to see the OC troops, and he had agreed with me that if all went smoothly for the rest of the voyage, he would give a good report of their conduct. Captain Church, the master of the ship, was very relieved to have the matter so resolved.

After my return to the UK, I submitted a personal report to the effect that the men's conduct had been exemplary throughout the voyage, and I am happy to say that no further action was taken with regard to the 'mutiny'. However, I was left with an uneasy feeling regarding the role of those who had harangued them.

Of course, the length of the voyage gave me plenty of time to think about my future career. I had been little more than a boy when I left my uncle's firm and joined the RAF. Suddenly I had been catapulted into a very harsh adulthood by the relentless momentum of war, and for all those years I had done nothing else. It was hard to realise that all that was now behind me, and I was finding it well-nigh impossible to unwind and relax. I had forgotten the 'normal' feeling of physical security around one. No counsellors or therapists in those days! I was facing the unknown.

The hard brilliance of the tropical sunshine faded as we sailed into the northern hemisphere, and at length the misty greyness of the English coastline impressed on me the reality of my homecoming. In the evening we docked at Liverpool, and bade one another farewell. I entrained for London with some other officers. It was a memorable journey for me, as it was the first I had made without the blackout since the beginning of the war. Seeing the lights everywhere brought home more than anything else that the war was really over. I reported to the Air Ministry, and was sent on leave.

I still could not get rid of a feeling of disquiet that somehow the world was not yet the safe place we fought so hard and long to save. Perhaps the celebrations for VE and VJ day had helped dispel such thoughts from those in Britain. In the Far East we never seemed to feel that hostilities were really at an end – for us they were not. The threat of Communism had not yet been appreciated by the West, but the description of that darkened room lurked uneasily in my mind. I felt uncertain about my future. I loved flying, but in peacetime was a Service career the best option?

CHAPTER ELEVEN

PEACEFUL BERKSHIRE

I knew I had come to a crossroads in my life, and I had to think long and hard about my future career. I had wanted to be a veterinary surgeon since early boyhood. I have a great affinity with animals, especially horses and dogs. They will come to me of their own volition, and I am never happier than in their company. As a boy, of course, there was no chance of my being able to afford all the years of training needed to become a vet, and there were no grants or loans to help in that regard. Even post-war, I knew that it was still impossible to realise such a dream.

Of course, I knew how much I loved flying, but had no indication of the tremendous part commercial aviation was going to play in the world. I eventually decided to continue in a Service career, in the pattern of life that I had come to know so well. This was despite the fact that one was not allowed to continue in the rank achieved during the war. I reverted to my substantive rank of squadron leader, but was given the acting rank of wing commander for the job I was to take on. Thus it was a double demotion. Like my brother officers, I found it difficult to gather momentum again.

My job was to be staff officer in charge of administration at Reserve Command HQ at White Waltham, Berkshire. This had become the largest command in the RAF, involving 22,000 Royal Auxiliary Air Force, 60,000 RAFVR Volunteer Reservists, and a substantial backing of regulars who organised the command, which took care of a great number of winding-down operations. In addition I was also responsible for a nearby camp with about 600 prisoners of war, mostly German. Many of them were pleased to get out and work on the local farms under supervision, and this proved to be a mutually beneficial arrangement with the farmers.

One of my more interesting extraneous duties was to be Command representative in charge of films for the RAF. Our civilian mentor was the great pioneer movie mogul D. W. Griffith, who was living in England at the time. He was most unassuming, and gave generously of his time and expertise for no fee, making certain that the RAF had the best films going. He also taught me an early lesson in money management, ensuring that all funds allocated for the purpose were held in interest-paying bonds while awaiting use. I much enjoyed my $2^1/_2$ years working with him.

The country was changing from six years of war, but we still had to keep the operational efficiency of the RAuxAF squadrons in being, as well as many reporting aspects of the RAFVR. To do this we used Reserve Command groups, balloon centres, and VR units of similar categories. Our run-down and cost-cutting were never enough for the Treasury, but we were all deeply conscious of the need for economy. A complete rethink of strategy was needed, as we thought there would never again be a threat from Europe.

Then, almost imperceptibly, we began to realise that a threat could come from our former ally, the Soviet Union. Our first real intimation of this was the way the Communists treated our Czech and Polish pilots, who had fought beside us so gallantly throughout the war. Many were put in jail, and even murdered. Not surprisingly, this caused many of those who got news of these events never to return to their native land. A lot of them had married English wives, and indeed loved Britain. In due course many took British nationality, and one could find no Anglophiles more loyal.

Apart from winding down on the service side, various civilian personnel were being forced to adjust to peacetime life, which many of them had never known except as schoolchildren. For those who had a trade it was relatively easy, but for others without the necessary clearly-defined skills and qualifications it could be very difficult.

At Maidenhead, which is near to White Waltham, a branch of the Royal Air Forces Association was inaugurated soon after I went there in 1946. As serving members were also welcome, I joined. The branch asked me if I would like to be its president. I felt very honoured, and said I would be delighted to accept. I remained president for just on 50 years, until the branch had to be closed, as no young people were interested in joining such associations. Age had taken its toll of the stalwarts who had kept this wonderful branch going for many years, and as their numbers and health diminished, we could finally keep it going no longer.

Hundreds of returning ex-servicemen, and their wives and families, have been helped not only materially but also by the warm and personal feeling of belonging to a large Service family. This is an intangible contribution which cannot be overestimated, and no one was ever made to feel a recipient of charity. This support and camaraderie continued through the years in civilian life, and perhaps it is at its greatest and most needed in old age. For their part, the aged veterans are those who work most tirelessly for those same charities.

I am afraid that, as far as the authorities are concerned, the ex-servicemen and their families are all too often made to feel very 'ex'! I have realised this all the more, as I have increasingly become a veteran myself. For instance, in the Maidenhead Branch we had members who had been part of the RAF group who watched the successful testing of the first UK atomic weapon at Bikini Atoll. They were dressed in tropical shorts and shirts, and the only advice they were given was to turn away if the glare proved too intense. Many of them died from leukaemia, and others are having related problems for which it is always difficult to get compensation, as it is extremely hard to prove that this event was actually responsible for their illnesses. It now seems that history is repeating itself, with the Gulf War syndrome.

In 1946 I lived in the mess at White Waltham. I have always loved the English countryside, and my appreciation of it was sharpened by having been away for so long. I resolved to indulge one of my long-cherished ambitions, and keep my own horse. There was a farrier in the village, and this decided me. He was a knowledgeable man, and he generously taught me much about horses.

Through a contact in Ireland, I purchased a fine mare, and had her sent over. She arrived by train at Maidenhead at 10.30 at night, having travelled in a special section of the guard's van. How times have changed. I was informed of her arrival, and was asked to collect her as soon as possible. A friend drove me to the station, and my batman (who had been a stableboy before joining the RAF, and was very thrilled at the prospect of having a horse at the base), rode the three miles on his bicycle.

Jenny was a beautiful black mare about four years old. She seemed to look at me enquiringly, as if to say, 'Now what?' Luckily, she had a halter and rope, and so, as it was a reasonably warm evening, I decided to mount her bareback and ride her back to her stable at the mess. Somehow, I found two bits of string which I attached to each side of her halter, and, with the batman leading on his bike, we got to her new home. Jenny was tired, and viewed the whole episode with disdain. Next morning I had to pinch myself when I woke, and began to wonder if I had dreamt it all, but there Jenny was, refreshed and completely at home.

I saddled her up, put on some reins and headgear, and Jenny and I had our first proper ride together, accompanied by Bobby, my Labrador, who seemed to enjoy the proceedings as much as I did.

However, he returned tired, for he was unused to quite such a mileage, or such an intense walk, even for a dog with his stamina. Bobby was the largest Labrador I have ever seen. He had been bought by my mother after the war, when her dear old golden retriever died. Bobby soon dominated my poor mother, and the only way she could stop him barking was to allow him to sit up at table when she was eating, and give in to his every whim. When I went on leave and saw this pantomime, I could scarcely believe it, for my mother was a strong character, and no stranger to owning large dogs. Unthinkingly I said to her, 'You can't go on like this, dear, I will take him with me and train him.' Before I knew it, my mother had me out of the house, with the dog on a piece of string (because he would not tolerate a lead), on the way to Surbiton station. I reached Waterloo, and then had to get Bobby across London to Paddington, for the train to Maidenhead. Bobby always looked somewhat belligerent, and this, combined with his size, was disconcerting to strangers, and I had a job persuading a taxi driver to accept us. Bobby had arrived about three weeks before Jenny, and I had already established a routine of long walks. Jenny's arrival was a godsend, but I think the mess began to wonder what I would bring in next.

In time it became obvious that I needed a larger horse than Jenny, and I bought Golden Crest. He was a magnificent gelding, about six years old, with a chestnut mane, and about sixteen and a half hands, whereas Jenny was fifteen three. I made sure Jenny went to a good home, and we parted friends. Golden Crest had a wicked sense of humour, and would enjoy tipping me off gently if I leant forward carelessly to open a gate. He would never run away, but would look down at me and, if a horse could laugh, at that moment he laughed. Bobby would lick my face, and seemed to ask, 'What are you doing down there?' He and Golden Crest became bosom friends, and Bobby was a great companion. He had just needed wider horizons.

I was fortunate at this time to meet Nigel Mould, a young artist making a name for himself with his portraits of dogs. He came to stay at our mess, just after he had drawn Princess Margaret's dogs. I asked him to draw Bobby, and he did a lovely portrait, but he was not satisfied, as he said it was not exactly Bobby. Whilst Nigel was watching him, Bobby heard my footsteps outside and looked up expectantly. Nigel touched up Bobby's eyes on the portrait, and remarked with satisfaction, 'That's it. That is just what I wanted!' In that fleeting moment he exactly caught the look in the dog's eyes. Over 50 years later Bobby still gazes down at me, with that special look I knew and loved so well. I'd like you to know, Nigel, how much pleasure that picture has given me.

Golden Crest, Bobby and I went out every day before breakfast, and I managed to keep Golden Crest in good shape with extra rides on Saturdays and Sundays. We got to know every inch of the countryside together, and covered many miles. Whatever the time of year, it was always beautiful.

I had two years there, and then I was posted to El Adem, to command its RAF station, and so it was back to the desert once more. I had to sell Golden Crest, but he also went to a good home. Bobby returned to my mother, two years older and a changed animal, which she was proud to take out on a proper lead. I knew he would miss Golden Crest, and I missed them both.

CHAPTER TWELVE

BACK TO THE DESERT

I arrived at El Adem, a few miles south of Tobruk, on 28 September 1948. What a contrast from the lush greenness of the Berkshire countryside. By one of those extraordinary twists of fate, I was back within a few hundred yards of where I had had my camp with No. 89 Squadron's Beaufighters at Bu Amud. The old airfield was now deserted, and the crashed Messerschmitt signpost had been removed. Indeed, Bu Amud had gone back to the desert.

El Adem was a strategic base roughly mid-way between Cairo and Tripoli, used as a staging post for aircraft overflying the desert. We had a twin-engined Anson, which I flew for desert rescue. I am happy to say that it was not often called upon for this task, but it was useful for visits to HQ and for 'shopping'. El Adem was a permanent station built with bricks, and there was even a squash court. How different from wartime days! There was a lot to be done. The station strength was about 600, plus 900 German prisoners of war who were my responsibility. It may seem odd, but this was still their classification at that time. They had not yet been processed for release. They gave little trouble, and we played them at soccer on a regular basis, ensured their health was of the highest order, and included them in the general running of the station.

Walter, the mess barman, was a German, with a wonderful voice, and I had a medical surgeon, a Welshman, who also had a fine voice. At times we would enjoy these two singing. The desert air, so silent and clear, seemed to lend itself to music, and we had a repertoire of Gracie Fields' songs, German *Lieder* such as *Schatz Ich bitte Dich heute Nacht*, and some of my favourite Welsh songs. We had a wind-up gramophone, and a fair collection of records, mostly classical. In the evenings we would sit and enjoy Handel's *Water Music* and many similar masterpieces in those unlikely surroundings.

Prior to my arrival there had been much pilfering. I decided to pay a visit to the local sheik with an interpreter. The sheik, Suleiman (Solomon), was tall, strongly built, and of aristocratic appearance in his flowing white robes. I imagined him to be in his thirties, and he spoke a little French, so we managed to communicate. He hated Italians, and showed me his hand which they had held up against a wall and shot a bullet through to ensure he obeyed their instructions. Needless to say, this had exactly the opposite effect: Suleiman and his tribe became the scourge of the Italians and Germans alike.

After several meetings, I think he began to feel that I too loved the desert, and he slowly came to trust me. On one occasion he suddenly said to me, 'Commandante, there will be no more pilfering. I have ensured it will happen no more.' I thanked him, and indeed there was no more. I only heard afterwards that he had issued instructions to this effect to all local Arabs, and the penalty for disobedience of his edict was the traditional one of chopping off the left hand.

One day Sheik Suleiman arrived at the station in a state of great anxiety. He told me that one of his young camels had fallen down a nearby well. Of course I realised the seriousness of the situation, for, should it die there, their entire water supply would be contaminated.

These wells are a brilliant engineering achievement, left by the ancient Romans from their days of occupation. Cyrenaica was then a 12- to 30-mile (19- to 48-km) deep and many miles long agricultural belt known as the 'granary of Rome', irrigated from underground cisterns and wells. In spite of their great age, some of these cisterns are still in use. The basic concept is that water is allowed in, but there is little or no evaporation. They are stone, and the entrance from the surface is about 6 ft (1.8 m) down into an underground chamber of room size. I went down into one of these birs, as they are called, and was amazed at its size. It was about 15 ft (4.6 m) by 12 ft (3.7 m), and about 12 ft deep, and I was assured that this was only a small one. The top opening to the surface of the sand was only about 30 in (.75m) square. When these were first built nearly 2,000 years ago, the engineers in those days must have had some indication where the water supply was. The entrances to these wells are kept carefully covered, not only to prevent evaporation, but also to prevent an accident such as the young camel falling in. The sheik was furious that someone had left the cover off, but his overwhelming concern was to keep the water pure.

We had a long-armed Coles crane, but I had to confirm that its weight would not crack the walls underground. We let a man down on a rope, who then drew a diagram in the sand to show our engineering officer and me where he thought it would be safe to operate the crane. We placed our crane on the chosen spot, and swung its arm over the hole to let him down again. He bundled the camel up firmly with rope, and it popped out like a cork from a bottle. Fortunately it had not sunk

Top: The author's grandparents, 1937.

Left: The author's parents, William and Ruby David.

Above: The author at 4½ years old.

Top: The First Flight. Dennis accompanied by his mother, in G-EBIZ, the red-painted 504K of Captain Phillips' Cornwall Aviation Co. The company gave first flights to many others who were later famous, including John 'Cat's Eyes' Cunningham.

Middle left: About to fly the Blackburn B2 at Hanworth in May 1937, in which Dennis made his first solo flight.

Bottom left: Ready for take off – the first fighter flight on a Hawker Fury at Sealand.

Bottom right: Portrait taken on the outbreak of war.

Dennis All the very best my old friend
Bee. 20.3.99

Top left: King George VI visits Lille Seclin, 1939. Talking to CO David Atcherley of 85 Squadron, 10 minutes after speaking to Dennis. Line up of aircraft, Gladiators, Blenheims and Hurricanes.

Top right: As Dennis prepares for The Battle of Britain, a sketch by Rothenstein, Church Fenton, 5 June 1940.

Above: Schoolboys in pilot's uniform! Early days in France. Note the early Hurricane (left) with the two-blade prop.

(Photo courtesy 'Bee' Beamont)

Top: 'Out of Ammo' by Geoff Nutkins. Already out of ammunition after previous combat, Dennis dived to the rescue of Squadron Leader Oliver, the CO of 85 Squadron over Northern France on 11th May, 1940. He forced the German pilot to break off his attack.

Bottom: 'Saved by a Friend' by Geoff Nutkins. Australian Pilot Officer John Cock was seen being shot up as he descended by parachute. Dennis fired a short burst at the attacking German fighter, destroyed it and went on to drive off a second Messerschmitt Bf109. He returned to circle John Cock,

LIE IN THE DARK AND LISTEN.

BY NOEL COWARD.

LIE IN THE DARK AND LISTEN.
IT'S CLEAR TO-NIGHT SO THEY'RE FLYING HIGH,
HUNDREDS OF THEM, THOUSANDS PERHAPS,
RIDING THE ICY, MOONLIT SKY,
MEN, MACHINERY, BOMBS AND MAPS,
ALTIMETERS AND GUNS AND CHARTS,
COFFEE, SANDWICHES, FLEECE-LINED BOOTS,
BONES AND MUSCLES AND MINDS AND HEARTS,
ENGLISH SAPLINGS WITH ENGLISH ROOTS
DEEP IN THE EARTH THEY'VE LEFT BELOW.
LIE IN THE DARK AND LET THEM GO;
LIE IN THE DARK AND LISTEN.

LIE IN THE DARK AND LISTEN.
THEY'RE GOING OVER IN WAVES AND WAVES
HIGH ABOVE VILLAGES, HILLS AND STREAMS,
COINTRY CHURCHES AND LITTLE GRAVES
AND LITTLE CITIZENS' WORRIED DREAMS;
VERY SOON THEY'LL HAVE REACHED THE SEA
AND FAR BELOW THEM WILL LIE THE BAYS
AND CLIFFS AND SANDS WHERE THEY USED TO BE
TAKEN FOR SUMMER HOLIDAYS.
LIE IN THE DARK AND LET THEM GO;
THEIRS IS A WORLD WE'LL NEVER KNOW.
LIE IN THE DARK AND LISTEN

LIE IN THE DARK AND LISTEN.
CITY MAGNATES AND STEEL CONTRACTORS,
FACTORY WORKERS AND POLITICANS;
SOFT HYSTERICAL LITTLE ACTORS,
BALLET DANCERS, RESERVED MUSICIANS,
SAFE IN YOUR WARM CIVILIAN BEDS,
COUNT YOUR PROFITS AND COUNT YOUR SHEEP
LIFE IS PASSING ABOVE YOUR HEADS,
JUST TURN OVER AND TRY TO SLEEP.
LIE IN THE DARK AND LET THEM GO;
THERE'S ONE DEBT YOU'LL FOREVER OWE.
LIE IN THE DARK AND LISTEN.

ITALY-BALKANS-N.AFRICA-EGYPT-LEVANT-IRAQ-PERSIA-

AIR FORCE NEWS

E.&W. AFRICA-SUDAN-ADEN-RHODESIA-MADAGASCAR-GIBRALTAR

JANUARY 30, 1945.

KEY BURMA PORT 'FELL' TO RAF PILOT

AKYAB, vital Burma port and one of the greatest prizes of the campaign to date, was «captured» by a RAF pilot.

He was 26-year-old Group Captain W.D. David, D.F.C. and Bar, a former Battle of Britain pilot, of Surbiton, Surrey, who landed on an Akyab air strip to make the dramatic discovery that all the Japs had fled.

When British and Indian troops reached Foul Point they found themselves separated from Akyab by four miles of treacherous water and they were prepared for a tough amphibious operation against the enemy.

South-East Asia Command had laid careful plans for the action. Landing craft were to launch British Commandos and Indian troops at three points on the opposite bank.

While preparations were being made G/Capt. David was flying over Akyab. No ack-ack greeted him, and dropping lower to investigate he could observe no signs of the enemy.

Finally he landed on one of the port's airstrips. From natives he learned that the Japs had pulled out on New Year's Day.

"Stole The Show"

The news seemed too good to be true. The assault troops landed as planned, but they found no enemy awaiting them. As a "Time" correspondent cabling the report commented, "a gas-engined bird stole the show."

Group Capt. David's discovery came as a dramatic climax to two years of bitter fighting for this Burma key-point.

The capture of Akyab gave the Allies a port with 20-ft of water and a system of air strips from which they can bomb Rangoon, only 320 miles away.

Top left: Dennis and John Cock in 1983, attempting the recovery of the Hurricane that John had parachuted from over Portland Naval Base.

Top right: The Free French pilots were thrilled to have General de Gaulle in their midst in 1942 at Crosby-on-Eden. Dennis pictured to the right, front row. Henri Lafont is extreme left, second row.

Bottom left: 'Lie in the Dark and Listen' by Noel Coward. Written by the author himself and presented to Dennis in Ceylon.

Bottom right: *Air Force News*, January 30, 1945. News of Dennis 'capturing' the Burma port of Akyab – after discovering it deserted by the Japanese.

Top: Akyab – (left to right) Headman in white shirt, Gen. Christison, Dennis, Paddy Bandon, and the white flag Dennis had first noticed. Photo taken in front of the L5 the General landed in. *(Imperial War Museum)*

Above left: 'JAPS GONE'. British prisoners send a message to the skies, Rangoon 1945, visible on the roof of one of the huts.

Above right: Viscount Trenchard. Boom! At the time this photograph was taken he had lost his sight.

Right: Group Captain 'Hughie' Edwards VC, taking over from Dennis when he left for Java

Top left and right: Two photographs of the almost unrecognisable remains of the Vampire Dennis crashed and walked away from, Western Desert, 1950. Note the melted wing.

Middle right: The author with King Abdullah and Sir Alec Kirkbride, the King's UK adviser.

Bottom: King Abdullah's Royal Standard, presented personally by the King to Dennis, who was OC of the RAF detachment in Amman. *(RAF Official Crown Copyright Reserved)*

Top left: Dennis with Glubb Pasha after taking him for his first flight in a meteor jet, 1950.

Top right: Nero, one of Field Marshal Rommel's army dogs which became the

Bottom: Sharing a joke. Dennis with Paddy Bandon and Chief of MoD Information at Pitreavie Castle.

Top left: Sir Leslie and Lady Fry.

Top right: Tanks in the streets of Budapest, October 1956.

Above: Captured Russian tanks. The people of Budapest claim their victory.

Left: A rare diplomatic picture. With Colonel Ksapenko (USSR) and Colonel Drobacs (Yugoslavia), in Hungary

00010

Igazolom, hogy W. D. DAVID UR.
ANGOL LÉGÜGYI ATTASÉ ÉS NEJE
70 AB 78 DT. 565 rendszámu
gépkocsival közlekedik.

Felkérem az összes illetékes hatóságokat, hogy a nevezett diplomata számára a zavartalan közlekedést biztositsák és szükség esetén nyujtsanak neki segitséget.

Budapest, 1956 nov 17.

/Dr. Münnich Ferenc/
Magyar Népköztársaság
Belügyminisztere

Удостоверяю, что г. В. Д. Давид
Воздушный Атташе Великобритании
и супруга
пользуется машиной № ДТ 565. 70 АБ 78

Прошу все соответствующие органы обеспечить названному дипломату беспрепятственное передвижение и в случае необходимости оказать ему помощь.

Будапешт, 17 ноября 1956 года.

Др. Мюнних Ференц /
Министр Внутренних
Дел ВНР

BRITISH LEGATION (CONSULAR SECTION) BUDAPEST

Великобританская
Миссия
в Будапеште

Всем кого это касается

Настоящим удостоверяется, что предъявитель сего документа, подпись которого прилагается дипломат Её Величества Министерства Иностранных Дел Великобритании и Северной Ирландии, путешествует по делам службы между Будапештом и Веной и взад по распоряжению правительства Её Величества Министра Иностранны Дел. Министр Иностранных Дел, от имени правительсрва Её Величества, просит всех, кого это касается разрешать предъявителю сего

В.Д. Давид. Г. Ж. Смит

[его жене и детям] свободно и беспрепятственно путешествовать, не чиня ему (им) никаких препятствий к проезду и предоставляя им все возможности и удобства согласно общепринятым международным узаконенениям и обычаям

29 октября 1956. года

BRITISH LEGATION CONSULAR SECTION 30 OCT 56 BUDAPEST

Консул

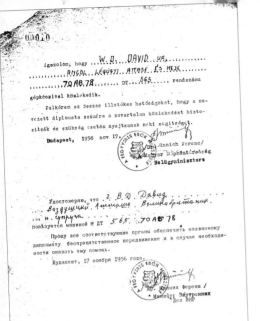

Top left and right: Faked passes used for extricating the convoy from Hungary, October 1956. Document 565 was written in Hungarian and Russian.

Middle left: Stalin's Boots; after the statue had been pulled down the Soviets tried to cover the whole plinth.

Bottom right: The Hungarian flag with Hammer and Sickle removed from the centre, thereby recreating the old national flag.

Bottom left: Dennis David being interviewed on arrival at the Austrian border by western media having led out the first convoy from Budapest since the start of the uprising. Note the broomstick tied to the front of his Vanguard car, with Union Jack nailed onto it, his only defence and identification!

Top: Dennis David, 1960, in front of a Canberra.

Above: NATO reception: (left to right) Lt. General Duilio Fanali, Admiral James S. Russell USN, General Savi, Chief of Staff, Aeronautica Militare and Dennis.

Left: Dennis signing the book on behalf of RAF Tangmere after accepting the Freedom of the City of Chichester, 1960.

Top left: The Queen talking to Dennis David in the line up of the guard of honour in Westminster Abbey when her Majesty unveiled the memorial stone to Winston Churchill, Battle of Britain Day 1962. The ceremony overran and on the Queen being warned the fly past was consuming a worrying amount of fuel while waiting, she remarked with a smile, 'If you will mix up Westminster Abbey, Winston Churchill, and the Battle of Britain, what can you expect?' (Courtesy Pathé News)

Top right: March 1981, Dennis invested with the Knightly Order of Vitez by Archduke Arpad Habsburg, Hungarian royal ruler in exile.

Bottom: From the filming of 'Aces High'. (From left to right), Group Captain Tom Gleave, Dennis David, Peter Firth, Group Captain Douglas Bader, Malcolm McDowell, and in the cockpit Simon Ward.

Top left: Major Chuck Shave.

Top right: Herman and Mrs. Ans Arens (on right) with, extreme left, Dr. Melville Bell Grosvenor, Chairman of the National Geographic Society and Sir Vivian Fuchs.

Middle left: 'Macky' Steinhoff with the author.

Middle right: Four British Battle of Britain Eagles at the Alamo, (left to right) Brian Kingcombe, Dennis David, Desmond Hughes and Johnny Cunningham.

Bottom left: Dennis awarded a medal from the Freedom Fighters, with two of the Captains of the Order of Vitez in the UK. On the left is Janos Szakaly and on the right, Dr Andrew Zsigmond de Lemhény. Behind Dennis is the bullet-ridden flag of Hungary.

Bottom right: Author with former Free French pupils at the 1991 Paris airshow. All old friends together.

Top left: (Left to right) AVM Ron Dick, the author, Hans Ekkehard Bob's son, Hans Ekkehard Bob and Col. David McFarland, in front of a model of the Wright Bros. aircraft at Maxwell AFB.

Top right: At Maxwell AFB, 1990, with Wolfgang 'Bombo' Schenck.

Middle left: Dennis with Fritz Losigkeit

Eagles by a local firm of outfitters. Maxwell AFB, 1990.

Middle right: Gathering of Eagles, 1987. Final night at Maxwell, (left to right), host officer Major John Wegner, Dennis, Nicky Barr, Colonel Dave McFarland.

Bottom left: (Left to right) Hajo Herrmann, the author and James B. Stockdale.

Bottom right: The author with Ken Walsh, 1987.

Top left: Dr. Heinz Lange and his wife Lo.

Top right: Oberleutenant Ulrich Steinhilper and Dennis at Biggin Hill, Kent, 1990.

Middle left: General Trudy Clark.

Middle right: Lester and Dora Strother.

Left: The final party of 1990, at Hendon, to celebrate the 50th Anniversary of the

Top left: Raising Funds for the Battle of Britain Museum in 1980. Thirty veterans signed 1,000 copies of prints of Hurricane and Spitfire paintings. These raised £30,000 for the Museum.

Top right: The author with the other 24 pilots who featured in *So Few*, at a Rolls-Royce party, 1990.

Bottom: Dennis David with Hurricane

out of its depth, and had sustained no injury from its fall. We unbundled it, and it rushed over to its anxious mother. The young camel vociferously told its mother of its awful experience, but was soon suckling contentedly. The sheik was thrilled, and I felt the RAF was well in favour.

Sheik Suleiman belonged to the Zenussi, a nomadic desert tribe, whose wealth is tied up in their camels, sheep and goats. Urban Arabs are despised by them, and they call them 'Town Arabs', a term of derision. The Zenussi have strict codes of honour, and once you are their friend they never waver. In their presence you never use the left hand for greeting or eating, for this hand is used in one's own personal toilet. They are great poets, as well as very practical, and have a mystical attitude to life which fascinated me.

Several weeks after the camel episode, there was drama indeed. The sheik's only son was rushed to us. The unconscious form looked like a little bundle of rags. He had obviously lost a lot of blood, because he had picked up a Red Devil, a wicked explosive device left by the Italians as they retreated in 1942. The aim was to incapacitate any Allied troops who came across them. Many warnings about them had been given over the years, but this child had picked one up. They looked like red ballpoint pens, obviously attractive to a child, and this one had blown up, severely damaging his arm. We rushed him to our sick bay, where our young Newcastle doctor immediately administered a plasma drip, and dressed the wound, saving the boy's life. It was a happy coincidence that we had, in fact, only received the plasma a few days before.

The sheik had by this time heard of the accident, and he was desperately worried. Soon we were able to tell him that all was well, and that his son's life was no longer in danger. He instantly said, 'You are now my Blood Brother.' He asked the interpreter to find out when I could visit him in his tent, as he wished to thank me there. On my arrival I was a little disconcerted when the interpreter was told not to come in with me, although I realised the reason when the sheik's mother appeared and served us tea. She was not wearing a veil. There was no higher compliment he could have paid me, and I realised that I was now truly considered a member of the family.

Arab tea is very refreshing, and is basically a mixture of strong tea with mint leaves. It is poured from a great height into small cups from an elegant long-spouted pot, and they never seem to spill a drop.

Thus a great friendship was cemented, culminating in a day when we went out alone together on a couple of beautiful Arab horses. To me they seemed small, but he said they were very strong, and would carry me with no problem. After a day's riding my horse had never even sweated, and seemed quite fresh. The Arab thoroughbred tends to have one vertebra less, hence its compact appearance. The bridle, saddle and stirrups were obviously durable, and seemed to be designed to suit the comfort of the horse as well as of the rider.

From the saddle, Suleiman suddenly raised his rifle and shot a running hare, killing it with one bullet to the head. I could scarcely believe my eyes, and congratulated him. He said, 'It is nothing, we grow up with the rifle.' They are also blessed with wonderful sight. Suleiman continued to grow in my admiration and respect until the day I left.

I felt I owed him more than simple thanks. It is amazing how two kindred spirits can communicate and share experiences with no great need for a common language. I thought he would enjoy a flight in my old Anson, and a different view of his world which he loved so much. He was delighted at the suggestion, and could not get over the beauty of the sky and clouds from this unimagined vantage point. We flew over some clouds with the sun shining down on them, and he was lost for words. He kept repeating three Arabic words, meaning 'How beautiful, how gloriously beautiful.' I was glad he seemed to like my world above the clouds as much as I did his.

Not many Western people like camels, but I had come to love and trust these animals during my previous time in the desert. A good working camel will go for ten days without water, and will cover up to 40 miles (64 km) each day. The white camels cover up to 60 miles (nearly 100 km) a day, but can only go without water for eight days. There is a cautionary Turkish proverb, 'By all means pitch your tent, but first tie up your camel.' They are prone to wander off. Apart from the Arab contribution to mathematics, it is often forgotten that they invented the coil, and used it to ensure that female camels had their youngsters at times which would not interfere with their working lives as beasts of burden or riding.

At El Adem, one never knew what was going to happen next. One day the weather closed in over the whole of the Mediterranean, and as El Adem was the only airfield accepting aircraft, we had quite a cross-section seeking shelter. By far the most interesting were the two carrying the Monte Carlo Ballet Company, returning from Cairo where they had been the guests of King Farouk.

The movements officer rang me up to say that his section was full of beautiful women. Delighted as we normally would have been, this filled me with dismay. We already had 26 extra aircraft in, and we were hard-pressed trying to allocate accommodation and facilities. Somehow we managed it, but over 400 extra mouths to feed presented no small problem. None of us had any previous experience of ballet dancers' appetites, and we could not believe that these delicate-looking girls could demolish heaped platefuls with the alacrity they did. We regarded ballet dancers with new respect! They were with us for a few days, and we were all sorry when the weather lifted, although the catering staff heaved a sigh of relief.

One day I was told that a Dakota of Mercury Airlines, carrying civilian passengers, had lost its way, and landed on a disused airfield 40 miles away just over the Egyptian border. As this was foreign territory, it could provoke a tricky international incident, and I decided it would be wise to take a team of armed men with me when I set off to see what had happened. I also took extra fuel. By the time we reached the aircraft the Egyptian police were already there. They were understanding when I explained that I wanted to get the aircraft en route to El Adem as quickly as possible. I think the police were pleased for someone else to take responsibility, and so the incident was quickly and amicably ended.

I enjoyed my stay at El Adem, which was all too short. During the summer we swam from the beach by Tobruk harbour. There were countless ships sunk in and around this area, but the swimming conditions were well-nigh perfect. Gradually these wrecks were being salvaged. During the war this place had been of great strategic value, for it is a large natural harbour, and was already important even in Roman times. It is interesting that the Tobruk area was also almost the dividing longitude line between the Western and Eastern Roman Empires. How strategic places tend to repeat their importance over the centuries!

Whilst I was at El Adem many old friends visited, including the legendary Douglas Bader. He flew his silver Proctor 'Willie Uncle' (G-AHWU), supplied by Shell Oil, for whom he was then working. Douglas was always a stimulating character, and it was good to see him so happy with his new employers, for whom he was full of praise.

Of course, I had to have a canine companion. This time it was one of Rommel's Afrika Korps dogs, which had been taken over by the RAF. Nero was a very large thoroughbred Alsatian, who never put a paw wrong the whole time he was with me. He had obviously been impeccably trained, and did not seem to mind flying. Like Alex, his one aim was to share time with his owner, which is the right relationship between man and dog.

From time to time, I had to report to Malta, as this was our senior RAF HQ. En route there in the Anson we refuelled at Benghazi. It is hard to think that in those days I was flying at around 130 mph (208 km/h), and frequent refuelling stops were essential.

On one occasion at Benghazi I had to have the Anson checked for ignition trouble. As this took some time, I investigated caves I had seen from the air, which a local had explained to me were the caves of Leyte. They were vast, and I found it fascinating that the water in them was clear and without a trace of salt, whereas other water in that area was brackish. It covered the floor, and seemed to be part of a large underground lake. I saw several blind white crayfish, about 10 in (25 cm) long, similar to those found in the Nile hundreds of miles away. I asked the local expert about them. He was vague, but said he understood that the whole desert had water under it. Perhaps this explains the birs I mentioned previously. *Bir* is part of the Arabic name for many places in the desert, meaning that there is a well there. Who knows, ancient Cyrenaica may one day return, and the whole desert will be farmed again.

My next posting was to be OC Flying Wing at Deversoir by the Suez Canal. This station had Tempests, but was shortly to be re-equipped with three squadrons of de Havilland Vampires, the RAF's first operational jets outside the UK. We were all looking forward to the chance of working with these exciting aircraft.

On 7 November 1949 I flew the Anson to Deversoir – there was no other way to get there – and off-loaded Nero to a waiting friend, then flew on to Fayid to report. After satisfying the customs officials, I returned to Deversoir, unloaded my kit, and pacified Nero, who had begun to wonder what was happening. My accommodation of the semi-permanent variety was adequate and reasonably cool. We were lucky to be on one of the lakes, so we had good swimming.

Within a few days the Vampires began to arrive. There was no official instruction for the hand-over of the jets, nor any training, so we just strapped in and started the de Havilland Goblin engine. We had received a dual Gloster Meteor jet, but this was unserviceable.

We did have somebody who had flown jets before, and he warned us what to expect, such as apparently slow acceleration on take-off, and a long low approach. All the pilots were reasonably experienced, and the transition was achieved with no casualties. We carried out several tests, and the Vampire stood up to them all, proving to be a first-class desert aircraft. Sand had no effect on the Goblin engine. Even if a considerable amount of sand was allowed to be sucked in, only vitrified glass beads came out, and the engine kept running. We quickly transferred the operational requirements of the Wing from the Tempest to the Vampire, and never lost a day's capability. We had a good station commander but, like me, he had to learn all about the Vampire from scratch.

We regarded our biggest problem to be the possibility of the Heyl Ha' Avir, the newly formed Jewish air force, attacking not only Egypt but also us. We also had to take very seriously the prospect of a mighty thrust by the Soviet Union down through the Middle East to the Gulf oilfields. Liaison with the other Services thus had to be of a high order. We had several Tewts (tactical exercises without troops) and in joint operations I was lucky to be with the Coldstream Guards. The Guards regiments are well-known for their precision on ceremonial occasions, but they are also superbly trained in soldiering.

The Vampire was an exciting aircraft to fly, and particularly agile. We all became proficient in attacks on surface targets, and my average error with unguided rockets was 7 ft (2.1 m). We thus presented a formidable attacking force. Of course in those days there was no computerisation, and it was the skill of the pilot that counted. Unfortunately, my accuracy was not fully appreciated by the Army when I led a demonstration attack on a group of trucks filled with petrol and placed as a target. My first salvo of four 60 lb (27 kg) rockets scored a direct hit, and blew the target to pieces. The remaining Vampires then fired into the blazing inferno. Many of the Army remarked to me afterwards that they were glad we were on the same side, and they all went very quiet. None of us had seen weapons like this previously.

King Farouk of Egypt had just been made an honorary air commodore in the RAF. To celebrate this, he asked several of us serving in the Canal Zone to his palace for tea. The word 'tea' gives the wrong impression of what was a splendid occasion. The King, resplendent in his RAF uniform, met us all personally, and was a gracious host. We then sat down at many tables, and were presented with commemorative menus. Even reading the list of items gives no idea of the sumptuous feast provided. The menus were decorated with a picture of his palace and were printed in both Arabic and English. We were all served with English tea, and of course the King was fluent in English. Sadly, he had allowed himself to become grossly overweight, and one felt self-indulgence had wasted a good man. His handshake was firm, and he had come to the throne very popular with his people. Nevertheless, it was not long after this that he was deposed, and he went to live in Italy.

One of my most pleasant duties was to entertain the King of Jordan. We were detached to Mafraq, a large airfield in the desert, not far from Amman, the capital, and on the due date King Abdullah arrived with his entourage. We had no idea what to expect, and it was a great relief to find that the King spoke perfect English, and had a lively and enquiring mind. He seemed well-versed in British affairs, and I was told afterwards that each week he read the *Illustrated London News* from cover to cover. He also had an English civil servant, Sir Alec

Kirkbride, who was a tower of strength and a trusted adviser.

The King was a real man of the desert, and like all such Arabs loved the land. His knowledge of plants was outstanding, and when he discovered that I had grown to love the desert, he passed on some of his knowledge. Sir Alec suggested to His Majesty that he might like to inspect some of our aircraft. A fly-past was arranged, and I took Sir Alec up in our now serviceable Meteor T.7. The monarch wanted to fly, but was forbidden to do so, so I took up some of his entourage instead, and the whole visit seemed to be a big success.

The legendary desert fighter General Glubb Pasha was also present. He commanded the Arab Legion, a force intensely loyal to the monarch. This force had largely British officers, and although small it was a potent outfit. It was agreed that we should carry out affiliation exercises with them whenever possible.

General Glubb Pasha's interest in and love for the Arabs and their way of life was such that he learned to speak every Arab dialect, thus endearing himself to all Arabs. He was very interested in aviation, particularly in our jets, and I took him up in the Meteor T.7 for his first flight in one. Having learnt how to operate the airbrakes, he frequently did so, and seemed to enjoy the shuddery reduction in speed.

On two occasions I went to King Abdullah's palace, which was a very imposing building – particularly after our tented accommodation at Mafraq. The first visit was a great honour. The King had decided that he wished to present the RAF with his own personal royal standard. General Glubb Pasha had informed me of this, together with two or three members of No. 6 Squadron, which formed the majority of the detachment, and were part of the Deversoir Wing.

King Abdullah had obviously been very impressed with his visit to the detachment, and the General told me this was the first time he had ever known him to present his personal standard to any non-Arab country. The 16-ft (4.9-m) pole to which it was attached presented me with a considerable problem when conveying it out of the palace. The monarch presented it to me personally, with due ceremony, and shaking my hand, after taking it first from an aide. My mind was racing, wondering how I was going to carry it out with suitable dignity on my own part, for, apart from the great length of the pole, it was extremely heavy. I think it was made of ebony, and the standard itself was richly-embroidered heavy silk. It was altogether most imposing, and we in the RAF felt deeply honoured. I must admit that I was able to enjoy it more in retrospect than at the time, for my overwhelming feeling then was great anxiety lest I should hit one of the many beautiful chandeliers!

Today this standard is one of the prized possessions of No. 6

Squadron. At the time of the presentation the King said he would be delighted if some members of the squadron would attend the palace to dine with him, a great honour which of course we were delighted to accept. A date was arranged, and I and my fellow officers dressed up in our finest uniforms. Our initial reception was impressive enough, but when we went into the dining room we saw that all the plates and cutlery were solid gold! Each chair had behind it a fierce desert warrior, dressed in the uniform of the Arab Legion, who watched attentively over his charge. The whole occasion remains an indelible memory. The sheer brilliance of that display of gold is impossible to describe, and even 'dazzling' seems an inadequate word.

King Abdullah was a much-respected monarch, and a good friend to the United Kingdom. I was greatly saddened by the news of his assassination a while later. He was shot, despite his personal bodyguard, while he was on his way to prayer. He was the great-grandfather of the present King Hussein of Jordan.

The whole Jordan area is steeped in history, and the ruins of more than one Crusader fort still rise above the desert. I was surprised to find that the stone door of one of these forts still moved on its axis. A principal architectural method at the time was the inverted hanging chain – a graceful flowing arch which looks good to this day. As a desert warrior himself, King Abdullah was fascinated by the destructive power of our 60-lb (27-kg) rocket heads and four cannon which could be loosed off by a Vampire. He also found its speed hard to comprehend, because we could cover a ten-day overland camel journey in 40 minutes.

After completion of our exercises with the Arab Legion, the wing was concentrated at Deversoir, to prepare for possible action. Even in those days the Gulf area was a constantly shifting balance of opposing powers, which we felt could be a threat to peace. The situation is really no different today.

One morning, taking off in my much-loved Vampire I had just reached 400 ft (122 m) when there was a thump behind me, and the fire warning light came on. I pressed the fire-extinguisher button with alacrity, and the light went out. I mentally congratulated myself on dealing so promptly with this emergency, but then the engine lost almost all power, and the engine controls ceased to respond, because the electric power cables had burnt out. I looked behind on hearing a roaring noise coming from that direction, and could see nothing but flames. I realised the situation was desperate, for with every second the heat was becoming more intense, and the flames had already burnt through the parachute pack on my back and were singeing my flying overalls.

I turned left and managed to glide in at high speed, for by then I found I had no power at all, and made a wheels-up landing in the desert. Just before I touched down I felt all the flight controls slacken off and become non-effective. My Vampire eventually slid to a halt, and I made all haste to get out, as by this time my parachute had been burnt off my back, and my flying overalls were already on fire. Apart from a full load of fuel and ammunition on board, the oxygen bottles were right behind my seat. I managed to leap out, and had not gone more than six paces when the oxygen bottles blew up. The fire rapidly became a raging inferno, and had I been a second or so slower I would not have lived to tell this tale. The heat was so intense that it melted much of the aircraft, which became just a puddle of metal in the sand!

I could scarcely believe my ears when an Army warrant officer drove up in his Jeep and asked politely, 'Would you like an iced lemonade, Sir?' By then 20-mm ammunition was exploding all over the place. We both retreated hastily to a safer position, and I can to this day remember the delicious taste of that iced lemonade. He had been taking it to some gunners nearby when he saw my Vampire in trouble and followed it to my crash. I later learned that I had caught fire as I overflew an explosives depot, where the general feeling was 'Please let him keep it flying a bit further on past us!'

There had been several Vampire fatalities, and it was never understood why even experienced pilots had never jumped. I was debriefed particularly on the aspect of the failure of the controls in the last moments. It was concluded that the flexible fuel pipes to the engine had frayed through wear and desert conditions, thus causing the kerosene to be sprayed outside the combustion chambers, instead of inside them. My fire warning light had gone out because the whole circuit was burnt out. In a few minutes the flight controls would also have been destroyed. Though it is every pilot's instinct to stay with his aircraft, and try to get down somehow, after my crash Vampire pilots were ordered to leave their aircraft immediately should a fire occur.

I was the first pilot to survive such an event. Hopefully, the investigation following mine, and the subsequent action taken, helped to save lives.

CHAPTER THIRTEEN

HELPING 'THE FATHER OF THE RAF'

On 10 March 1951 my flying tour came to an end, and I became due for an administrative posting. It was my good fortune to renew service under Sir Charles Steele, who had been my AOC in Malta. He was now AOC-in-C Coastal Command, and I was posted as staff officer in charge of administration for the Northern Coastal Command Group at Pitreavie Castle, near Dunfermline in Scotland.

This entailed responsibility for the Northern Atlantic, and all the area up to and including the Baltic. It meant watching the numerous Soviet submarines and fishing fleets, and generally policing the entire area. We were also part of the North Atlantic Treaty Organisation (NATO), and of a joint Royal Navy and RAF Headquarters. Not least, there were the civilian responsibilities for those who get into distress at sea. In those days we also supervised mountain rescue in Scotland. My admiration for the Royal Navy and the Royal National Lifeboat Institution increased the more I got to appreciate the work they did, and in particular the weather conditions they did it in.

Pitreavie Castle was an old Highland fortress, but it had not escaped Cromwell's attentions, and the son of the owner was said to have been hanged on his orders. My greatest delight over this posting was to re-establish my friendship with the Christisons, who lived nearby. Christie was on the point of retiring, as General Officer Commanding-in-Chief Scottish Command. Such a post entailed being Governor of Edinburgh Castle. Another friend in the same area was Group Captain Lord Hamilton, who was Master of Holyrood, a much-esteemed title. The history of Holyrood goes back hundreds of years, and Holyrood House is one of Scotland's finest palaces.

Alistair MacLean – of the already noted birthday party in Java – was now running the Edinburgh Tattoo. The Edinburgh Festival was already world-renowned, and the Tattoo, its most famous and traditional event, certainly makes the heart of every Scot beat with pride. I have always held Scotland and the Scots in high regard, and this posting greatly enhanced those feelings. Perhaps there is a particular affinity amongst fellow Celts, as we seem to have many traits in common. Awkward and stubborn for sure, but loyal to the death.

I cannot understand how the Scots got their reputation for being mean with their money. One of my extraneous duties in Scotland included being a member of the Council for Soldiers, Sailors and Airmen, which used to meet regularly once a month. I was amazed how much welfare Scots gladly gave to their own troops, both serving and ex-service men and their families. This made a big impression, and I have tried to get other authorities to continue on the same lines. Sir Charles Steele was a great champion in such matters.

We were also responsible for operations and administration for the RAF in Northern Ireland. It was obviously important not to get involved politically in any way, in view of the delicate situation existing there at the time. It has been my good fortune, throughout my life, to make friends with a cross-section of nationalities, religions and beliefs, and I have always thought of them as just my friends, and always as worthwhile people in their own right. I have had many interesting discussions with all of them, and my only wish is that we could all live in harmony together.

I used to visit Northern Ireland every month, for a few days at a time, to see how things were progressing. We were fortunate in having good men in command, and our problems were few and far between. It was important that we were very even-handed in all our dealings with the locals, many of whom I got to know and like. To this day, however, I can never understand how some of these delightful people could live such religiously segregated lives. In one of the places I visited it was pointed out to me that the Catholics would shop on one side of the street, and the Protestants on the other, and some residents were said never to cross the street in their whole lives. I did notice, however, that the very young children tended to like one another, and when possible would play together. Tragically, a change seemed to take place as they grew older, and their lives became segregated.

Skipping ahead some years, in the 1980s I was on safari in Kenya. Amongst those sharing the holiday with us were a young man and his girlfriend from the Republic of Ireland. One felt at once that they were on their guard, sharing the trip with English tourists, but discovering that I was very proud of my Welsh ancestry dispelled some of their reserve. Paddy, the young man, and I soon got on well together, but the girl was very wary of us all. Paddy and I talked at length about 'The Troubles' in Ireland. I was interested when he told me the story of the colours of Drogheda (pronounced 'Droyda'), which was the part he came from, and which are black and red. Red for the blood of the Irish shed in 1649 by Oliver Cromwell, 'when the hills ran red', and black for the mourning that ensued. This is thought of to this day, and one must live in hope that eventually the horrors of the past will be consigned to the past, as the British have done with the much more recent and vivid horrors of Germany and Japan.

My years in Scotland were happy years, back with old friends, and making new ones. I made a visit to Tarland to meet Lady MacRobert, who lost four brilliant sons in the wartime RAF. She was a magnificent lady, and despite having lost her husband as well as her sons, had by no means become a recluse, and entered very much into the life of the community. Tarland is renowned for its large estates, and in particular for its fine breed of Highland cattle. Long-horned, and well-known for their shaggy coats, they are smaller than other cattle, but very strong and sturdy, and I found them placid and friendly.

Our station at Kinloss, north of Tarland, remains to this day the home of the RAF mountain rescue team. Like the lifeboat crews, all the members of these teams, service and civilian, are volunteers. I was surprised to learn how often their services were called upon, in inclement weather, averaging several times a week. Of course, the advent of the helicopter made an enormous difference.

There is an unending fascination in the story of the Loch Ness Monster. Anyone in that area will have his own particular tale, and there is always the sneaking feeling that there is 'something' in those waters. Even today, when driving near that loch, one cannot help looking across the surface of the water just in case one might see something.

About this time General Christison became due for his retirement. He had always been a keen conservationist, and had done research into the agricultural history of the land in the Border Country. He found that, over 150 years ago, monks had successfully grown fruit in orchards they planted in a small valley near Melrose. Because the westerly wind blew there in the winter, there was little or no damaging frost. Knowing that the productive age of apple and similar fruit trees is 30 to 35 years, he felt that this project would see out his old age, although the locals were more than a little sceptical.

His long-time batman worked with him, and in due course he was marketing his crops in Edinburgh. He then became more adventurous, and diversified into pears and plums and later into soft fruits. His season would start with black and red currants, gooseberries, strawberries and raspberries, going on to plums and damsons, right to the final autumn apple harvest. His produce became famous for its excellence. A near-neighbour kept bees, which was mutually beneficial, as they pollinated the fruit blossom, and ensured a good fruit harvest, and lots of honey for the neighbour.

Christie had come to notice that those of his military friends who had no other interests when their Service careers ended had usually not lived long after their retirement. A case in point was Christie's friend General Slim, who received the Japanese surrender at 10 am, and was sacked six hours later. Although the order was rescinded, he died shortly after his retirement. In the event, Christie himself outlived his orchard. When he was in his nineties the trees felt they had reached their allotted span, and they began to die off. Eventually he felt that, having got so far, he might as well make one hundred! He reached his century, but died shortly afterwards.

As my administration tour came to an end I was selected for the Air Warfare College, at Manby in Lincolnshire. This is sometimes called the University of the RAF. Students spent a year studying all aspects of the Service's flying roles: bombers, fighters, coastal and transport. Mine was one of the last courses to fly all these roles. The course lasted a year, and the Treasury was always seeking to have it terminated, as it cost £80,000 per pupil, which in the 1950s was a lot of money. I was delighted to be one of the 'chosen few'. Manby was a prewar station, so we were all housed in brick-built accommodation. As the airfield was small, we tended to fly from a dispersal field nearby. The training was intensive, and we had two overseas officers, one Canadian, and the other an American, who later became the General Commanding US Air Forces in Europe.

During the year I was able to keep up my sport. In the Middle East I had captained the Combined Services squash team, and had been able to play at the Gazero Club in Cairo with many first-class competitors. During 1953 while I was at Manby I had the honour of captaining Lincolnshire, when we beat all the surrounding counties.

On graduating from Manby in May 1954 I joined the staff at the Ministry of Defence (MoD) in London as an assistant to the Chief of the Air Staff, Training. He was none other than 'the Abandoned Earl' Paddy Bandon. My post was primarily concerned with training crews for the forthcoming V-force.

This force was a big step forward for the RAF. The USAF, which had been formed in September 1947, had already created its Strategic Air Command (SAC), under General Curtis LeMay, and was fast converting it to all-jet. The RAF decided to form a V-Force, a separate wing of bombers within Bomber Command to complement the American SAC. It was a new concept for us, requiring different planning and training. Apart from the first pilot and captain of the aircraft, and the usual second pilot and navigator, a whole new breed of aircrew officers had to be trained. They were called air electronics officers.

The V-force was composed of three types of large four-jet aircraft, the Vickers-Armstrongs Valiant, the Avro Vulcan and the Handley Page Victor. About 100 of each aircraft were ordered (it must be remembered that the Cold War preoccupied the free world in those days). I was not lucky enough to fly the last two types, but the Valiant was ahead of the others in timing, and in December 1954 I managed to fix trips, as an MoD official, in production Valiants on test from the manufacturer's airfield at Wisley in Surrey. These trips totalled over five hours, and I was able to fly from the second pilot's seat. One of the leading company test pilots was Brian Trubshaw, whom I got to know at that time, and who later became chief test pilot on Concorde.

Though it was slightly less advanced than the other two types, the Valiant was an exciting aircraft. We routinely flew at 50,000 feet at just below the speed of sound, and it fascinated me to see F-86 Sabre fighters, the most advanced in service at that time, unable to match our speed or height. I remember thinking what a superb aircraft the Valiant was, and how advanced.

They were all aesthetically beautiful aircraft, but it was a time of rapid change, exploring new aerodynamic shapes. To try to minimise risk, all three differed significantly. The Valiant was the most conventional, and was therefore intended to be developed first. It had slightly swept-back wings and tail, but the later Victor had a graceful curved (so-called crescent-shaped) wing and a horizontal tail on top of the fin, and in its original form was powered by Armstrong Siddeley Sapphire engines. Most striking of all, the Vulcan was a tailless delta (triangular wing) aircraft, powered by Bristol Olympus engines.

Vickers did a great job with the Valiant, and did indeed get into production first, against an order for 108. These followed three prototypes, the third of which was made much stronger in order to permit low-level attack, where it would be much more difficult for it to be detected by hostile radar. I knew nothing of this, and it was only much later that it was discovered that some of the production order should have been of the strengthened Mk 2 version. In February 1964 it was decided that, to escape radar detection, the V-bombers had to fly at low level. As they were all of the weaker Mk 1 type, within weeks dangerous cracks were appearing, and the whole Valiant force had to be grounded.

All these bombers were capable of being part of a nuclear deterrent, but although their range and capability were considered very impressive at the time, the advance of technology continued apace. Higher-flying and faster aircraft were already on the drawing board. However, the trusty V-force was a frontline defence of our country for many years, until after the Falklands campaign, and well into the

1990s many were used as tankers for refuelling jet aircraft in the air.

When I was at Manby I met George Edwards who was the chief designer of the Valiant, and later of Concorde. He told me at the time that they now had abundant power, and I can remember him looking at a large building and saying, 'We could drive a house along.' Development of this massive power continues to this day, but of course with power comes speed which generates more heat on the metal, and is possibly the greatest hurdle for designers.

I was lucky to have a first-class officer who prepared an outstanding paper for the Air Staff to consider, which covered all aspects of training for the V-Force aircrews. This paper was so good and comprehensive that I forwarded it in its entirety. I was particularly anxious that the officer concerned should receive due credit for his forward thinking. Imagine my disbelief when I found this paper had been taken over by a senior official, rewritten and endorsed as his own, before sending it on to higher authority. I felt I could not let this go without comment, but, alas, voicing my very strong feelings about this matter achieved nothing except to be very detrimental to my prospects for future promotion.

After a few weeks in the job, someone rang me up saying 'Dicky here, Dennis, do you remember me?' I thought fast, and knowing that it certainly would not be Lord Louis Mountbatten (Dicky to his friends), and the only other Dicky I knew was from my days in the Middle East, and he was now Chief of the Air Staff! I dismissed this as unlikely, and decided it must be one of my friends playing some kind of joke. I therefore answered flippantly that he could pull the other one. 'No, Dennis,' came the amused reply, 'it really is Dicky, the CAS!' I practically leapt to attention at my desk, and could still scarcely believe my ears. He enjoyed my discomfort, and politely requested that 'when I had a moment' – he had a wicked sense of humour – would I pop round to see him? I drew a deep breath, and told 'God' I would do so. The enormity of a mere wing commander (all those years later I still had not achieved the rank I held in wartime) being rung up by a Marshal of the RAF, who was CAS, is very hard to explain to the layman. Such a thing just never happened.

Lord Dickson, as he became, was a direct descendant of Lord Nelson, and a popular and competent CAS. On my way to see him I called in to see Paddy Bandon, to report my summons. He laughed and said Dicky had already spoken to him, and thought I would be surprised. Dicky received me as an old friend, telling me "'Boom' is in trouble." 'Boom' was the nickname Lord Trenchard had earned, through his deep booming voice. He was 'The Father of the RAF', which he had caused to be founded on 1 April 1918. Previously he had been in charge of the Royal Flying Corps. As a Marshal of the RAF he never retired, and continued to serve until his death. This recognition is afforded to all marshals of the RAF, admirals of the Fleet, and field marshals.

He had now reached his eighties. As a young man he had fought in the Boer War. A brilliant polo player, he was given command of the Australian Light Horse, but soon suffered severe injuries to his lung and one leg. Recuperating in Switzerland, he watched the Cresta Run, and thought this was something he might do. The Run then consisted of a one-man bobsleigh, and after seven runs Boom found he was regaining control and mobility in his injured leg. Eventually he won the Cresta Run.

Qualifying as a pilot in 1912, he became one of the first officers of the Royal Flying Corps, and, even in those pioneering days, he could foresee the tremendous role air power would play in future warfare. For ten years after World War I he continued to run the RAF.

He was popular with the Treasury, for he was able to police the wild North-West Frontier of India with aircraft. This meant that, following tribal warfare or other fighting, instead of the British having to keep thousands of troops in the area, one aircraft would drop leaflets on the town warning the inhabitants to get out, as they were going to be bombed, and a few hours later some aircraft would fly in and administer justice! As well as saving lives, it also saved a lot of money.

Another illustration of his intuitive vision was his comment on the installation of the Royal Navy's heavy guns at Singapore. He always said these would never be used, as they were facing in the wrong direction. Nobody believed him until he was proved to be right, and the Japanese army drove south by land. In 1929 he relinquished the post of CAS mainly because King George V asked him to be commissioner of London's Metropolitan Police. As a small boy I saw his tall, commanding figure on a white horse at a ceremonial occasion, and this made a lasting impression on me. Little did I think that I would ever meet and work with him.

One of his early innovations was to put radios in the police cars, thus forming the first 'flying squad'. As a result, the criminal underworld sent him a telegram saying, 'Every bastard born in London should be called Trenchard.' He showed this to the King. To his horror the King then handed it to Queen Mary, who read it without any change of expression. She then turned to Lord Trenchard and with a lovely smile remarked, 'My dear Lord Trenchard, what a very large family you would have.'

Now at last I was to meet my boyhood hero. Dicky had explained to me that Lord Trenchard was having difficulties with his biography.

Initially the work had been undertaken by Hilary Saunders, one of the official war historians, who had known him for many years. Alas, Hilary died, and Lord Trenchard was put in touch with another author, with whom he was unable to establish a comparable understanding. Lord Trenchard had impaired hearing, which after World War II had led to severe deafness, and by this time he had lost his sight as well. He turned for help to his old Service, and Dicky asked me if I would help sort out this delicate situation. I rang Lord Trenchard at once.

I went to his flat near Sloane Square. Lady Trenchard opened the door and said, 'You must be Wing Commander David. Hugh is waiting for you inside.' I was ushered into 'the presence', and found a tall and erect man, still looking very good. He had mastered the art of looking straight at one, and it was hard to believe that those eyes could not see what they were looking at.

He told me of the problems with his memoirs. What seemed so sad to me was that this great man was reduced to having to ask for help, when all his life he had been such a dynamic leader. From the moment she opened the door I felt that Lady Trenchard was a very special person, and it was clear that she was going to be the linchpin in sorting the memoirs out.

I could see that there had been a clash of personalities between Lord Trenchard and the new author. Bruce Lockhart was a busy MP, and seldom available when Lord Trenchard wanted him; he simply did not have the time to go through piles of documents. I contacted the well-known historian Arthur Bryant, whose views were valuable and strengthening, and had he not already been so committed he would have taken on the task himself.

The key to moving forward proved to be William Collins, of the publishing house. Lord Trenchard and I went to his office. He had just returned from Kenya, where he had stayed with Joy and George Adamson to sew up *Born Free*, the best-selling story of Elsa the lioness. He was full of tales about his visit, such as the night when the fully-grown Elsa decided the one bed she wanted that night was the narrow camp bed he was already occupying. She snored the night away, while he hardly dared breathe. On telling Joy Adamson next morning, she said, 'I wondered where she was, she is rather inclined to sleep around!' We listened fascinated, problems of the biography momentarily forgotten.

Eventually Mr Collins managed to retrieve all the documents and memorabilia, and signed up a promising young author, Andrew Boyle. He took on the job of finishing the biography, and it was published by Collins in 1962. Although this was a very time-consuming task for me, in addition to my normal work involved with training the V-Force aircrews, it was a most rewarding episode. I grew very fond of Lord and Lady Trenchard, and after the problems of the book were resolved I stayed on with Lord Trenchard as his aide, which was in fact a milestone in my air force career.

Early on, before I got to know him more personally, he made a very unexpected comment to me. 'Old David,' – as he always called me – 'you will probably suffer from being connected with me. Others have, and I do not think you will be an exception.' He was very aware that by no means everyone agreed with his uncompromising opinions, and the manner in which he was never content to settle for anything other than the best that could be achieved. I replied that I would keep my eyes open, but that I was sure any possible unpleasant consequences would be more than compensated for by the opportunity to work with him. I was already aware that the position of honorary aide to the founder of the RAF was a much-coveted one, and inevitably there were disappointments among those who had not been asked. As I have already written, the CAS's telephone call had come as the greatest surprise, and there was nothing I could do about what followed.

Lord Trenchard hid his blindness and his deafness admirably. He hated his hearing aid, and his great joy was in switching it off, sometimes with embarrassing consequences. One such occasion was in a prestigious club, where after a conversation with a particularly garrulous gentleman, Lord Trenchard turned to me and remarked in his resounding voice, 'I never COULD stand that man, Old David.' Unfortunately 'that man' was still standing next to us.

Lady Trenchard played a consummate role in preserving her husband's independence, yet watching over him with great concern. However devoted they were as a couple, he must never feel cosseted by an over-anxious wife. It was comforting for her to know that a younger officer, who admired him greatly, was also very supportive of him.

All this time, not to dwell on his frailties, Lord Trenchard was playing an active role as a director of Unilever. Many times I would accompany him on his almost daily journey to Unilever House in the centre of London. On Service matters he would use me to set down his thoughts and ideas for official papers. I would then take this material and write it up, for his approval. Often he would say, 'Take it away and sprinkle some full stops and commas over it with a pepper pot, Old David.' I would then take the finished draft to him, and he would ask me to guide his hand for the signature. I was deeply conscious of the trust he invested in me, in view of the highly confidential nature of some of the letters.

It was with great sadness that on 10 February 1956 I learnt of Lord Trenchard's death. The funeral was a very moving event, for the coffin was carried by no less than six marshals of the RAF, and our whole Service felt a great sense of personal loss. I kept in touch with Lady Trenchard, and she visited me when I was air attaché in Hungary. My affection and admiration for her increased each year I knew her. I felt that with the passing of Lord Trenchard a pioneering era had come to an end. It had been a time full of formidable personalities and unforgettable characters, and cliché or not, they were made of a stuff we are unlikely to see again.

CHAPTER FOURTEEN

'CAPITALIST VODKA'

After Lord Trenchard's death, I continued my job associated with the training of aircrews for the RAF's new V-Force of strategic jet bombers, which I found very interesting. I was, however, very aware of the atmosphere that had been engendered by my outspoken stance concerning my young officer's report on the V-Force. It was April 1956, and I still had some time to go in my posting, but I had begun to think very seriously about leaving the RAF while I was still young enough to have the prospect of making another career. When I was asked to go and see the senior posting officer I wondered vaguely what it was about, but nothing could have prepared me for his opening question, 'How would you like to go as air attaché to Hungary?'

I indicated that, of course, if that was where they wanted to send me I was perfectly willing to go . . . but when was this to be? The normal training for an attaché posting is about 18 months as, apart from the language of the country, there are matters of protocol, gaining a general knowledge of the duties involved, and so on. I was therefore even more nonplussed when I was told 'as soon as possible, as the post is vacant'. 'As soon as possible' in fact meant 'yesterday'.

My shock and disbelief at this latest bombshell must have been obvious, for the posting officer went on to explain the delicate situation that had suddenly arisen. It seemed that our air attaché in Budapest had been caught by the secret police bringing various goods, such as watches, across the border in and out of Hungary illegally. Despite all the emphasis that was put on being aware of surveillance in such postings, in the normal course of training for the job, my predecessor had been blissfully unaware that he had been watched and recorded 24 hours a day. One day he was stopped by the dreaded AVH (Allam Vedelmi Hatosag), the secret police, when he had the illicit goods in his car. He was confronted with all the records and photographs that had been meticulously kept of all his trips and activities. They then said that they wanted the minutes and full details of the MoD (Ministry of Defence) meeting he was to attend in London in a few days' time. They were in an unassailable position for blackmail, and of course, he had no alternative but to ask the RAF to recall him immediately, giving some indication as to why.

I found it hard to grasp the full implications of the task I was being asked to take on. One thing stood out like a beacon: I must fight for as much time and the best preparation I could get. We eventually reached a compromise of five weeks, which seemed woefully inadequate, but I can only say that my tuition was of the highest calibre. I was thankful for the expert instruction I received, but, alas, this haste meant that I still had little or no knowledge of the Hungarian language. It is in any case a difficult language, and I knew that any knowledge I had of other European languages was useless, despite attempts to reassure me with remarks to the effect that, as I knew a bit of French, I would manage all right. The only language Hungarian is vaguely related to is Finnish. I knew I would just have to do my best to remedy my linguistic deficiency when I got there.

In addition to my special briefing with MI5, I underwent the usual photography and radar surveillance training. In those days Hungary was behind the Iron Curtain, and the Cold War was very much in being. My whole attaché training was thus intense and compressed.

Luckily the only major change in uniform required was the purchase of aiguillettes, which I bought off my predecessor as he no longer needed them. These consist of heavy gold-braided cord, with two 'gold' metal pointed pegs on the ends, and they are worn looped round the arm and over the left shoulder, with the two pegs hanging down in front. This is for the ambassadorial duties. For royal duties they are worn on the right shoulder. Until I needed them I had no idea what significance they had, but learned that when aiguillettes were used originally they were made of ordinary rope attached to two pegs to stick in the ground. They were worn by *aides de camp*, and were used to tether the master's horse. I loved the story of their origin, and viewed my extra gold braid with renewed interest, and only wished I had a horse to tie up!

I also bought my predecessor's black Humber Hawk. I had never had such a fine car in my life, and it proved to be a good friend during my time in Hungary. My predecessor had chosen the Hawk, as this was the vehicle most often used by the British authorities serving behind the Iron Curtain.

My preparation came to an end all too soon, and I set off for Hungary via Germany and Austria. I had purposely chosen this route so that I could pass by Louvain (Leuven), some 20 miles (32 km) east of Brussels. It was over Louvain, in May 1940, that I lost my special friend, Chris Mackworth. I said a little prayer for him as I drove through the woods of Louvain on that day in May 16 years later.

It was a long and tiring journey but, after a couple of overnight stops, I reported to our embassy in Vienna, and collected instructions from the military attaché there. Apprehensively, I drove on to the Austro-Hungarian frontier at Hegyeshalom, and I remember a feeling of reluctance at saying goodbye to the Austrian border authorities, which they seemed to understand. A chillingly forbidding sight lay ahead of me. An eerie kind of no-man's land covered the short distance between the two frontier posts, but what different worlds it spanned. Cheerful, harmonious, welcoming Austria was left behind, and I drew up at the guardroom beside the massive locked gates into forbidding Hungary.

The guards were very correct, and their thoroughness was marked, especially the way they covered the car while they operated the actual gate. They had been expecting my arrival, so there was no difficulty in this respect. This was literally the Iron Curtain, for Hungary lay behind a steel fence as high as a tennis court's perimeter, and stretching as far as the eye could see, punctuated roughly every 200 metres (220 yards) by watch-towers with armed guards ready to shoot at anything they deemed suspicious. As if the fence and watch-towers were not enough, the minefields, laid along numerous furrows, were also evident. I was waved through the gates and they clanged shut behind me. Already I knew my life here was going to be different.

After a few miles, I came to the town of Mosonmagyaróvár. Here for the first time it was possible to see Hungarians going about their normal business. They were mostly connected with farming, and practically the only form of transport was the horse and cart. I had been told that all Western diplomatic cars were monitored when they passed through towns, so it was no surprise to see police noting the number.

After successfully navigating my way through the large town of Györ some 25 miles (40 km) further on, and having seen only an occasional truck with Soviet soldiers, the Hawk suddenly came up behind a large Soviet convoy, full of troops, with a field kitchen. I passed a few vehicles before a bend in the road gave a long view ahead. The vehicles stretched as far as I could see, so I just sat behind one truck full of troops. The young soldiers were amused, but their tough senior NCO spoke to them and they no longer looked at the Hawk. After some 15 miles the convoy turned left, and the road was again clear.

This slow progress delayed my arrival at the British military cemetery a few miles west of Budapest. There our military attaché, Colonel Noel Cowley, was waiting to meet me, and escort me to the air attaché's residence. He knew about the problem with my predecessor.

I was excited to be in this wonderful city. Most of the houses were dilapidated, and many were still bullet-scarred from World War II. There was even evidence of the Turkish occupation of over three centuries before, and a mosque which seemed in better condition than most of the other buildings. Soon the road ran along the west bank of the broad Danube, and we climbed steeply to Kelenhegy Ut (street), almost at the summit of the 770-ft (235-m) Gellért Hill, where my residence stood.

It was of nineteenth-century vintage, solidly built. The frontage, facing west on to the street, was unexceptional, but at the rear the French windows in the dining room opened out on to a balcony from which the view was quite breathtaking. It looked steeply down to the Danube, with the seemingly endless city of Pest on the far side, and I could see all eight of Budapest's bridges crossing the river, all of which had been severed in World War II. I had previously read the history of the oldest, the beautiful Lanchid suspension bridge, which was begun in 1839 to the design of Englishman William Clark, by the order of Istvan Széchenyi, a leading figure in the Hungarian age of reform. Construction was completed by his son Adam Clark, who carried out numerous grand engineering projects in Hungary, married a Hungarian girl, and lived there for the rest of his life. The Lanchid bridge fascinated me, and throughout my time in Budapest I always tried to use that bridge to cross the river.

The household staff were introduced, and the head of household, a very beautiful blonde, welcomed me to my new home. I also inherited a chauffeur and a second maid. I had been warned that the head of household and the chauffeur were officers of the AVH, and that the assistant maid, like all the staff, was required to report to the AVH in detail on the air attaché. This fact seemed never to have occurred to my predecessor. I decided that I would discharge the housemistress and chauffeur as soon as I could reasonably do so, and meanwhile I would be ultra-careful. Only much later, during the course of the Revolution, when I discovered the incredibly detailed file that had been kept on the previous incumbent, did I realise how frequently and how successfully the housemistress had compromised him, while the smooth chauffeur had been the one who had so diligently photographed everything that the attaché had ferried in and out with his car!

My first duty was to report to my new boss, Leslie Fry, who held the post of Her Britannic Majesty's Minister, as we did not have an embassy but a legation in Hungary, and he officially represented the Queen. The attachés ranked as counsellors, which is one rank below minister. Each air attaché behind the Iron Curtain was fortunate in having an assistant air attaché, a specially selected warrant officer. I was sad to learn that mine was about to leave Budapest, having completed his tour of duty. He had done a magnificent job holding the fort prior to my arrival.

Leslie Fry, in addition to his Foreign Office background, had had a long military career, and had, of all happy coincidences, been an officer in one of the Gurkha regiments. After having been fortunate enough to have been with them during my postings in the Far East, I have the greatest respect for anyone connected with them. It was a very unusual background for such a Foreign Office official, which alone I felt marked him out as a unique head of mission. In my new role in the diplomatic world I reported to him above all, and in fact the Foreign Office took precedence over the RAF.

In view of the manner of the departure of my predecessor, I viewed my first meeting with Leslie with some trepidation, and he too, I feel, must have wondered just who was being sent out at such short notice. At once, from our first meeting, I felt that here was a man I could completely trust and respect, and he quickly put me at my ease with his great warmth and kindness. As we became better acquainted, he paid me the great compliment of giving me a free hand in my work. The only stipulation he made, and one which I wanted also, was that I should tell him exactly where I was going, and what time I anticipated being back. He also required of the staff at large that he be informed immediately any time I was overdue.

Shortly after this I had the pleasure of meeting his wife Penelope. Little did I think at the time what an incomparable help she was to be to the whole mission throughout the testing days that were nearly upon us. Amongst other things, fortunately, her interest in medical matters and the knowledge she had so gained was to prove invaluable. Right from the start, we laid the foundations of a warm friendship that has endured to this day. Later, I was more than delighted when Leslie was most deservedly knighted, and so glad it was an honour in which she could share. Sadly, he died in 1976 and is sorely missed by her and his many friends.

When a new attaché joins his post he at once has to make several 'calls' on his opposite numbers, West and East. This was interesting, and took priority over most other matters until I had done the rounds of all my fellow attachés. It meant a visit to the respective embassy in full uniform, with sword and aiguillettes. This was quite a business, particularly as the warmer weather had arrived, and Hungary was a country where the wearing of summer uniform was not permitted. Add to this the need for formal meetings with strange people, most of whose languages I did not speak, in unfamiliar surroundings, and it could all be quite worrying. In the event, each call was a pleasant and interesting occasion.

The visits to the Western attachés were fun. The French produced some superb wine, and the Italians some beautiful old Chianti. The Americans, both the military and the air attaché, were particularly hospitable. Then it was time for me to visit the Eastern bloc.

First the USSR: they had no air attaché, and their military attaché, Colonel Ksapenko, was very correct, yet made me feel welcome. Caviar and a very smooth vodka were provided. Although he could speak English fairly well, on my first visit he had the Second Secretary of the Soviet embassy to interpret. I was well aware that the interpreters were pretty sure to be connected with the KGB. Colonel Ksapenko was an impressive man, who was helpful throughout, and his very confidence showed that the British attachés (I was always accompanied by our military attaché on these calls) were being given top treatment. The visit went off well, and we both felt that a friendly atmosphere had prevailed. No doubt the fact that neither of us was a true intelligence officer helped. Colonel Ksapenko had served in the Soviet artillery, and we were both having our first experience in the diplomatic world.

It gave me a strange feeling as I discovered during our conversations that the Russians knew all about my service background, and I was congratulated on the number of enemy aircraft I had destroyed during the war. Apart from this we discussed the weather, and other non-military topics. Whenever the conversation ventured towards political or military subjects I noticed a distinct change in the way the interpreters always discussed the questions, and became more guarded in reply.

The Second Secretary showed he had a dry sense of humour. Ksapenko replied to a question about his time in the artillery during the war. He had been talking about the need for attachés to get on together, saying that we had been allies in the war. I asked him about the tremendous battles on the Eastern front. Colonel Ksapenko was frank in his reply, and the Secretary seemed proud to translate his answers. Ksapenko said that he had been with his unit fighting almost continuously on the retreat to the established line of defence, and had been in the great battle of Stalingrad. He wryly said that he had walked many miles from his initial location before taking up defence positions for the Stalingrad battle. Subsequently he and his unit had chased the still formidable German army all the way to Berlin, a lot of the time on foot. He then said quietly, 'It was a long way.' The Second Secretary laughed with us at Colonel Ksapenko's huge understatement. All in all I liked the Russians, as they had been frank and inclined to be friendly. Both men were completely assured, which showed me they were not without influence, and I could see the importance of these early formal meetings.

At both the Polish and Czech embassies I was made to feel very welcome, particularly at the former. The new Polish attaché, Army Colonel Bieriolierski, seemed glad to meet a member of the RAF, as he had served in the RAF as a fighter pilot during the war. He had been a warrant officer in the famous Polish Fighter Wing, which was distinguished for its bravery. He was always appreciative of our viewpoint, and was prepared to speak out for the British when things got rough in the ensuing months.

The most interesting 'call' was made on the Chinese military attaché. This was unhurried and, with great charm and dignity, we were made to feel completely at home. Having got to know some Chinese in my time in the Far East, I had grown to like and respect them. The Chinese now, of course, were under the regime of Chairman Mao. The military attaché was very slender, and obviously a sick man. I got to like him very much, but sadly he soon succumbed to his liver complaint. His replacement was equally friendly, and surprisingly was nearly 6 ft (1.8 m) tall, and well built. One thing was obvious throughout my time in Hungary: the Chinese and the Russians did not trust each other.

The Yugoslav attaché, Milan Drobacs, was a wonderful man. He had been a partisan fighter like his ambassador, and had an incredible gift for languages, as well as a passion for football. He always seemed to be trusted by the Russians, who dictated attaché policy for all the Iron Curtain states.

It then became my duty to return all these 'calls', in the attachés' rooms in the British Legation. I provided scotch and wines, and although some partook of the scotch, most seemed to prefer wine. All went well until the return 'call' made by the Soviet attaché and the Second Secretary. I thought it might be a nice gesture to provide a little vodka in addition to the scotch, knowing it was an especial favourite of the Russians, as well as plenty of ice-cold white wine. Things got off to a good start when Colonel Ksapenko gave me a packet of Russian cigarettes, which I had admired during my call at the Soviet Embassy.

As it happened, it was a particularly hot day, and we were all arrayed in our best winter uniforms including swords and aiguillettes, and the Russians were festooned with medals. I had with great difficulty managed to obtain some vodka from a friend in the American Legation. I was not altogether certain as to its origin, but it had very colourful labels. My Soviet guests seemed very appreciative of the gesture, and in the absence of any small vodka glasses, I poured it out into small wine glasses. We all four raised our glasses and knocked them back in the true Russian manner. No words can describe the instant result. We were all rendered speechless, except the Russian interpreter. He cast an admiring glance in the direction of the lethal bottle. I felt as if I had swallowed liquid fire, and I could see Ksapenko felt the same. Our faces flushed, and we broke out in beads of perspiration! He looked at the bottle and, when he had regained the power of speech, remarked with a laugh, 'Capitalist vodka!' It seemed a most apt description. We all roared with laughter, and thankfully started to put out the fires with the chilled wine – except the interpreter, who enjoyed a second glass of capitalist vodka, much to my amazement. This was an unlikely start to a congenial friendship with my opposite number, Colonel Ksapenko.

In 1956 the diplomatic situation was delicate, and we were all careful not in any way to offend each other. There was much giving and accepting of hospitality. Normally the ambassadors kept to their own circles, but at times we as Counsellors joined in.

The Queen's official birthday party was held at the British minister's residence, and was a big affair. Leslie Fry, our head of mission, entertained the president of Hungary, and I was given the duty of looking after the Soviet ambassador, Yuri Andropov. It was a fascinating occasion. I had been told in my MI5 training that this ambassador did speak some English, but I did not expect him to be so open with me, nor his English to be so good. Luckily he was accompanied by Colonel Ksapenko, who was still prepared to laugh with me over the capitalist vodka, and had obviously told his ambassador of the incident.

I had also learnt that Andropov had been Soviet liaison officer in the Arctic ports during the war. He had been filled with admiration for the British seamen who had braved the icy seas and the heavy attacks by the German bombers and U-boats, to bring supplies to the Soviet Union. These convoys were often decimated, and many badly damaged vessels only just managed to limp into the ports, and there was great loss of life. They received merciless punishment from the Luftwaffe, which was based in Norway. In fact the USSR had a special medal struck for those who took part in the convoys, as a mark of gratitude for their heroism. It is sad that the British government forbids these British seamen to wear it as a gallantry decoration in their own country.

I had had misgivings about dealing with Andropov, but contrary to my expectations, I found him easy to get on with. I was helped by Milan Drobacs, who spoke perfect English, and Andropov was understanding about my lack of Hungarian. He seemed quite content to converse directly in English without an interpreter, which was unusual in those circumstances. Moreover, he seemed prepared to talk about a wide range of subjects. For instance, he was interested in certain British writers, and to my surprise he said that he particularly liked Oscar Wilde. When I asked what it was about Wilde's writing that especially appealed to him, he said, 'The way he describes a drawing-room and captures the feeling of that time.' For good measure, he also said he enjoyed Charles Dickens. Every diplomat from the Eastern Bloc I ever spoke to who professed to read English said that Dickens was their favourite author.

Andropov proved to be a most interesting man. On every occasion I was to meet him over the next two years I found him to be the same polite, calm man, who was always a presence to be reckoned with. He was clearly a very powerful person, apart from his undoubted position of authority, for it was apparent that he was the man who dictated Eastern Bloc policy in Hungary. He was very courteous, and well turned-out, while never in any way appearing to be overdressed. I got on well with him from the start, no doubt helped by the fact that his Second Secretary had given me a sound report. This early meeting with him was to stand me in good stead.

At that time we had no idea of Andropov's real importance in the Soviet hierarchy, although something made me feel at the time that he was more than just an ambassador. This of course was to be confirmed when, many years later, I learnt that he was in fact one of the most powerful men in the Soviet Union, the chairman of the KGB (Komitet Gosudarstvennoi Bezopasnosti, Committee of State Security in all the Russias). Later he was to become president of the Soviet Union.

Matyas Rakosi also came to this party. As First Secretary of the Communist Party in Hungary, this man was all-powerful in Hungary at the time, and had the odious title of 'Stalin's most apt pupil'. He was deeply unpopular, and had made many enemies. He was a leading light in Hungarian political circles, and the champion of the Communist cause in that country. He had given the AVH a free hand to do as they wished with the people of Hungary. I soon learned about their excesses in torture, and it was Rakosi who finally set in motion the events of the unrest described in this book. He wanted to be so feared that any opposition would be utterly cowed. His cruelty was matched by his personal greed, and when the time came for this wretch to leave Hungary later in 1956, and proceed to Moscow, nearly a full trainload of loot accompanied him. This one-way journey took place just after the Hungarian Revolution flared up.

My first sight of him confirmed my worst conception of someone who was totally evil. I was sorry for our First Secretary, Kit Cope, who had the task of escorting him. At that time Rakosi was supremely self-confident. Although a Jew, he had actively helped to inflict suffering on fellow Jews, and many of the thugs who were the infamous AVH torturers were the same men, and women, as those employed by the Arrow Cross, Hitler's Gestapo in Hungary in World War II. Many of them were of Jewish origin, which greatly surprised me. One had to realise that such people had attained their positions of power by being not only ruthless but brilliant as well. Rakosi spoke about six languages fluently.

He had one great enemy, Marshal Tito of Yugoslavia, who had grown to loathe him. In July 1956 a more lenient line was seen to be introduced from Moscow in relation to Hungary. It was said that Marshal Tito had complained about the hideous excesses of Rakosi and his band, and had demanded changes. Whatever the reason, Rakosi suddenly lost his secure look and confidence; he seemed ill, and had three separate facial twitches going at once. In brief, he was scared, and 'resigned' on 18 July 1956. He officially pleaded ill-health, mentioning 'hypertension'. Admitting some of his mistakes, he wrote:

> 'After the 20th Congress of the Communist Party of the Soviet Union and the report to Comrade Khrushchev, I clearly realised that the gravity and effect of these mistakes were more serious and extensive than I had previously thought . . . If the rehabilitation of Rajk and others was slovenly and suffered from interruption, if criticism and self-criticism as well as the liquidation of the cult of personality were slow to progress, if the fight against sectarian, dogmatic views and methods was not positive enough, then I, the First Secretary of the Party, have to accept serious blame . . .'
>
> [Quoted from *Szabad Nep*, the official party-line paper, 19 July 1956]

Kit Cope, whom I just mentioned, was our First Secretary. He had fought with the partisans in the war, and consequently got on well with the Eastern Bloc officials who had also been similarly involved, and was thus a particular asset to our Mission.

The social side of my appointment was quite onerous, but nevertheless had to be met, as it was necessary to carry out all one's obligations and accept hospitality at other embassies. After earlier polite and more formal or professional meetings, I found conversation got on a more friendly footing with some of my Service counterparts at diplomatic occasions.

I was always pleased to see Ksapenko, and there was also a Soviet four-star general, Kossikov. He was a real Cossack, and every inch a serviceman. There was a problem with the Soviets in particular, however, for they were very keen on their vodka toasts, and the glasses, though small, had to be drained in one. I could not risk offending by not complying with the custom. Some nights I had to attend two cocktail parties before an official dinner, and I quickly learned that by drinking a glass of milk before I went out it was possible to overcome any bad effects.

Of course as far as possible I 'toured' the country, and kept an eye on Soviet and Hungarian aircraft, particularly those at fighter bases. I would drive about 30,000 miles (48,000 km) a year. There were no real surprises, but the Soviets were installing a new type of large air-defence radar, and that was of interest.

Hungary is a great food-producing country, and is a delightful mixture of mountains, forests, plains and the enormous Lake Balaton. It also has some well-used rivers, especially the legendary Danube and the Tisza. There are large agricultural areas, but at that time methods of farming were primitive, and the horse and cart was the most universal means of transport in the countryside. Although the Communists had tried to implement the collective-farming system, the local peasants were not whole-hearted in their involvement and, in spite of many threats, could not be coerced. I grew to love these independent-spirited people, with whom I felt a great affinity. Like the British, when everything went wrong they could laugh about it, and they had a keen sense of the ridiculous, as well as a fierce national pride.

All the time I was gradually getting to know the ropes, for there was much to learn, which ordinarily would have been part of the lengthy training before a posting. Leslie Fry and his wife could not have been more helpful. For instance, there is the important point of protocol that the minister represents the monarch. Accordingly, whenever he is officially entertained in your house, such as at a formal dinner, the minister is automatically seated at the head of the table. It was typical of Leslie's thoughtfulness that he rang me prior to the first time he visited me officially, to ask if I was aware of this. Also, in these matters, I am forever grateful to my Foreign Office mentors who guided me so thoroughly in the short time before I left the UK. Amongst those I met there was a civil servant official who took a tremendous responsibility off my shoulders, as I was able to submit all letters and reports to him, knowing that he would expeditiously channel them in the right directions.

The time came when I was able to remove the unwanted staff at my residence, and engage their replacements. I set about this task with care, as it had to have the approval of the Hungarian authorities. I was well aware, of course, that the staff would be required to report on my movements and life-style anyway. This was a point one always had to bear in mind. In order to be sure everything was done correctly, I asked the consul at our Legation, Joan Fish, to set things in motion for me. I explained that as far as possible I would like to employ older people, who were in need of employment but still competent to do the job. Perhaps people with aristocratic backgrounds, who had lost everything but would have some knowledge of official entertaining. Working in an attaché's household would give them a home, as well as a degree of security. Thus I acquired an interesting household staff.

For example, my butler, Edward Liszy, had been a minister in the Horthy Government between the two world wars, and I have a warm memory of him as a grandfatherly figure. He could trace his family back to AD 1100. He suffered from damage to his wrists, where he had slashed them with a razor. He had been driven to this during 'questioning' by the AVH, who subjected him to all sorts of torture. A favourite was what they called 'The White Goose'. They placed a broomstick at the back of his legs and then tied his hands together in front of his knees after passing the broomstick in front of his elbows. This had the effect of making a man fall all over the place, particularly when the AVH then tied his feet together as well. They continued to put him through this 'game' for hours, and his limbs became unbearably painful. A variation of this pastime was to lean their victim against a red-hot stove while he was in this tied-up position, while they amused themselves watching his frenzied efforts to get away. When their victim managed to fall clear, he was pushed against the stove at another angle. It was after one of these sessions that Liszy tried to commit suicide. A chance inspection by a guard stopped his demise, but for the rest of his life he lost the full use of his hands, as tendons were severed.

I helped Liszy to escape from Hungary during the Revolution. He reached South America, and I later heard that he married another Hungarian out there, from all accounts a rich lady who shared his passionate love of horses.

In many ways, my new head of household staff was like a second mother to me. I kept in touch with her until her death many years later. She was directly related to our own royal family. In a communist state such people suffer. Some were absentee landlords with little interest in their responsibilities, but most cared deeply for their estates and people. Communism does not discriminate, and many suffered undeservedly. She told me how the Communists had taken over her beautiful home and large estate simply by seizing her elderly mother and standing her against a wall, threatening to do unspeakable things to her unless all the property was signed over . . . so they signed, and they watched helplessly as their beautiful thoroughbred horses were ridden away. She and her mother had to leave their home, and start life again as best they might.

I quite liked the housemaster, a small rather timid man named Szabo. His wife was part-Russian and a fine woman, and they had six children. They lived in the basement, together with another woman who was also supplied by the state, presumably to keep an eye on the house and its occupants. My predecessor had tried to get rid of them, but they were a pleasant enough lot, and I knew they would stay whatever I did, so I felt it best to make them feel accepted as part of the household. This policy paid dividends, and a state of harmony established itself.

My new chauffeur was an ex-army officer, who had suffered in his service career, but had recovered sufficiently to regain his ability to drive, although severely handicapped. He lived in a nearby town, as did the daily maid.

One more all-important member of the staff was the cook. She was understandably terrified when the house was surrounded by fighting at the time of the Revolution. I gave her a bottle of scotch to fortify her through these difficult days. She apparently slept for 48 hours, and then reappeared with an empty bottle and a vacant look. Her general demeanour was so funny that, even with all the disasters going on all round me, I could not help but be amused by the whole episode. I have always thought this was an excellent way to see out the start of a revolution.

My new household staff seemed happy enough to be in a Western diplomat's house. They slept in and seldom ventured outside, unless they were accompanying me or my family for shopping or some other venture. They became very scared when the AVH decided to visit in one of their cars outside my home, which they did from time to time. We all knew the AVH cars, and their registration numbers.

I always knew when a member of the staff had to proceed to the AVH offices for their regular 'questioning', for they became very nervous and unable to look us in the face. Poor old Liszy was particularly upset about this, especially on one occasion when the AVH tried to get him to sell me a diamond ring. If I had bought the item they would have tried other ploys, and eventually would have been in a position to blackmail me. Liszy was greatly relieved when I said I was not interested. It was a very good ring, worth several thousand forints (then about 33 to the UK pound) and I was offered it for a few hundred forints. Of course they had just taken it from its real owner.

As will be gathered from the number of staff required, my house was a large one. As equivalent in rank to a counsellor in the Legation, my allowances were geared to this, but I found they barely covered all the expenses.

The Hungarian capital comprises the old town of Buda on the right (west) bank of the Danube, joined by bridges to the more modern and industrial city of Pest on the other side. In the middle at one point is the Margit *sziget* (island), a green oasis forming a lovely location for houses and good hotels. Budapest has been likened to a beautiful woman who has suffered so much she has grown old before her time, but I say the bone structure is still superb.

It is amazing that Hungary has kept its identity, given the many times it has been invaded. The Turks were there through the sixteenth and seventeenth centuries, and they have left their mark, for they were excellent administrators, and particularly good at planning the education of the young. The Austro-Hungarian Empire had been a powerful force in that part of the world in the early part of this century. After World War I its eventual collapse left Hungary out on a limb. The way Hungary was treated in the Versailles Treaty was unnecessarily harsh, in my opinion, and this has been the cause of a great deal of unhappiness in that part of Europe. Much human misery resulted from the territorial divisions which split many families into cross-boundary segments.

The months between my arrival in May and October 1956 passed quickly. Early on, our military attaché and I were invited to see shipbuilding on Lake Balaton. This is a beautiful part of the countryside, surrounded by mountains, and popular as a summer resort. The lake is enormous and shallow and, because of this saucerlike topography and the high winds which can quickly arise from the surrounding hills, it can be dangerous. It is a beautiful opalescent green colour, which I was told is due to the minerals in the ground.

It was a windy day when we left Balatonfüred in the official boat. This was made of aluminium and to an excellent design, but it was not suited to a short sea, which is what the crossing soon became. Most of the passengers were sick, but we were not affected. After an hour of careful handling, the skipper managed to cross the lake safely, and we visited the shipyards, where similar boats were being built. Hungary has a lot of shallow deposits of bauxite, from which aluminium is produced, and this new industry was using the metal to make hulls for their boats. I had already sailed on Balaton with a wooden boat, which I must confess was more to my liking. I was relieved to hear that on our return journey we were to use a conventional boat.

As we were being shown over the yards, I could not help but notice a stunningly beautiful blonde, who suddenly seemed to be with me all the time. I had been warned about such ladies, and realised I was being tried out by the AVH to see if I would fall for her wiles. At lunch she sat next to me, and was very attentive; I could feel her knee gently moving against mine. It was like a James Bond film, and I found it slightly embarrassing. I was, however, fascinated by her perfect English. She had a ready command of all the idiomatic phrases, with no trace of an accent.

On the way back to the other side of the lake I was able to have a quiet word with her, as by this time she had ceased to try and entrap me. I asked where she had learnt her English, and was flabbergasted when she said 'Sutton High School'. I understood more when she said that her father had been on the embassy staff in the UK. It was all a lesson to me in how thorough the Soviets could be in their forward thinking, to take full advantage of the background of such an outstandingly beautiful young woman all those years later. Just the sort of information that the Foreign Office would be interested in too, and which attachés were expected to pick up. When we came to part she shook my hand and said, 'I am glad it ended like this.' I heaved a sigh of relief.

Another official invitation turned out very differently from what had been planned. I was asked to join another attaché for a boar shoot in the Barconi forest, which was a favourite sport in Hungary. Their national dog is a Vizsla, which is similar to the Weimaraner to look at except that its coat is a beautiful russet tan all over. It is incredibly brave and loyal, and, in order to save its master, will attack a wounded boar without hesitation. I was allotted a Hungarian *Jaegermeister*, with a Vizsla bitch which had obviously whelped recently, and we set off. After a while a large boar, with his sow and six piglets, crossed our path. I could not possibly have brought myself to shoot any of that little family, and was glad to see it go on its way. Later I was presented with a magnificent stag, but again refused to shoot, not even raising my gun. I could only gaze in wonder at this majestic animal. For the second time the *Jaegermeister* and his dog gave me an inquiring look, but seemed to understand that there were some strange Englishmen who went on a hunting expedition but did not want to kill anything.

I was more interested in seeing the Vizsla's litter, as I had been impressed by the wonderful behaviour of the mother, and had complimented the *Jaegermeister*, which delighted him. He said the puppies were for sale, and took me to his small home in the woods, and in a little shed proudly showed me the litter. Sleeping at the bottom of a heap of enchanting golden puppies was the king puppy, and I asked if I could buy him. The sale was agreed, and I returned to Budapest with the youngster who was to become the best friend I could ever hope to have. At the time I could hold him in the palms of my hands. Immediately we got into the car he made himself comfortable on the seat beside me, with his head on my lap, and went to sleep. I lost my heart to him from that moment, and for the rest of his life. Little did I foresee all the adventures we would share together.

I called him Betya after a tribe of 'Robin Hood' bandits who once lived in the Barconi forest and were supposed to have robbed the rich to give to the poor. I had never known the Vizsla breed before, and Betya was a special dog. He was completely fearless, and when he first saw the Danube as a young puppy he went straight into it and swam across it, several hundred yards. The Vizslas are renowned for loving water, and I had difficulty coaxing him out of it. I recollect he slept all the way home after that exercise. The Vizsla has since become a favourite gun dog, internationally, as it points and retrieves and has a very good nose.

I have already mentioned the miles I covered 'touring' (as it was euphemistically called) the countryside, which was one of the most important aspects of my job. As very little information abut Soviet and their satellite forces was exchanged or reported in those days, the task fell to the attachés. The chief aim of these trips was to find out about Soviet and Hungarian forces, particularly the former. One had to be very careful, for invariably one was followed. The AVH would shadow me with varying degrees of efficiency. Usually the 'tails' were good, and in such a small country it was well-nigh impossible to shake them off. My official car was an old RAF Standard Vanguard, which was a good old workhorse, well maintained and tough enough for the many rough roads in Hungary. Main and secondary roads were good, and high-speed travel was possible, assisted by the almost total lack of private traffic. The airfields and barracks, which had to be 'viewed' whenever possible, were spread all over the country.

On some days, when I was not being followed or observed, particularly by armed sentries, it was possible to view and even photograph aircraft and installations. I soon found that a photograph was by far the most accurate way of recording information, and I tended to concentrate on this aspect of my task.

I often recalled my final briefing in London, when I was told, 'Of course, Group Captain, you are not asked to do anything dangerous, and I must say you are on your own. If you are caught, we would disclaim any knowledge of your activity, but any information you can get could be invaluable . . . now let me see, we are particularly interested in . . . .' I could not help thinking at the time that these were the words of true politicians. Now I was actually carrying out the tasks, and having to avoid armed sentries, trying to make sure I was not being followed by the AVH, and above all being on my own apart from my faithful assistant from the Legation. It seemed a trifle one-sided. There were the inevitable 'narrow escapes' during these ventures, and I grew very fond of the reliable old Vanguard. It was good over rough ground, for its suspension had been strengthened.

One day I was watching Tokol, a Russian airfield on Csepel Island, south of Budapest, in the Danube. Through my binoculars I saw a happy crowd of young Soviet air force officers. They had obviously just left a lecture, for they carried books and writing materials. They behaved just as all happy carefree youngsters do: one tripped a fellow in front, who in turn knocked his hat off. A good-natured mêlée ensued, until a senior officer came along and with a laugh called them to some form of order. This single incident made a great impression on me. It showed morale was obviously high in the SAF, which was what we called the Soviet air force (actually it is the VVS). From what I had been able to witness so far the SAF was good, and the flying I had seen was of a high standard. The personnel, and especially the aircrew, appeared excellent. Discipline was strict, but there was obviously much respect for authority. This was not necessarily the case when the political officers were around, and the atmosphere was strained.

Such people were always present whenever I was allowed to meet any Soviet officers, which was itself a rare occurrence. The same applied when I met Hungarian army or air force officers. In time, as I seemed to meet the same people at official functions, I gradually was able to pick out the commissar-type political officers of both services. They were usually more confident, and quite often one saw a senior officer looking very uncomfortable in the presence of a more junior officer of the commissar type. After a time I tried to avoid speaking to anyone when these unpleasant people were about.

I was interested to meet Colonel Ference Nador, the Hungarian fighter ace, and we became as friendly as it was safe to be. By this time my knowledge of Hungarian was improving, though I was by no means able to converse fluently in it. I had also picked up a smattering of Russian, so, together with a bit of French and much sign language, some communication was possible. I found Nador to be a man of great character, with a charming wife. He had flown Spitfires, which he loved, before going on to Soviet-built MiG jets. We had little chance of private conversation, as the commissar types always hovered close. Nevertheless, slowly but surely a friendship was formed. When we met, we did not discuss jet aircraft but, for the benefit of the commissars, reminisced about the wonderful flying characteristics of the Spitfire. We enjoyed a glass of wine, and what might otherwise have been a dull occasion was often lightened.

I found that the best time for my 'tours' was about five in the morning. This at first seemed to catch the AVH unawares, and I was sometimes able to 'view' my intended target before breakfast, although I noticed that my car was monitored whenever I passed a police station. During my seemingly casual visits near to Soviet installations, equipment and aircraft, it was sometimes possible by careful planning to obtain useful intelligence data, despite armed sentries patrolling the fences.

Gradually I gained proficiency with the lens on my Leica camera, so much so that, on one occasion when I was on a 'picnic' on a hill some five miles from a Soviet base, I was able to set up my camera on firm ground, and take a line-overlap of the entire base using some 20 separate shots. The camera and the bulky lens were carried in the bottom of the picnic basket, which was never unpacked unless a careful check had been made of the surrounding area to ascertain that no AVH or service sentries were about the place. For this particularly successful trip I had made four unsuccessful sorties. It was painstaking work, requiring endless patience, and it could be likened to trying to solve a crossword puzzle without having any clues. I often found that seemingly irrelevant facts could turn out to be most important. Service attachés were not alone in this work, for all members of the UK Legation were encouraged to remember or gather anything they heard or saw which might be of interest. Leslie Fry was wonderful in the way he built up his staff in these affairs, and the groundwork was to pay dividends.

I had to send my own reports, which were of a more technical nature, to the Air Ministry in London. Other reports, particularly those pertaining to the local political scene, were passed to the minister, Leslie Fry, and there were times when he would ask me to look out particularly for certain details. The military attaché and I co-ordinated our own trips whenever possible, thereby avoiding duplication. There was very little co-ordination with any other Western embassy or legation attachés, although some information was exchanged. Later, during the Revolution and its bloody aftermath, the US air attaché was away from Hungary receiving medical treatment for a broken ankle, so I helped out the US assistant air attaché whenever possible.

CHAPTER FIFTEEN

TROUBLE BREWING

From April 1956, in the six months leading up to the Hungarian uprisings in various parts of the country, there was a general feeling of unreality. Rakosi and his thugs continued their evil practices. Innocent people were dragged from their homes in the middle of the night, and were never heard of again. In one case I heard of, a young couple were taken and their very young baby just left. Luckily a neighbour heard the baby's cries, and looked after it, for the parents were never seen again. I tried to find out what their crime was, but from all accounts they were a very law-abiding couple. One person who knew them said they were just too good-looking and nice for the AVH to tolerate.

Leslie spent many hours trying to help such victims, and his personal efforts did result in some being saved from a terrible fate. He spent much time explaining to me why we could not do more, and was adamant that contact with Rakosi and his henchmen had to be maintained. Gradually I began to understand that there was no alternative to this policy, though I hated it. I was always careful never to speak to a Hungarian if there was a chance that I was being 'tailed' at that moment. Such a conversation would immediately invite a visit by the AVH and, no matter how innocent the individual, their protestations of innocence were very unlikely to be accepted. Service attachés were always of particular interest to the AVH. This was normal practice, but their main concern was to track down any Hungarian who spoke to us.

Rakosi's second-in-command, Erno Gero, was another vicious Stalinist who had grown to be hated. He was an intellectual, who was reputed to smile only when someone was suffering, and as I had with Rakosi, I felt an overwhelming sense of evil whenever I met him. Needless to say, they both took good care of themselves, and were never without armed guards. The original feelings of relief and optimism felt throughout Hungary at the departure of Rakosi were quickly dashed when it was learned his successor was to be Gero. Undoubtedly, both Rakosi and Gero were responsible for much of the disaffection and resentment in the country. Their callous indifference to people's suffering and their support of the AVH's reign of terror and torture, which seemed even to intensify in Gero's day, certainly played a large part in setting the scene for the uprising that broke out in October 1956.

It is small wonder the Hungarians hate being occupied by foreign troops. This has been their lot since Roman times, when the two settlements, one on each side of the Danube, marked the birth of Budapest. Later came the invasions of the Huns after the death of Attila, followed by Charlemagne, and then the Turks. Later still came the Austrian Habsburgs (enlisting the aid of the Russians, who have invaded Hungary three times), and of course the Germans in World War II. It is truly amazing the way Budapest has remained Magyar, and throughout all this the people have shown their determination to remain Hungarian. They were always prepared to sacrifice their homes and lives, if need be, in order to keep their heritage intact for future generations.

The AVH installed a camera in a shop on the other side of the street opposite the entrance to the British Legation. The lens of the camera was positioned in the letter 'O' of 'patyloat' (dry-cleaning shop), so that everyone entering or leaving the British Legation was monitored and photographed. The camera was removed by the AVH as soon as the trouble started in the Uprising. I knew about this camera and arranged for anyone who wished to see me to do so at meeting places away from my house or office. I never used the same place more than once, and any such meeting was automatically cancelled if I was unable to shake off any followers. I tried never to involve locals in any of my work, because they were always at such an unfair disadvantage. Whenever I wanted to do anything of an official nature I used the state machinery and state personnel, who were cleared for contact with the West. Other work I tried to tackle with my assistant or on my own, and this policy was to prove invaluable.

So far, of the Hungarian leaders I have mentioned only Rakosi and Gero, for they were the two most responsible for the oppressive rule in Hungary. In contrast, the prime minister, Andreas Hegedus, was a colourless and relatively unimportant man. President Istvan Dobi was likable, but usually vague owing to an excessive consumption of alcohol. In a Communist state it was the First Secretary who held the reins of power. He alone controlled the Party, and had Moscow's backing, which automatically lent him the support of the armed forces. Thus the whole Communist hierarchy can be likened to the Al Capone days in the USA, when the great gang leaders survived by virtue of the strength of their own bodyguards.

AVH members were well paid: a captain had a salary ten times that of a factory supervisor. They also had special shopping facilities, and they had the use of cars, a luxury denied to ordinary people. Above all, it was the power granted to them that attracted the worst type of individual, who really enjoyed inflicting pain on helpless people. In the forthcoming Revolution all types of AVH were given some of their own treatment. Many escaped to the West, posing as refugees, and some went to ground when they saw an opportunity of leaving the ranks of the AVH without being discovered. Any that were spotted were dealt with as they deserved, but the majority fled to the Soviet forces' camps, where they awaited the application of Soviet might which was ultimately to crush the Revolution. The AVH were some of the most hated men and women in Europe, and with good reason.

The summer of 1956 drifted into autumn. Outwardly everything seemed much as usual, but it was possible to detect an air of uneasy calm. The food riots in Posznan, Poland, sparked off a lot of comment, and this curiously coincided with a slight lessening of the press censorship in the national papers. It was strange to be able to read even a mild criticism of the Communist regime in Poland, especially about something as basic as a shortage of food. There are firm links between the peoples of Hungary and Poland, founded on mutual trust over the years.

A Polish general, Josef Bem (1794-1850), had led the Hungarians to victory against the Habsburgs in 1849 in their fight for the country's independence, and there is a fine statue to this Polish warrior in Bem Square in Budapest. The Hungarians had been incensed that the Soviet forces had forcibly suppressed the Polish food riots, triggered by the price of sausages. Actually minimum force had been used, and the troubles ended abruptly when food appeared again in the markets at acceptable prices. I had noticed that the Soviets seemed to respect the Polish fighting ability, and were careful when dealing with them. Another reason that minimum force was used in Poland and the maximum in Hungary was that Hungary's boundaries abut the West and Yugoslavia, as it then was, whereas Poland was surrounded by Soviet satellite states.

Following the support given to the Poles by the Hungarians, particularly from the student factions, in newspaper articles, and open letters whenever such access to the media was possible, some Polish students came to Budapest to thank their Hungarian friends formally. That it was possible to read such news in state-run newspapers was something which had not been allowed for 12 years. It was like the first spark to a touch-paper, and the effect on young and impressionable minds is hard for people from the West to understand, where freedom of expression is taken for granted as a normal right of the individual. Wherever I went, whether in Budapest, or about in the surrounding countryside, I heard excited comment about these articles. They seemed to fan the flame of nationalist pride that still glowed, despite all the persecution the people had endured.

During 19-21 October 1956, the Polish Party's Central Committee leaders had won concessions from Moscow. Initially the Hungarians could scarcely believe the news, and it was all openly discussed with the visiting Polish students, who were understandably delighted.

On the afternoon of 23 October I noticed more people on the streets than usual, in fact too many for the AVH to take on. I have always been interested in observing people, and the very nature of my job had honed this sharply, so I decided to mingle with them. Some outspoken Hungarian speakers started to gather crowds around them, and they began to shout, 'Why should not Hungary gain concessions? Why do we have to suffer from the Rakosis and the Geros?' At first there was much laughter and cheering. I asked some of the people at one of the gatherings why they were not afraid of AVH retaliation, and on all sides I got the answer that there were too many of them for even the AVH to deal with. They added that these bullies would be too frightened of any confrontation with an angry crowd that was too big for them to haul away victims to their torture chambers.

I joined the crowd at the Petofi statue, where speeches were being made and poems read, some by famous actors, which was something typical of the Hungarians at a time of great nationalistic emotion and pride. Sändor Petofi was a national hero, a Hungarian poet who did much to inspire his country in 1848 with his famous poem 'Arise Magyars'. He will always be quoted with great pride and reverence.

I saw that some Polish students had joined the crowds, and I moved on, joining another group around the Bem statue, before going to the British Legation to report to the minister. Despite the laughter and the cheering, I was feeling increasingly apprehensive, wondering when the regime would take violent action to stop things getting out of hand. At the time the atmosphere was like a happy family outing, with everyone enjoying each other's company. Everyone was well-behaved. There was no drinking; their heads were intoxicated enough without the aid of alcohol. The only thing that reassured me was the size of the crowds, which seemed to increase throughout the afternoon of 23 October, as more and more people poured into Budapest from outside the city.

Gero, we later learned, was really scared as he realised how the AVH was being increasingly outnumbered. He called the Soviet commander in Hungary for assistance, in a state of near-panic. As the massive Soviet armed forces were spread around the country it took some time for them to gather in sufficient numbers in their correct locations. The regime did not trust the Hungarian army and air force units, with good reason. As future events were to show, great numbers of Hungary's own troops joined with the Freedom Fighters, as the young revolutionaries came to be called.

Another little-known fact was that the Soviet troops in Hungary had grown to like the country, as many of them had been there for years. Some were even related to Hungarians, owing to the partitioning of Hungary after World War I, when great tracts of her lands were lost to the then Balkan states. Some parts went to the Soviet Union and, like troops everywhere, some postings could be arranged.

That evening, 23 October, I was dining with the American assistant air attaché in Pest when, towards the end of our meal, the phone rang. It was the US Legation to say the crowds were gathering in unprecedented numbers, and something seemed to be brewing. Of course we all dispersed to see for ourselves what was going on. As I drove through the streets of Pest, they were full of people laughing and talking excitedly. I left my car and joined one of the largest gatherings, in Heroes' Square, which is a large open square, in the middle of which are statues of the kings and national leaders of Hungary. Some of those of the kings had been melted down to build a monstrous statue of Stalin, and this huge monument was the most hated in Hungary. It added insult to injury when one recalled what beautiful and revered statues were destroyed in order to construct it. People tried not to look at it, and many are reputed to have spat in Stalin's direction if they knew they were not being watched. Now I found everyone jubilant, for they had just managed to topple this hated symbol of their oppression, and were in a state of euphoria.

It had been a difficult task. Initially they had attached ropes to Stalin's head, and tried to pull him down with the aid of several trucks, but to no avail. Magically some oxy-acetylene equipment was obtained, and the backs of the statue's knees were cut through with the flame. Only then did the crowd manage to pull it over. It had just fallen when I arrived.

To my surprise many people spoke to me in English. I asked one man about this and was told how they had longed to communicate in English for years, but using the language would have meant immediate arrest. In the following days I found young people who would have been too young to have learned English before the years of oppression, but still had some knowledge of the language. I asked them how they had learned it, knowing it was forbidden in all schools, and they said their grandmothers taught them! I feared even then that the AVH would have spies in the crowds to note those whom they deemed to be the ringleaders.

The crowd had thrown caution to the winds, however, and told me that they wanted to drag Stalin to the Danube to drown him and his memory for all time. Once again they were frustrated in their desires. Joe proved to be too heavy to be moved, so they started breaking him into smaller pieces. Many years later I was vividly reminded of all this by the scenes and atmosphere at the destruction of the hated Berlin Wall. I was given a small piece of Joe, which I later had sawn in half to give a piece to Leslie. We both kept these as souvenirs of a remarkable night that was to change history.

I left the rejoicing crowds reluctantly, but felt I should see more of what was going on in the city. A sense of great unease and apprehension was uppermost in my mind. I drove to the radio station, as I had been told that the people were intending to broadcast to the West that they wanted to be free of Gero and Co, and that they also wanted free elections and the removal of Soviet forces from the soil of Hungary. There was indeed a very large crowd there, and they were still in good spirits, despite the fact that the AVH had managed to muster a formidable guard outside the station, and there was consequently no chance of the crowd's optimistic demands being met.

As I drove away from the radio station I passed a convoy of Hungarian T-34 tanks on their way there. They were not at action stations; their turrets were open, and their commanders were waving to the crowds. By contrast, as I drove past the Houses of Parliament on the lower river road I passed a large convoy of AVH. They were parked, but let me pass. I noted they all looked scared and apprehensive, which was not surprising, considering the overwhelming numbers of the crowds throughout the city.

I got home, phoned the duty officer at the Legation, and made a full report of what I had seen. Shortly afterwards I was telephoned to tell me what had happened at the radio station after I had left. The Hungarian tank reached it, and the officer in charge walked up to the building, calling on the AVH to give themselves up, and to let the people tell the world what was happening in Hungary. The AVH replied by firing into the crowd, killing the tank officer and a young girl. Her body was picked up and passed back over the crowd, and the body of the tank officer was also shown to the crowd. The sight of those two, the first victims of what was to become the Revolution, caused the time bomb of suppressed emotion to explode. The mood of the people turned to anger, and a renewed determination to rid their country of the Soviet forces, and to deal with Gero and the AVH themselves.

Suddenly rifles and guns from the Hungarian Army barracks nearby were being distributed to the crowds. My informant told me that thousands of workers had arrived in Budapest from the many industrial plants on Csepel Island. These men and women had arrived with arms, and they all wanted to fight for their country's freedom. Conflict then began in earnest, with especially heavy fighting at the radio station. Soviet troops arrived, and set about the task of trying to subdue the Hungarian Army at Kilian Marie Theresa barracks, which were gallantly defended by Colonel Pal Maleter and his small force. I passed this news to the Legation, and they told me there were also reports of fighting breaking out in the cities of Debrecen, Szolnok and Szeged.

Everywhere it seemed that the AVH and the Soviet army were engaged in fighting of a far more serious nature than they had bargained for. The opposition was clearly tougher and more determined than they had expected. They were trying to subdue a country that was fighting for its freedom.

Events moved fast, and were difficult to follow in those early days, for the situation in various parts of the country changed by the moment. Those who took up arms included factory workers, tram and train drivers, miners, students and people from all walks of life. They were supported by men from the Hungarian army and air force, but a great number of young men and women, many still in their early teens, seemed to be in the forefront of much of the fighting.

They soon began to be referred to as the 'Young People'. They fought with incredible bravery. I spoke to some in and around Budapest, and was always impressed by the fact they knew exactly what they were fighting for. Despite Soviet-indoctrinated schooling throughout their lives they had learned to hate the regime, where everything good was reported to have come from the Soviets, and everything bad from the West. They realised the evil perpetrated by Rakosi, Gero and their cohorts, and loathed them.

News had reached Budapest of the arrival of Rakosi in Moscow with his trainload of loot stolen from Hungary. This was somewhat of an embarrassment to his Moscow masters at that time, and reports later intimated that much of the loot was 'confiscated and distributed' by senior Soviet officials. Such news only intensified the fury of the Hungarians. If they could have found Gero he would have been torn limb from limb. It was at about this time that the young revolutionaries came to be called the 'Freedom Fighters', a name that was to embrace all those who fought to the death to liberate their country. It was to remain forever their epitaph, and it was richly deserved.

A great new symbol of their cause began to appear everywhere.

The Hungarian flag, red white and green, always a symbol of pride to the nation, had for years been desecrated in their eyes by having the Hammer and Sickle emblazoned in the centre of it. Now flags appeared all over the place, and wherever they were seen there was a large hole in the middle where the hated emblem had been cut out. When they were first displayed on buildings they were greeted with cheers.

A favourite weapon of the youngsters was their home-made 'Molotov Cocktail', which was a lemonade bottle filled with petrol and primed with a detonator to be thrown at a tank in the hope of causing it to catch fire. With unbelievable bravery they would get as near as they could in order to try to hit the exhaust, when the petrol would ignite. Several of the Soviet T-54 tanks were 'cooked up' in this manner, and many of the youngsters died. The wonderful Magyar humour is typified in the story about two kids aged 13 and 14 comparing notes after some fighting. The 14-year-old boasted to his brother saying, 'I was in the heavy anti-tank unit in the Uprising, while you never served in anything more than the light anti-tank units. We had two-litre lemonade bottles, your lot never used anything above the one-litre cocktail.' There were many similar jokes, and I remarked to a Hungarian once how, like the British in a tight corner, they still seem able to find humour in adversity. He replied 'Perhaps we learnt it from you!' Perhaps it all stems from our shared Celtic roots in ancient times.

The fighting continued in Budapest for some days. It was fierce at times, and I only managed sporadic forays about the city, and then only on foot. I got photographs of some of the fighting, but this was difficult in the dull light. One never knew when there would be a sudden spray of bullets flying around. On one occasion I had flattened myself into a doorway, which I felt was rather inadequate cover, when two Freedom Fighters hurried past with their guns at the ready, and gave me a cheerful wave. Their youthful confidence somehow brightened the whole day.

As in other British diplomatic legations, we had a powerful wireless transmitter/receiver. This allowed uninterrupted communication with London throughout our time there, entirely due to Leslie's foresight and persistence. With great determination he had managed to stop certain Treasury officials from removing the equipment, for reasons of economy, only a short time before. I wondered just how much would be saved by not having wireless. Now we were the only direct communication link with the West throughout the Revolution, and were thus able to tell the free world what was happening in Hungary.

Progressively, the situation got more serious, and Leslie ordered all British staff and their families to come and live at the Legation.

Luckily the building was fairly large, for not only did we have to feed and sleep the staff and families, but many businessmen had been stranded in Budapest when the fighting started. In addition, the number of newsmen increased as the story got out and made headlines throughout the world. Initially the pressmen stayed in hotels, but as fighting became widespread and intense, the British press representatives were also housed in the Legation. Our W/T operator was getting somewhat exhausted by the constant flow of reports he was having to transmit.

Despite Leslie's efforts to persuade the pressmen to keep inside the Legation, their job was to get news and pictures, and they continued to do so until one of their number, Noel Barber, was shot in the head by a Russian sentry. Sefton Delmer managed to get him back to the Legation, and Penelope Fry worked on staunching the bleeding, and taking what precautions she could, in her usual capable way, to minimise the effects of shock. He was semi-conscious, but she kept him alive until the Hungarian doctor we used for the Legation managed to get through on his bicycle, a brave effort indeed. He had to put 40 stitches in Noel's scalp. Undoubtedly, Penelope saved his life.

The pressmen were first-class, and apart from their eagerness to get stories, co-operated wholeheartedly with our 'house rules'. No one groused, although conditions were difficult for us all. Accommodation was cramped, and feeding arrangements were not easy, though we were glad to have our own NAAFI (Navy, Army and Air Force Institute) supply in the basement, so there was no shortage of food. Morale was high, and no small credit is due to Leslie and Penelope and the Legation staff for the way the Mission kept functioning in those difficult days. As numbers increased, people slept in offices and along corridors. All this meant a much increased workload for the British consul, Miss Joan Fish, whose dedication to duty was of the highest order.

Events were difficult to follow. The Legation had many visitors, not now watched by the AVH camera, which was removed on 23 October. All the time we got the same request from the Hungarians, they just wanted the free world to be told the truth about the Uprising. Many said they would fight to the death, rather than allow another Rakosi/Gero regime to run their country. On 24 and 25 October, there were two changes in government. Imre Nagy replaced Andreas Hegedus as premier, and Janos Kadar replaced Erno Gero the following day. Everyone was delighted to see Gero go, but initially it seemed another case of Communist musical chairs, and not much regard was paid to it all. Both Nagy and Kadar had been in power before. Nagy had been premier in 1953-55; he had been expelled from the Party in 1955, but was readmitted in 1956. Nagy was of the post-Stalinist New Course, and generally considered to be a Nationalist Communist. He enjoyed considerable support among the people, and gradually became a leader to be recognised.

Colonel, later General, Maleter, the gallant defender of Kilian barracks in Budapest, signified the military leadership, and was chosen by the Freedom Fighters to lead Hungary in the Uprising. Nagy quickly reconvened Parliament, and started a reform programme, which included a lot of reorganisation. Kadar had been a minister, and was a Central Committee member until 1951, when he had been arrested in connection with the Rajk case (a moderate Communist who was unlawfully arrested and killed). Kadar was tortured in prison by the AVH, outrageously from all accounts, but was released in 1953 and returned to government when Rakosi was removed in July 1956. Although Gero had been a great friend of Rajk, he had been quite happy to help in his arrest, torture, and eventual murder by Rakosi and Co, which was normal politics for those days. It gives one some understanding of why the revolution of the people had to happen, there was so much hatred against the Stalinists. Once Khrushchev felt secure enough he made some drastic changes, including the removal of Rakosi.

The fighting continued, and by 26 October the AVH were the prime prey of the Freedom Fighters. Whenever they were found they were killed unceremoniously. I took many photos at that time, which tell the story eloquently. Some of the most moving show where some of the young fighters died in the streets. There are flowers, and sometimes candles or a flag. Any AVH who was killed was left to lie where he fell.

The news that Her Majesty's Minister had referred the Hungarian case to the United Nations was a great morale raiser for the Freedom Fighters. Many came to the Legation just to thank the British for passing on the truth. Our W/T at the Legation remained the one sure link with the West throughout. I went about Budapest as much as the fighting would allow, and it was easy to see that, whereas the people had been fatalistic about fighting to rid themselves of their hated oppressors, now they knew the United Nations had been officially informed they were full of hope.

I learned a lot about the AVH as their headquarters had been stormed by the Freedom Fighters. Files on the diplomats were found, and their whole method of tapping diplomats' phones and their close surveillance were exposed. I was shown the meticulous file that had been kept on my predecessor. It was a salutary experience to read it, and see the chilling accuracy of the reports of his every action. Records captured included accounts of many horrendous deeds carried out by the AVH, and it all strengthened the Hungarians' determination that it should never be allowed to happen again.

In time I got to know some of the Freedom Fighters who seemed to be on duty near the Legation. They always let me pass, and even offered an escort, which I declined as it was important that I should appear as neutral as a diplomat could be. I felt apprehensive at the great spirit of optimism that prevailed everywhere. It seemed uncharacteristic for the Soviet Army to be quietened down in this manner. A Hungarian officer told me on 27 October that he thought the Soviet tank crews had run out of ammunition. They had not re-armed after the main fighting, and were keeping a low profile. The battles had been harder than they expected. Both sides were tired, and some of the Soviet troops I saw looked gloomy. Some were talking openly to the people who asked them why they fired on helpless workers and children. They replied they were obeying orders, but some said they did not like what they were doing. There was indeed a true incident in which a Russian tank actually fired on AVH thugs who were mercilessly shooting down women and children, and those trying to rescue the wounded. Gradually all the tanks withdrew from Budapest to the outlying areas, some even flying the new Hungarian flag with the Hammer and Sickle insignia cut out of it.

The fighting which led up to a near lull period had done incredible damage to the city. Glass was everywhere, as tank main armament had been used extensively by the Soviets, and anti-tank fire by the defending Hungarians. In the battle around the barracks many Soviet tanks were destroyed, not to mention overturned trucks, trams and cars, and hastily erected barricades. Another real hazard was the live tram wires, which had broken from their holders, giving off a firework display of electric sparks.

There came a period of relative calm, after which the pressing need was distribution of food. Any shopping or collection of food during the fighting had been out of the question, but now farmers from outlying areas delivered masses of food, vegetables and animal carcasses, all free of cost for the hungry people. This was a spontaneous act which typified the feeling in the land, and the Hungarians helped each other wherever and whenever they could. At last they were about to regain their freedom from dictatorship and oppression. Political prisoners were freed, but so also were ordinary thieves and criminals. These criminal types immediately made their way to the West, hoping to cross the frontier to Austria and freedom. It seemed they could not change their ways, and many were soon back in prison, this time in the

West. Alas, many of them gave Hungarian refugees a bad name in parts of Europe, the USA, Canada and Britain. In contrast, most of the real political prisoners wanted to stay and continue the fight.

I travelled around Budapest, but was sad to see all my worst fears being realised; the Soviet troops had only withdrawn to the outskirts of the city, and the tanks occupied the airport. Hundreds were parked along the runways, with sentries everywhere. Hungarian army servicemen confirmed that the Soviets were bringing in great numbers of tanks, and thousands of troops. I reported this ominous news to Leslie, who included it in his report to London.

During those days an inscription was carved on the Petofi statue 'October 23 1956'. This simple memorial was to record the sacrifices of young and old who had fought so bravely for their country's freedom. Within a few days of the new regime taking over, this reminder was removed, but it will never be erased from the memories of all the freedom-loving Hungarians.

Leslie thought it would be wise to take advantage of the lull, which we both feared was only temporary. It was agreed that I should try to take a convoy of wives and children to safety in Vienna. The Legation had become far too crowded, and this would relieve the pressure on it. In any case, it seemed a good idea to get as many as possible to safety, if it could be accomplished. Incidentally, as the numbers taking shelter in the Legation had increased, Leslie had asked the Foreign Office what he should do about the cost of his 'hospitality'. The answer came back promptly that he was to keep an exact account of what each 'guest' owed the Legation, and see that the amount was recovered! As it happened there was no problem, everyone was only too grateful for the way they had been given secure shelter and food at such a time, and paid up readily.

I was keen to get moving as soon as possible, especially knowing that the Soviets were massing more and more forces in the country from the East. Early on 30 October I led the convoy away from the Legation, and Leslie and Penelope saw us off that grey and gloomy morning. Just around the corner another street battle started up, but it was fortunately not in the direction we were going. I was amazed at the eventual size of the convoy, 39 vehicles in all (I started with 16). As the news got around that the British were organising a convoy, most other embassies and legations added a car or two. In the event, I set off with British, American, French and Italian women and children, as well as numbers of displaced businessmen from Austria, the Netherlands, Czechoslovakia and Canada, to name but a few. My main concern was that there were a number of pregnant women in various cars. Many of these wonderful young wives drove themselves, and as we progressed I came more and more to admire their cool courage.

Normally it would not take more than two hours to reach the Austrian frontier, but on this occasion it took my convoy nearly four times as long. This was because we were constantly encountering hold-ups and checkpoints; I counted more than 25 of the latter. Some were Soviet, some AVH, but over half were Freedom Fighters. It was a worrying time for me, as I could never be certain of the mood of the next group to be encountered.

A very frightening hold-up point was a Soviet T-54 tank, which was completely blocking the main Vienna road about 20 miles (32 km) west of Budapest. Its turret was closed down, and it slowly traversed so that its 100mm main gun pointed directly at my car. It seemed gigantic. I stopped, with the whole convoy drawing to an anxious halt behind me.

I got out and held out the big Union Jack flag which I had nailed to a broomstick, and which I had tied to the bumper of my trusty old Standard Vanguard. There was no reaction, so I walked up to the tank feeling smaller with each step I took nearer to this monster. I wondered what I could do. I could hear amazing whirring noises from the machinery inside, but there was no sign of anyone to whom I could speak. Somewhat ineffectually I knocked on the side of the tank and asked, 'Excuse me, is there anyone there?' Needless to say there was no reply. I then walked round the tank, and on returning to the front I saw a small slit had opened through which I could see the eyes of the driver looking at me.

I was dressed in civvies, but tried to look authoritative, and gestured for the turret to be opened. This worked: a hatch opened and I asked the tank commander in my poor Hungarian if we could proceed as we were a convoy of dependants of diplomats in Budapest. As in all my dealings with the Soviet forces, the young officer was very correct, and intimated that I was to wait where I was. Little did he know I only guessed at what he was saying in Russian. He spoke on his R/T set and obviously got permission for us to move. He then showed more of himself from the turret, and pointed in the direction of Vienna. I said 'Nasdrovie', he saluted, and I nodded. I went back to my car, and all 39 of us drove carefully past.

I had much more trouble with the AVH checkpoints. They wanted to throw their weight about, and were obviously smarting from their defeat in Budapest. They seemed to have formed an 'AVH safe area' about 25 miles (40 km) from Budapest, and straddled the Vienna road, blocking it completely. They tried to make me turn the convoy back, but I became angry and called for an officer.

Eventually a dispirited captain appeared, and I introduced myself as

Ezradez David (Colonel David). This and my diplomatic passport had the desired effect. I also possessed two passes made out by myself and the British consul at the Legation the night before. We used every official-looking stamp we could find, and with the help of a Russian-speaking visitor we created an impressive-looking clearance paper. I also possessed a 'mislaid' pass signed by the Minister of the Interior, which allowed me to go about the country. This pass had been removed from the AVH headquarters when it had been taken over by the Freedom Fighters, and was given to us as a souvenir. It was also signed by the AVH ministerial chief, and all we had to do was fill in my name in Russian in the blank space. Thank God, it worked!

The Nationalists were all anxious to help in any way they could. They ranged in age from early teens to about 60 years old. All were armed and seemed well-acquainted with their weapons. Many of the Freedom Fighter barriers were manned by Hungarian army or air force personnel in uniform.

A serious worry on the trip was the necessity of finding a place where everyone, especially the pregnant women, could 'answer a call of nature'. After some three hours of driving, in those frightening conditions, and with the intense cold, this was obviously becoming urgent. Fortunately we came to a long stretch of good road with trees on either side. There were no checkpoints in sight, so I stopped and the convoy did likewise. It was then an amazing sight. Without any briefing, all the women and children went into the woods on one side of the road, and all the men disappeared into the woods on the other side. It was a case of instantaneous and necessary action.

When everyone was back in their cars, I went down the convoy trying to reassure them that we were doing well. Once again I was impressed by the women of all nationalities. All were outwardly calm and courageous. I had arranged that the last vehicle in the convoy was the Legation truck which had a high canopy, so that it was easy for me to see that the convoy was intact. It had been arranged that if ever there was a straggler, the truck would stop to help, and then I would know something was amiss. The truck was driven by the Legation's ex-Royal Marine guard, a magnificent fellow who was a tower of strength in the convoy. In the back of his truck he had a collection of stranded businessmen, some of whom were from Iron Curtain countries, but everyone got on well together.

At last I led the convoy over the Hungarian frontier at Hegyeshalom. We crossed the road adjacent to the minefield and came into Austria at Nickelsdorf, where we were met by a host of cameramen and reporters. They all wanted news, for we were the first people to get out of Hungary since the uprisings had started. We desperately wanted a rest, but managed to do what we could for the newsmen. I recorded a tape for Ivor Jones of the BBC, which was broadcast unedited on UK radio. Eventually we left the Austrian frontier post, and drove on to Vienna. On the way, just out of Nickelsdorf, at the side of the road to Vienna, I saw Austria's few tanks lined up facing east. It was a morale-boosting sight, but it brought a lump to my throat, for these small old tanks would have been no match for the Red Army's T-54s, but it demonstrated the spirit of the gallant Austrians.

As I drove, partly to keep awake, I turned on the car radio, tuned to the BBC Overseas Service. The first thing I heard was the signature tune of the popular serial '*The Archers*'! I could hardly believe it.

In Vienna I called at the British Embassy and made my report to the ambassador, Sir Henry Wallender. He and all his staff were most helpful, and quickly took over the task of caring for the British families. Before allowing the convoy to disperse I had checked with all the other members that they had somewhere to go in Vienna. It was a great relief to be able to relay to the ambassador a true picture of events in Hungary. He sent an immediate dispatch to London, and I was promised clerical help the next day to send some reports to my own Service chiefs in London.

My hard-working and very conscientious warrant officer, Jock Falconer, was a Scot and the most courageous and reliable of assistants I could ever have hoped for. Once he had settled his wife and family comfortably, he rejoined me at the Embassy, for there were many reports and official letters to prepare before we could finally get to bed. Throughout all our time together in Hungary nothing was too much trouble for Jock. Somehow he coped with all the office work and endless reports, as well as being a fine partner on the touring trips. Jock and his family were a great asset to the Legation.

About midnight I at last got to my hotel, more than ready for my first quiet night's sleep in some time. My head had hardly touched the pillow before the telephone rang. It was the news agency Reuters. They were very understanding, realising that it had been a long and difficult day, but were anxious to get a complete report from me, on tape. This took about an hour, and I kept almost falling asleep. A lot of this interview appeared verbatim in most of the newspapers of the free world.

CHAPTER SIXTEEN

'SEND US BANDAGES'

The following day was occupied in non-stop work with our official business, and also in making arrangements to get the families back to the UK. At last on the morning of 1 November Jock and I left Vienna in the trusty Vanguard, heading a little convoy of two other vehicles. One was driven by Kit Cope, who had been on leave, and the other was full of newsmen. Once again I had our Legation truck bringing up the rear. Again a great number of checkpoints had to be negotiated, but somehow it seemed a much easier journey without the women and children to colour one's decisions. There were fewer AVH barriers, and the Soviet sentries seemed more decisive and confident. The Nationalists were still optimistic and sure of their position, and all along the road the locals waved, greeting our little convoy with smiles. Alas, I felt that many of them thought we were a sort of advance guard from the UN.

We made Budapest in four hours, and found things much as they had been when we had left two days earlier. The main difference was the total absence of Soviet tanks, for all had been withdrawn to Ferihegy airport and Törökbalint. Ferihegy was the city's airport, some 15 miles (24 km) from the city centre on the Pest (eastern) side. Törökbalint was about the same distance away on the Buda side, and was an excellent defensive site because of the terrain. It was chilling to note this deployment, for it meant that the Soviet Army was not leaving the country, as so many had hoped.

The people were still optimistic, and the Hungarian Nationalist government headed by the new prime minister, Imre Nagy, was utterly different from the 'extreme left' order under Rakosi and Gero. The demands for a multi-party system, representing all shades of opinion, were being met. They also believed that, as the United Nations were taking up their case, they would have massive support from the world community. Alas, I had a great sinking feeling in my heart, as I could see at once that suddenly the Hungarian news was being downgraded in all the international press to the status of being very much a secondary story on inside pages, because just at this moment the Suez crisis had burst upon the world. The international press was immediately focused on this, so it forgot its repeated criticism of the Soviet action in Hungary. It could not have been more disastrously timed from Hungary's point of view. Of course, the truth will probably never come out, but was it just coincidence that Kim Philby was very much involved in the affairs concerning the Canal at that crucial moment? I had no idea he was around at that time, but later on, when I learned more about the two disasters that had occurred so close together, and more about Philby's nefarious deeds and his great manipulative skill, it seemed like the missing piece of a jigsaw.

On 1 November 1956 Imre Nagy, as Hungary's prime minister, declared his country's neutrality, and asked the free world to recognise this, and the fact that Hungary had left the Warsaw Pact (the Iron Curtain countries' equivalent to NATO). The people went about the work of clearing up after the fighting. Shopfronts and windows had been smashed or blown out all over the city. Time and again I saw valuable goods, beautiful jewellery, clothes and even groceries, in the shattered shop windows. It was all there for the taking, yet there was never any looting or thieving of any description. It is wonderful to be able to report this, for there have been many stories to the contrary. I was there and I saw it for myself, and it made a deep impression on me. It says a lot about the character of the Hungarian people.

Throughout these days of false freedom, the Soviet troops were quiet and kept a low profile, and did not fire unless actually fired upon. I drove about the city as much as I could, and ventured into the surrounding areas where possible. On one occasion, while exploring towards the east, I drove into a large Soviet contingent. I was not held up, but was left in no doubt that I should return to Budapest immediately. On my return to the Legation after these drives, I could only report an ever-increasing build-up of tanks, troops, personnel carriers, trucks, guns and other military equipment. It was all looking more and more ominous.

On 3 November, after obtaining Leslie's permission, I managed to arrange a meeting with a high-ranking general, who now held a most responsible position in the new Nationalist hierarchy. I had met him at several official functions, and we had formed a respect for one another. There was never any question of military or political discussion during our previous meetings, which had touched only on harmless topics. I would never have insulted his intelligence by raising any controversial subject, knowing we were always in the company of a political spy.

The general was very pleased to see me, despite being incredibly busy that day (which was to prove his last day of freedom). He gave me a private hearing which lasted an hour. Initially we had to rely on an interpreter, which caused inevitable delays, but after a while we managed to talk to each other directly. I answered his questions, and he was glad to have confirmation that the British Legation was sending the truth to the West, and that our W/T set was still working. He was most grateful for the stand Leslie Fry had taken, and asked me to convey his thanks.

He asked me also to pass on a request from the new government to exiled members of the old Horthy regime (pre-Communist Hungarian government) to stay away. He said there had been offers of help from these people, but confirmed that their previous self-indulgent love of the good life, in such places as Monte Carlo, whence they returned to their estates only when they wanted to take more out of the country, would not endear them to the people, and Hungary did not want them back. These rich estate owners had shown little or no interest in their estates in the past, or in the staff left to run them, and their behaviour had laid the foundations for the Communist take-over. These 'exiles' were very different from those landowners who had spent their lives looking after their beautiful homes and estates in Hungary, and had paid the price when the Soviet Communists triumphed. He wanted the completely fallacious reports that Horthy supporters were behind the Uprising denied in no uncertain terms.

I asked him what he felt had caused the Revolution. He confirmed that there seemed to be no organised conspiracy. It had just evolved, and he, as so many others, had been caught up in the events. He also confirmed that he thought that the cruel and repressive Rakosi/Gero governments had caused the tempers of ordinary people to be raised, until some felt they could take no more. I received similar answers from people in all walks of life, whenever I asked this question.

I told him about the Soviet forces I had seen massing just outside Budapest, and told him about my journey to and from Vienna three days previously. He made notes, and said his intelligence showed there were eight or possibly nine Soviet armoured divisions in Hungary at that time, and added that further Soviet infantry units were coming into the country all the time from the USSR and surrounding satellite countries. He was in no doubt how ominous this all was, and asked my opinion. I could only confirm his feelings.

He then said that the more optimistic ones in the government thought the Soviets were building up their strength to add weight to the forthcoming talks which were due to take place that evening between senior members of the Hungarian government and the Soviets. This was the first I had heard about talks, and I asked if I could be told what they were for? The general said he had his doubts about the real purpose, but added, 'Our premier, Imre Nagy, trusts the Soviets', and he thought there was sincerity in the Soviet request. Imre Nagy would attend, together with his senior members of government. These included General Maleter, defence minister, who was the acknowledged military leader of the Freedom Fighters, and the general to whom I was speaking. I said the Soviets would undoubtedly be smarting from their temporary defeat at the hands of the Nationalists, and as these included all walks of life, the situation would undoubtedly be delicate. He agreed, and said, 'The Hungarian army and air force are behind Imre Nagy, and the whole country is in agreement with our declared neutrality.'

He was calm, and took me to one side before I left his office, quietly adding, 'The Budapest newspapers are enthusiastic about the future, and we have already achieved much, but I am not fooled by this Soviet build-up of forces. Please let the West know our plight. If all goes well tonight, then Hungary will want co-operation and help from the West. If not, then please see that the West sends us bandages.'

This was said with quiet dignity, and was a very moving moment. Throughout our meeting I had seen that he had liked my Players cigarettes, so I placed a new packet on his desk before shaking his hand and bidding him farewell.

As I left his office in the Houses of Parliament I somehow knew I would never see him again, although all round me the people were still happy and full of hope. It was going to be a difficult journey to the British Legation. My eyes were already misted, and it was not easy to see very well.

As I left the building, a Soviet general delivered a formal note to Imre Nagy in which reference was made to the size of the Soviet forces in Hungary, and also ordered a conference for that evening at 20.00 hours to discuss the situation. No reference was made to the talks arranged earlier. Imre Nagy and his generals were to be amongst those present. This peremptory behaviour did not pass unnoticed, and all the Nationalist forces were placed in a state of advanced readiness. As ordered, the Nationalist leaders kept the rendezvous with the Soviets.

There were no talks. Instead General Serov, head of the Soviet secret police, was there to supervise the arrest of all those gallant men. They were never seen in public again, and news of their deaths was eventually published.

I reported my meeting with the general to Leslie, and then, as I had a bad cold, and also had to meet some people, I decided to sleep in my own home instead of my office, after meeting my contacts. On that night of 3 November, I went to bed with a couple of aspirins. At 04.00 hours the next morning all hell was let loose as the Soviet forces thundered back into Budapest.

No one needed any explanation of what was happening. The crushing might of the Soviet forces was showing Hungary that there was going to be no second chance for them, and this time there would be no doubt about the outcome. I immediately telephoned Vienna, and told the staff on duty in the British Embassy there that they must wake the ambassador and tell him of the massive Soviet assault. He had asked me to inform him immediately if there was any significant change in the situation, and I assured his staff that there was no doubt that he must be woken up at once. I also recommended that any of our families still in Vienna should make arrangements to return to the UK as soon as possible.

I then telephoned Leslie Fry who, needless to say, had also been awakened by the onslaught. He asked if I had managed to contact our ambassador in Vienna, and was pleased to hear that I had already reported to the Embassy. It seemed unreal that one could get through to Vienna so directly and easily on the telephone, where all was peace and quiet, amidst all the mayhem which was going on outside my house. I was thankful that I had got through when I did, as not long afterwards in one of the fierce exchanges of fire just outside, I saw a Russian soldier deliberately shooting out my telephone cable, after which of course my house was cut off from the outside world.

As it turned out it was fortunate that I was not able to leave my house for some days, for in that time there was a succession of most unwelcome callers. Had I not been there undoubtedly my staff would have been whipped away by the AVH, and the house looted and ransacked from top to bottom.

The noise of the battle was horrendous. Although as a pilot I was used to aircraft noise, and to the deafening throb of the huge bomber raids we fought against in the Battle of Britain, I was not used to enormous tanks with heavy armament fighting pitched battles in the street just beyond the front door. The Soviets had installed a large 152 mm gun on top of Gellért Hill very near my house, and every time this opened up the whole house shook. Apart from this, there was also a machine-gun post and a smaller field gun at the end of the road, to guard any approach to the larger gun. Of course it all invited real interest from the Freedom Fighters by day and night. At times the noise seemed continuous, with mortars and rockets also playing a part. Fires were started which could not be extinguished, and parts of Buda looked like an inferno as I looked down on it from my house. Every window in the house was shot out during this time, and anyone who dared to peer above a window ledge was immediately shot at. For several days I crawled on all fours below any window I wished to pass.

My beautiful little Vizsla puppy Betya did not, alas, understand about curfews. He had just been house-trained, and was instinctively a very clean dog. One evening when I did not notice he got out to spend a penny. The Soviet soldier on guard by the machine-gun post just outside the house saw something move and opened fire. By nothing short of a miracle one bullet went right through the puppy's tummy from one side to the other, and, as we later realised, missed every vital organ.

Bleeding profusely, Betya crawled back into the house. I was horrified but, being unable to get any help, applied what first aid I could with the medical supplies I had available, doing my best to staunch the bleeding with bandages. For several days after that my chauffeur and I nursed him cuddled on our laps. Amazingly, he made a complete recovery. He also proved that dogs do have a sense of colour, because for the rest of his life, if he saw anything in a brown uniform, he would change from being the most placid of animals into a raging killer. Any shade of blue, whether light RAF or Navy, he did not mind at all. Later, when the battles were over, and things were reasonably quiet, and Betya had grown up, he chased a group of Russian soldiers down a street, to the delight of the watching Hungarians.

Of course, being the national dog of Hungary as well, he became known as the Freedom Fighter dog, but sadly, as a gun dog he was finished. Although very courageous in every other way, the sound of gunfire or thunder shut him into a world of fear that even I could not penetrate, as he searched desperately to find some small enclosed place where he could hide. He had a little disc of white hairs on each side of his stomach, where the bullet had entered and left. In his old age – he lived to 13 – when he met young dogs, they would stop to pass the time of day with him, with wagging tails. A glazed look would gradually come over their eyes, and I reckoned he was telling them about his war wound!

Another casualty in the household was the little son of Mrs Szabo, my housemistress. Although they were sheltering all the time in their quarters in the basement, by ill luck a bullet came through the window, literally parting his hair. I can still picture the line this superficial wound made down the side of his head. Of course everyone was shaken by the event, but it was once again a miraculous escape. Again I attended to it with some of my medical supplies, and all was well.

The fact that I had helped her with her child forged a special relationship with *Szabo Neenie* (Auntie Szabo) which, with her Russian background, was to prove invaluable in the days to come.

During a short lull in the fighting I heard some people come into my hall. I went down to investigate, and found three AVH starting to round up my staff to take them away for 'questioning', and probably eventually the firing squad. One was literally drooling in anticipation, and all the staff were visibly terrified. I was furious, and asked one of them what was going on. He stuck a machine-gun in my stomach, and said he was acting on orders of the new government. I pushed his gun to one side, and his expression turned to one of amazement, as I went for him in my poor Hungarian.

Mrs Szabo came from the basement to see what was going on, and joined in. Fortunately a Soviet officer then appeared on the scene. He was in charge of the AVH gang, and clearly did not like his task at all, from the looks he gave them. I asked Mrs Szabo to explain I was the British air attaché, and that my house was ex-territorial, and had diplomatic immunity. The Soviet officer soon understood, and ordered the AVH to leave immediately. I thanked him through Mrs Szabo, who carried on talking to him afterwards. He told her the AVH was arresting anyone considered to be 'a suspect'. He did not like his job as escort, but the AVH had to have Soviet protection.

It was awful to see the AVH in action again so soon. Many unfortunate people were being led off to the AVH 'questioning rooms', and I was powerless to help them in any way. Thankfully, because I was at home, at least my own staff were safe. They were petrified of these thugs, and it was heartrending to see fully-grown people so reduced by fear. I hung my uniform in the hall to point out to any other AVH that the house was forbidden territory.

We later had a Soviet officer and six men call, looking for somewhere to sleep. They were very tired, having been continuously on duty for some 36 hours, and were obviously glad to find a Russian-speaking woman to talk to. Mrs Szabo gave them some hot soup and sent them on their way, telling me she felt the officer was a good man, and we would have no trouble there. We had another visit from the AVH, who were also successfully sent away. By now we knew what to say, and Mrs Szabo's Russian was used to good purpose. She told me later she had told the AVH to be careful, as the Russian officers and men had been, and the house had their protection.

We began to get reports of Soviet looting in any unguarded properties they could find, and we were visited by three renegade Soviet troops. They obviously had not been fighting, they were far too fresh and plausible, and could well have been looters. As soon as they learnt I was a 'British colonel' they left, and there was no trouble. Once again I was thankful that I was there to safeguard my staff. Another thing which turned out to be in our favour was the Soviet machine-gun emplacement just in front of the house. Gradually these men seemed to become responsible for us, and their very presence kept away many AVH thugs.

Throughout all my dealings with Soviet military personnel it was extremely rare to find anyone, even the newest conscript, who did not behave at all times with the utmost correctness (except perhaps when off-duty they got at the vodka, and even then they never forgot discipline). At the same time, one group did appear menacing. These were the Mongol troops, who were ruthlessly efficient, rather like the Gurkhas but without the smile. They gave me a chilly feeling.

The Egyptian ambassador, whose house was just up the road, was not as fortunate as we were. He was hiding in the basement when the looters arrived, and finding no one about, they took clothing, jewellery and food belonging to the ambassador and his wife. Eventually, when the Soviet High Command in Moscow was informed, they tried to put matters right, as they desperately wanted to be friendly with the Egyptian government, as the Soviet influence in that country was being built up at that time. They sent the Egyptian ambassador many items of clothing, and a lot of jewellery. Unfortunately, none of it was theirs, and the ambassador's wife promptly rejected it. It was obviously loot from some other unfortunate. The worst *faux pas* was the delivery of large pieces of pork which, of course, neither of them could eat. The wife, a most attractive young lady full of spirit, left Budapest as soon as she could, vowing never to return. As far as I know she never did, and we missed seeing her at official functions.

I had noticed things were a bit quieter, and the machine-gun post had been removed from the road in front of the house, which all pointed to the fact that the fighting was dying down. My next lot of young Soviet soldiers had obviously heard about Mrs Szabo being Russian, and were just like any troops far from home. They were pleasant enough youngsters, and when I asked them what they thought the Union Jack was, which I had hung outside my house, Mrs Szabo told me they said it was 'a pretty piece of rag'! When I told them what it was and what I was, they were amazed. They said they had been told they were fighting the Fascists, and that the whole thing was something to do with the Suez Canal. Some of them also genuinely thought the Danube was the Suez Canal. To me it was very significant that all these troops were talking about the Suez Canal, and I knew I must report this as soon as I possibly could.

When I was able to get around again, I soon discovered that all the Soviet troops who had been in Hungary prior to the Revolution had been sent out of the country, and replaced with entirely new forces. In time the fact that my house was a diplomat's residence did sink in, but not before many Soviet troops had come to look upon it as a link with their own homes. All very difficult, and I had to point out to Mrs Szabo that her Soviet soldier friends must make their visits less openly. She saw the wisdom in this, and whenever she could laid on hot drinks and food for her fellow-countrymen only after dark. I suppose it was my food and drink, but it was a good insurance against the AVH. The staff were not afraid of the Soviet troops as they were of the AVH.

When the soldiers were being entertained downstairs by the Szabos, the staff came upstairs, so there was never any difficulty in this respect. The numbers visiting were always small, but gradually the visits themselves became more frequent. One day I noticed an armed Soviet sentry on duty at the gate of the house. Mrs Szabo was as intrigued as I was, and made enquiries. Apparently, one of our more regular visitors, an NCO, had decided that we needed protection. It was a kind gesture, but I had to ask for the sentry to be removed.

Soviet troops were always punctilious in their salutes, and I have to say that I always found the Red Army gave a good account of itself, both in battle and in more mundane duties. Their officers were well turned out, and were confident in their own ability, and their troops were young but well-disciplined. Because they were just ordinary soldiers, I could detect a feeling of distaste for the AVH thugs they had to protect.

Fortunately, it was standard policy for us as diplomats to build up a personal store of food, drink and medical supplies in our homes, as calls on such stocks could be great with the official entertaining we had to do. It was quite normal to give a full dinner for 16, a buffet for 30-plus and cocktail parties for 70-plus. Adequate stocks were essential when so far from Western sources. During the fighting there were many visits from young mothers in the vicinity, who chose their visiting times carefully to avoid the AVH. They wanted milk for their babies, and luckily I had a large stock of tins of condensed milk which helped to keep many young Hungarians alive in those difficult days. Even my stocks became depleted, however, as I was feeding 16 mouths every meal in the house, as well as the young children along the street, not to mention the visiting soldiers. They always repaid Mrs Szabo's hospitality with some of their Soviet army bread. It was wonderful, made with a rye flour I think, whole grain, and dark in colour, substantial, with a delicious flavour which I thoroughly enjoyed!

Some young families called during a lull in the fighting, and asked what I suggested they should do. They had young children whom they wanted to have a free start in life, and the recent visits from the AVH had terrified them all. Many avoided being caught by the AVH by slipping from house to house. It was an old and established practice, and everyone helped the escapees as much as possible. I could only advise these courageous young people that they would have to walk out, as any vehicle would be searched. It was still possible to get out of Hungary to Austria or Yugoslavia, as these frontiers had not been closed. Most of the youngsters did decide to go, and I could only make sure they had enough milk and other necessities for their immediate needs.

All manner of subterfuge was used to make unreliable neighbours think they were still at home. For instance, a pram would be left outside the door, and then taken in and put out again on another day. I always agreed to help on these cover-ups whenever possible. Some promised to let me know if they ever made it to the West safely, and I received several messages from couples confirming successful escapes.

Over 100,000 people made their way out of Hungary during those difficult times, and most of them had to walk out. They did not want to leave their country, but they could not tolerate another return to the Rakosi/Gero type of regime. Their main fear was the return of the AVH, and the renewed presence of these evil people had been a deciding factor.

After some days the fighting subsided enough for Leslie to send a couple of cars from the Legation to pick up a few of us who had been separated from the building when the onslaught began. Before leaving my house I made sure that Mrs Szabo had plenty of food, and that the Russian soldiers were still sending in their very sustaining bread. I trusted this stocky, tough and reliable woman, and as she had turned to me when her child was wounded, I felt we had built up a rapport.

I reported to Leslie, and told him my news. He confirmed that the Imre Nagy government had been replaced by the Kadar government. Apparently Janos Kadar had been ordered by the Soviets to take over the government on 4 November, at the time when Nagy and his team were arrested by the KGB party led by General Serov. This news had reached me at home by radio broadcasts. Of course the free radio had soon been replaced by a return to Party-type broadcasts.

The British Legation was still crowded, partly because we had a host of newsmen, who were a cheerful bunch, all firm in their resolution to condemn the way ordinary people in Hungary were being slaughtered. I personally watched a T-54 tank in one of the streets firing its big gun into the lower stories of a building to bring it down because a sniper was on the roof.

The Freedom Fighters had fought heroically, but they were outgunned and outnumbered on every side. As the days went by, what had been their two great mainstays of hope, that the West would come to their aid, and that the United Nations would come to see for themselves what was happening and take up their cause for freedom from oppression, began to crumble. The United Nations had been refused permission by the Soviets to send any delegates, and so feebly said there was nothing they could do. The West had been promising arms and support, especially through the broadcasts over Radio Free Europe, which had encouraged and inspired many of the Freedom Fighters. Then, in their hour of need, it stood by and watched the little country's bid for freedom pulverised by the overwhelming might of the USSR. All the time, the attention of the world was focused on Suez.

Words cannot begin to describe how rotten and ashamed it all made me feel. There was virtually nothing I could do, except help a few individuals where possible. One of my worst moments was when the telephone rang in my office, and it was a handful of youngsters still holding out in the post office. They said they hoped the West was coming soon, as they were down to their last few rounds of ammunition . . . and then the line went dead. All I could do was watch the Soviet armada of tanks rumble down the street.

Even with no hope of outside aid left, many still continued to fight as and when they could for the freedom they believed in so fiercely. In due course the Kadar regime announced an amnesty, but by this time the Hungarians had learnt in the hardest way to trust no one; many put away their arms in plastic bags and buried them, which I think gave them some feeling of security.

There was a significant and moving incident in the British Legation when the correspondent from the Communist newspaper the British *Daily Worker* decided he could no longer support his communist creed and formally denounced it. Leslie Fry was the first to congratulate him on a courageous decision, and said he was proud to shake his hand. We all felt the same. Ivor Jones from the BBC and Sandy Gall were still with us, and we knew the press would do all it could for Hungary when they got back home. Most of them left on 9 November to go to Vienna in a convoy, which reached Austria after a prolonged journey.

The fighting had died down, and the Soviet tanks patrolled the streets regularly, pointedly ignored by the people. A major task that had to be confronted was obtaining food. No trains had run for 19 days. The Soviet government had stopped food and medical supplies coming into the country from Austria. I never could find out why, for they were certainly needed, and needed urgently. Perhaps it was to prevent the West being in any way in a position to help.

The AVH were back in business, with their ghastly trail of arrests, interrogation and torture, but they needed the backing of the regime. It was hard to understand how Janos Kadar could allow them to act in this way when he himself had suffered at the hands of the head of the AVH, General Farkas Mihalyi (in English, Michael Fox), a particularly poisonous character. The only glimmer of hope was that Khrushchev trusted Kadar (as much as he would anyone), and had never liked Rakosi. Perhaps Kadar would be able gradually to wring some concessions from Moscow.

The aftermath of the Uprising was rigged trials, reprisals, deportations, and the carrying out of countless death sentences. Exact numbers are not known, but many thousands were removed, and their loved ones never heard from them again. No amount of enquiries succeeded in getting even an acknowledgement about these 'missing persons'. Later, trainloads of prisoners were sent to the USSR, and many little scraps of paper were found along the rail tracks with pathetic messages to loved ones in a last effort to leave their names before being consigned to oblivion.

The Soviets were in control of the towns, but some of the Freedom Fighters still banded together in the hills and forests, determined somehow to continue the fight for their country's freedom. They were great youngsters, and above all they wanted to talk, and for their stories of what their country had gone through to be told to the West, and for all the world to know what had been happening. Always the biggest villains to whom they kept referring were Stalin and Rakosi. I met many on my travels round the countryside, and my heart ached for them. Whenever they asked me what they should do, I felt helpless, and could only advise them to join the thousands of other people who were making their way out of Hungary on foot. I knew the main roads were blocked by the AVH, but there were still many other routes that one could walk along in relative safety.

On one occasion when 'touring' I saw a Hungarian pilot in air force uniform at the roadside, obviously looking for a lift. A young boy was with him and I stopped and picked them up. By this time I knew everyone had an unusual personal story to tell, and the pilot turned out to be a fiery Freedom Fighter. I warned him we would soon be coming to a checkpoint, and whatever he did he must keep any arms well hidden, if he had any with him. A short while later, I was horrified when, glancing to the back of the car, I saw him firmly gripping a revolver.

I shouted angrily, 'Put that bloody thing away!'

He rapidly complied, and to my great relief we passed through the checkpoint without incident. Some days later I had a message from the Foreign Office in England saying they had with them a Freedom Fighter who said he knew me, and could I help in verifying this? I told them to ask him what he used to keep his revolver dry, as I had happened to notice that he had a condom over the barrel! It struck me what an ingenious idea it was. I was delighted when the reply came back that his story was confirmed. He stayed in the air force, becoming Vitez (knight) General Janos Karaszy-Kulim, and now lives in Kent, England.

During the exciting few days of hard-won freedom, I had gone round picking up any information I could which I thought would be of interest to MI6. At one time I used the end of my nail file to unscrew a data plaque from a Soviet radar installation, and mentioned in my report that I hoped they appreciated it, as it had ruined my nail file. In their next postbag they enclosed a new nail file, with the point carefully stuck in a cork, with their compliments.

Khrushchev took over the question of dealing with Hungary himself. Many of the country's armed forces were disarmed, and in the case of the Hungarian air force most personnel were sent home and told to await further instructions. Their aircraft and some equipment were just left at their airfields under Soviet guard. I learned this first-hand when I was asked if I would see four Hungarian officers who had called at the Legation requesting to see me. I first asked why they wanted to see me. They said I was respected by the Hungarian air force fighter pilots, as they all knew about my combat record, and they would be very grateful for the chance to talk to me. They had come to see me on their own initiative to ask a senior officer's advice.

They were all quite experienced fighter pilots, flying the MiG-19. Their own commanding officer had been arrested by the political officer in their unit, and this action had done as much as anything to make them call on me. They were a dashing foursome, just like fighter pilots in any air force. It was strange to sit there and consider the irony of it all.

Here was I, a Western attaché who had been a fighter ace in World War II, talking to a bunch of Communist-trained MiG fighter pilots, who were asking my advice regarding their future. 'Please tell us what you think we should do, just as if you were our commanding officer.' I found it very moving. There was certainly a bond between us, perhaps because we had all shared some of our lives in the skies together in fast and exciting aircraft. Their speech, behaviour and even mannerisms were so akin to any RAF pilots. It was uncanny, and we were all so soon at ease with one another.

After hearing their story, it became clear that they would have to leave Hungary if they were to avoid being taken by the AVH. When I said this they reluctantly agreed, for I was only confirming what they thought. I knew the escape routes to Austria were closed by this time, but that the Yugoslav frontier was still passable. They intimated this is how they had thought of escaping, and I was able to agree with their plan. They said they would leave as soon as they could. I asked if they had sufficient funds, and they had all that side organised and food as well for their journey. They were unmarried, but were very concerned about reprisals against their older relations. After over an hour's talk, we shook hands, and I wished them well. They agreed they would send me a message if they made it to safety. Some months later a message did reach me from Italy, via a friend in Vienna, to say that all four had succeeded in getting away. I hope they are living happy lives today somewhere in the world, for they certainly deserve it.

I continued with other senior officers interviewing my quota of visitors to the Legation. Unfortunately, the British military attaché had been PNG'd (sent home as *persona non grata* – a standard diplomatic move used many times during the Cold War, with or without good reason) just before the Uprising, so we were short of staff and I had to look after things which would normally have fallen to him. There had been no chance of getting a replacement out. There seemed to be an unending stream of people finding their way to the British Legation, for all sorts of reasons. Some had decided to leave the country and just wanted someone to know their whereabouts, and leave their story and name with a British official. Many were just plain scared, and wanted advice.

One poor man stayed a few days to regain his strength. He had been arrested some years back by the AVH by mistake, but they did not let him go in case he talked. Instead they tortured him to make him confess to a crime he knew nothing about. They ended up nailing his penis to a bench with an ordinary hammer and nails, and then flogged his penis afterwards. He seemed an inoffensive and dear old man, but he was clearly very frightened and agitated, and with good reason.

Another visitor I interviewed impressed me greatly. He was Ference Beiber, a well-built man who had been released by Freedom Fighters from the jail complex for political prisoners affiliated to the Tatabanya coalmines. He had been fighting the AVH and the Russians ever since his release. He had worked for the British Council from 1946 until he was arrested by the AVH on 31 March 1950 when he was walking home from work. Two others arrested with him were subsequently tortured and imprisoned, but managed to escape.

At first Beiber was treated with every courtesy. He was then asked to sign a statement full of lies about the British Council. When he refused, his treatment gradually became more severe. After 14 days of refusing to sign, he was subjected to torture. The AVH wanted him to tell them secrets of the British Legation, which he could not as he had no knowledge of such matters. He kept telling them the truth: his only work in the Legation had been confined to the storage and supervision of the Council's film library.

The torture got worse. They beat him on the body for days, and on his testicles and penis; they pulled out his fingernails, and burned his body with cigarette ends. Then they used an electric soldering iron to write on his body, as well as using this as a poker to inflict incredible pain up his rectum and on other sensitive parts. After days of this treatment Beiber was filthy and covered with blood and vomit. He was then taken to another office where a senior AVH official produced a piece of pork, saying, 'We have just been to your home, raped your wife, and cut this piece of flesh off your baby son.'

This was the last straw. Practically deranged with pain and rage, Beiber broke free and got hold of the heavy typewriter in the office, which he slammed on the heads of his new tormentors. He was kicked to the ground and repeatedly beaten with rifle-butts. He lapsed into unconsciousness, and was left to die. He remembered little for months, but was formally imprisoned for life, being sent to the coalmines at Tatabanya to be worked to death alongside the other political prisoners.

The political prisoners were worked as hard as the ordinary miners, the difference being that they were purposely given less rest, practically no time on the surface, and above all very little food. Clearly, it was the intention of the Rakosi regime to kill them off. The ordinary miners took pity on these poor wretches, and somehow managed to smuggle food to them whenever the AVH were off their guard. Beiber was full of praise for these miners, who he said were wonderful, and very brave, for had they been caught they could easily have become prisoners themselves. He owed his life to them.

At last, during the Uprising, Beiber was released by the Freedom Fighters. He weighed 45 kilos (7 stone or 98 lb), whereas his ordinary weight was 76 kilos (12 stone or 168 lb). He said even the life in the mines was heaven compared with the AVH jails, with their habitual bouts of torture. He had quickly joined a band of Freedom Fighters and fought with determination to rid his country of the AVH.

I asked if there was anything I could do to help in any way, could I contact a relative? He said there was none. His wife had married again, and neither the wife nor the child were his any longer. He had made this break when his sentence was announced, to allow his wife to make a new life and free her from any contact with a man who had become marked out as a special AVH prisoner. All he wanted was for his story to be told to the free world, as he felt that the Rakosi regime had contained so much evil.

I promised that his story would be told in the West, and I have now done this in numerous lectures I have given, and in various official reports. I have seen many results of man's inhumanity to man, but Beiber's suffering must have been as great as that of anyone I have ever met. Throughout, he spoke in a flat voice with no emotion; perhaps all feeling had been beaten out of him. He said his life in Hungary was finished, and asked me about escape routes. With his history, I told him to make all haste. I told him I only hoped he would be successful in his bid to escape, for I could see he was by no means a broken man; he had great courage and integrity, and I hoped he would find a new life in the West. However, he seemed resigned to pessimism, for the AVH had done its work all too well. He cheered up slightly when he told me that he had killed several AVH in the fighting.

We shook hands, and he left my office. He promised to let me know if he reached the West. Alas, no such confirmation reached me. Perhaps he was shot on the way to freedom, for many shared this fate. If he has indeed survived, I hope he may hear that at every opportunity I have told his story, and perhaps he may feel that his prolonged suffering was not entirely in vain.

I had far too many similar interviews. In recent years I have met Vitez (knight) Janos Szakaly, who had been head of police (the regular police, not the AVH) and we have become great friends. He, too, was arrested, and was sent to work in the infamous Tatabanya mines. For four years he received treatment similar to Beiber, and like him he admired the courage of the ordinary miners in helping him survive, risking their own lives by smuggling in food.

There was a happier ending to my friend's story. When he was released in the Uprising he reached the UK. Together with many other Hungarian refugees here, he hoped the officials in charge of helping them find employment would be able to assist him. His first difficulty was convincing them that he was not a miner! David Hicks, who was already famous for his furniture, was looking for someone who was willing to learn the craft of antique restoration. My friend, who had always loved working with wood, gladly seized the chance, and became one of the top craftsmen in the antiques world. Indeed, he has restored furniture in some of the Royal establishments. He and his wife and family live quite near us, and they have in recent years been able to visit Hungary, which had previously been impossible. As yet there is little hope of his regaining the land and other property which was seized from him so long ago.

Toward the end of 1956 the Freedom Fighters managed to print some news in a paper called *Igazag* (Truth). The articles were well written by Nationalists, to counter the half-truths being widely circulated by the new regime. As the following two items are so poignant, I have decided to quote them verbatim. If the English translation does not always seem grammatically correct, it has to be remembered that the Magyar tongue is unique, and sometimes difficult to render in English. I have throughout my writing about Hungary used both the titles Uprising and Revolution for the events in 1956, as I have felt that they are in fact interchangeable. The first extract will, however, clarify more precisely how the people of Hungary look upon the two terms:

> Extracts from *Igazag* (Truth): the newspaper of the Hungarian Freedom Fighters. October – November 1956:
>
> *'Revolution or a Fight for Freedom'*
>
> We are of the opinion that the difference between a Revolution and a Fight for Freedom is that, while the aim of a Revolution is to change one group of people in power for another, the situation in a Fight for Freedom is that an *entire* nation rises up and uses all the means it can – including armed force – not in order to attain political power, which it considers of less importance, but in order to shake from its shoulders the heavy yoke of an oppression imposed on a whole nation.
>
> *'Heroic Hooligans'*
>
> Those who have seen the corpses of the young men and women in front of the Astoria Hotel, or in the Sandor Brody Street, cannot help being struck (apart from the paralysing tragedy of the scene) by the fact that so many of them were wearing thick crêpe-soled 'Teddy Boy' shoes, so many multi-coloured socks on feet that will never again tap to the strain of dance music, so many Teddy Boy trousers, all crumpled on their dead legs.
>
> Dear Heroes, dear dead Heroes, dear young men and women, we beg a thousand pardons for our blindness in not knowing that, apart from your fondness for 'swing', you possessed noble,

immortal souls, and you were ready to sacrifice your own lives – just for us! Your outward conceit evidently arose from the disdain you felt for the life to which the AVH and the Russian machine guns put an end. There, lying on the pavement, your flashy clothes and your superior airs have vanished for ever, along with the crease in your trousers, and the kaleidoscope patterns of your swanky ties.

CHAPTER SEVENTEEN

FAREWELL TO HUNGARY

As 1957 dawned, everyone knew that Hungary would never be the same again. Disillusionment with the false promises and propaganda of the West was complete. At the same time, never again would the ordinary people tolerate a regime such as that of Rakosi, and there were signs that the Kadar government was aware of this. Once the active fighting had died down there had been a lot of passive resistance and a lot of damaging strike action. In an effort to try and get the country back to work, concessions were being made to the workers if they returned. In the past, any striker was simply arrested and shot, and so even the AVH was not being allowed to behave quite as badly as they had earlier. A new relationship was emerging between the government and its people, for never again could Moscow take Hungarians for granted. Certainly they had earned the admiration of the world and, as far as I could gather from talking with various contacts, even the Kadar gvernment was proud of this new national stand. One Russian general I met, who spoke English, said, 'They [the Hungarians] are a brave people' – praise indeed from a high-ranking soldier of the USSR.

Gradually the strikes diminished, and there was a slow resumption of diplomatic life. During the remainder of 1957 we met members of the new Hungarian government as official functions were resumed. We found some of these officials were the same as we had known previously. The main changes seemed to have taken place in the top posts, and certainly in the AVH. The Hungarian service chiefs I met after the Uprising were a new lot: they seemed younger, and some were less stilted in their approach when talking to us. The new government was still far from secure, and it relied on the Soviet army for its very existence. When Kadar signed an agreement with Moscow to the effect that Soviet troops were to remain in the country for years to come, this was the final *coup de grâce*.

The Writers' Federation, a focal point of intellectual opposition, was suppressed, and trials by specially formed military tribunals were set up. Arrests were at their worst in July 1957, when over 8,000 were reputed to have been taken. These arrests were justified by such statements as 'Revolutionary elements are planning to take advantage of the fall of Malenkov and his associates in the Soviet Union to mount yet another effort to overthrow the Hungarian government.' All absolute nonsense, of course.

To bolster Kadar's prestige Khrushchev decided to pay a state visit to Hungary, with all the trimmings. Western diplomats were puzzled about the reason, but Leslie told me he had been informed that the Eastern Bloc's political reason for the visit was that Khrushchev wanted to attend the celebrations on 4 April. Though Hungary had been an ally of Germany in World War II, to most Hungarians the Germans became an oppressive occupying power, and 4 April 1945 was the day when they were 'liberated' by the Red Army. We all doubted this explanation, and Leslie told the Foreign Office as much, particularly as Khrushchev's responsibilities in the Soviet Union had been increased.

He arrived at Ferihegy Airport in an Aeroflot Tu-104 jet airliner, on 2 April 1958, and was met by a large organised deputation headed by Kadar. There were also countless police, workers, guards and AVH lining the route from the airport to the government offices. Some schoolchildren had also been bussed in to vantage points to wave flags. I do not know how much of this Khrushchev took in, but he made a great show of letting everyone know that it was Janos Kadar who was his favourite. On arrival they greeted each other like long-lost brothers, and Khrushchev was heard to congratulate Kadar warmly on the way he was running things in Hungary.

Khrushchev was in a good humour, and went about the city a lot before leaving on 8 April. He was obviously enjoying his visit, and pulled Kadar in whenever possible when talking to groups of people, making great play of the fact that Kadar was in good favour with Moscow. I met him at an official function, and also saw him at a wreath-laying ceremony at Heroes Square on 4 April. This also was a formal affair, but it passed without incident.

Khrushchev was a very squarely-built man, not tall, and although he looked fat this was far from the case. He was really powerfully built, and tough. He had a good handshake and gave the impression of being a happy tubby man, somewhat clown-like to look at with very wide trousers, but when I looked at his eyes they were piercing and ice-blue, very alive and burning with curiosity. He missed nothing that was going on about him, and I knew that I was in the presence of a very strong character.

After the visit everyone could see that he had built up the morale of the Communist Party in Hungary, so perhaps that was the main reason for the visit. Kadar's position was much enhanced, and he too showed signs of increased confidence, and a few more lenient measures were gradually introduced. I spoke to a dear old Hungarian lady who said, 'Whatever the reason for Comrade Khrushchev's visit to Budapest, it will undoubtedly mean less bread for the Hungarians.' She could not read or write, but her reaction to the visit was typically cynical.

There was another important state visit in 1958. The Polish First Secretary Wladislaw Gomulka spent some days in Hungary. In contrast to Khrushchev's, it was played down as much as possible, and Gomulka was allowed to meet only a few selected people. It was obvious that it was feared that the Hungarians would use this Polish visit to demonstrate. However, the occasion passed quietly, particularly as Gomulka made a joint declaration with Kadar to the effect that he supported the new Soviet policy for Hungary. After he left, all sorts of declarations were published in the press, but the people had long ago stopped reading such news. They disbelieved any government statements, and read papers only for the sports news. I met Gomulka and some of his delegation; he was not an impressive man, but he seemed warm and easy to talk to.

In June 1958 the Soviet news-agency Tass and Hungarian newspapers disclosed that Imre Nagy and General Maleter had been executed. It had been hoped that more lenient sentences would have been passed on these brave men, who had done what they rightly considered to be their duty for their country. On all sides one could feel only disgust for the Soviets, and for Kadar and his government. I doubt if there was ever a time when Kadar was more hated, and the situation in the country was very tense.

Many people talked to me about these executions, and all condemned them. Some wanted to get out their guns and start another uprising. I always countered these proposals, saying that Hungary had made her sacrifice in 1956, and that the Soviet army in Hungary was now immensely powerful, and would if necessary kill most of the population. It was this type of advice, together the knowledge that the West was not prepared to help in any way (as had been demonstrated in 1956, when even the United Nations were unable to take any action over Hungary), that dissuaded active resistance on the part of the 'silent' Freedom Fighters. At the time this was a sad line to adopt, but it was the wisest in the circumstances.

Of course, I was now experienced in my job, and always aware that I was being followed and reported on. I had not forgotten seeing those detailed files on my predecessor. Sometimes, when I was 'touring' and saw what I knew was a tailing car in my rear-view mirror, I thought of the words of the official who had briefed me before I left London: 'Of course, Group Captain . . . you are on your own.'

There were several occasions when I was nearly run off the road into a convenient ditch. More than once I was thankful for the fact that my car was powerful, and a great road-holder, and fast enough to outdrive my pursuers. I knew only too well of the sad 'accidents' in which the driver was killed, his car having unaccountably left the road and crashed.

During the height of the fighting I had been stopped on one of the bridges in Budapest and strip-searched by a corporal, despite all my protestations of diplomatic immunity (which obviously meant nothing to him), and my Russian protestations of *niet pushka* (no guns). Fortunately, it was quite true, and I was allowed to put my clothes back on and go on my way on what was a very cold night. Being stopped for no particular reason was a fact of life, and people learned to carry nothing that might incriminate them.

Leslie and I were keenly aware not only of being followed, but also of 'bugs' being concealed to catch any unguarded remark. Many a time we would have what might be termed a 'sensitive' discussion as we closely admired Leslie's plants in his lovely garden. With our heads well down, we knew no one at any possible vantage point could lip-read, even with binoculars! He and Penelope were known to be knowledgeable on gardening matters, so it did not appear unusual to admire his flowers.

One evening, when diplomatic entertaining had been resumed, I hosted a dinner party. After we had sat down at the table, one of my guests, unsuitably called Colonel Virag (Colonel Rose), proceeded to stick his finger through the middle of the flowers in the floral centrepiece on the table. On enquiring what he was doing, he said that he was looking for 'bugs' (the electrical kind). I remarked that it showed what one could expect at his own house.

Knowing that one's house is probably bugged as a matter of course, we regularly had to have it professionally 'degaussed', which was also done to the Legation premises. When the Foreign Office team were due to come and go over my house we saw to it that it was cleared for them. Their equipment was sensitive, and they needed the place to be very quiet. It was a good excuse to go out for a day's picnic. On one such occasion Betya nearly caused heart failure amongst the team. I had not taken him with us as usual, as we had a full car. Just as the men were deeply engrossed in their work, the door was suddenly thrown open with a bang! I was told afterwards their hearts were in their mouths, as they thought they had been caught by the AVH. Instead, they were confronted by a brown dog, very proud of his ability to pull the door handle down with his paw and imperiously throw open the door, but with a rather puzzled expression on his face as he seemed to ask, 'Where is everybody?'

Sometimes my official duties took a particularly enjoyable turn. One such occasion was when I had to look after the renowned violinist Yehudi Menuhin and his wife, when he came out to give a concert. What an interesting and delightful couple they proved to be. Needless to say, his concert was a great event. He charged the authorities the maximum he felt he could, and then saw that all his fee went where it would most help the ordinary Hungarian people. In conversation he made a most perceptive remark that, 'In politics it is as if the West is playing bridge, while the Russians are playing chess.'

He was the most unassuming person, and told me that he still practised up to eight hours a day: what a perfectionist. I took the Menuhins out to a restaurant where they could hear a cymbaline, in a gypsy orchestra. The Magyar gypsy violin music is well known, and my guests listened enchanted as the leader of the orchestra serenaded us at our table. Yehudi was most interested in the sweeping style, which of course is quite unlike classical violin. He complimented the violinist most graciously, and the man was quite overcome when Yehudi said with all sincerity, 'I wish I could play like that!'

Someone else I was more than delighted to entertain was dear Lady Trenchard, who came out to stay with me on a private visit. I had problems with her papers, as the Hungarians had never heard of a viscountess, and the title was difficult to explain. Eventually they said that they would be happy to put her down in her maiden name, and she could have papers to visit me as 'Mrs Bowlby' and come as my cook. Lady Trenchard roared with laughter when she heard this, and we both found it quite extraordinary and never really understood it, but it was so good to see her again.

In 1956 two-thirds of the Hungarian population were Roman Catholics. There had been countless battles between the State and the Church. Despite or perhaps because of the regime's displeasure, the churches were full on Sundays. Though not of the Catholic faith, I attended a mass in Budapest, and the church was packed, with people standing in the aisles. The music was beautiful, the organ backed up by an orchestra in the gallery. I could well see why one of the things the Communists feared most was the strength of Catholicism.

Cardinal Mindszenty's story is well known, and in 1956 he was regarded as the heroic saviour of the Catholic faith in Hungary. He was thrown into prison by Rakosi, where his treatment at the hands of the AVH was as bad as could be imagined. In October 1956 he was set free by the Freedom Fighters, and as there was still fighting in progress when he was released, he was taken to the nearby US Legation for safety. As it turned out, he stayed in the Legation for years, and he remained Hungary's symbol of faith. Fortunately this conformed with American policy as, perhaps surprisingly, it was a rule in our Legation that Her Majesty could not grant political asylum.

I had many friends in the American Legation, and it was arranged for me to attend a private service the Cardinal was giving for his mother. She was a dear old lady, dressed in simple black peasant robes. The service was very moving, and an occasion I will never forget. I had previously asked my host to ascertain whether the Cardinal would mind a Church of England member attending this private mass. The Cardinal replied that he welcomed all who believed in God. He was a wonderful man, with a face full of strength and character.

It was significant to me that the day I met the Cardinal was Christmas Day 1956. His deep love and respect for his mother was very apparent, and 'strengthening', which is the word that comes to mind whenever I remember this exceptional man.

The AVH kept watch on the US Legation continuously. While Cardinal Mindszenty was there, usually at least four of them were on watch, for many years. I met several US officials who told me that it had been put to the Cardinal that he should leave Hungary and go to Rome, for it would apparently have been a simple matter to get a Hollywood make-up artist to disguise him ready for the trip, to fool the AVH. He always refused, however, as he felt that his presence in Hungary helped the Catholics and all church-loving people, as indeed it did. He was symbolic of the Nationalists' faith, and of their desire for freedom.

I met many incredibly brave men and women throughout the time I was in Hungary, and they have earned my undying respect and affection. I met the ordinary people all over the country, from the simple peasant farmers and their families, to factory workers and intellectuals in the towns, young and old. It was a cross-section of the population, such as I would never have met had it not been for the exceptional circumstances of my time there. It changed my life.

Of course, I could never forget my role as a diplomat. I continued to meet Andropov at various functions, and though always aware of his powerful position, I equally felt there was hope for the Soviet Union if they had such men. On one occasion he told me that he felt a priority for the future of his country was education for the younger generation. On one of the rare occasions when anything political was mentioned, he remarked that the 'Soviet homeland and the satellites are like an enormous monolith. When Hungary had her troubles it was as if a brick had come out of place . . . we had to pat it back.' I can see his hands now, as he illustrated the act of patting it back. Recollecting those days, I could not help thinking, 'Some pat!'

On a later occasion he walked down a staircase with me at a function, and suddenly put his arm round my shoulder just as we were about to pass the Head of the AVH at the foot of the stairs. I could not help but notice the look of utter amazement on the latter's face, and could not resist saying, 'You see I have friends in high places.' To this day I have wondered at that seemingly 'spontaneous' gesture from Andropov. What was he trying to demonstrate, and to whom? He was a man who always did things with a reason.

Many years later I was flabbergasted to discover that not only had Andropov been head of the KGB all those years, but he had now become president of the Soviet Union. After giving the matter considerable thought, I wrote to Dennis Thatcher. I had met him and Mrs Thatcher prior to her becoming prime minister, and had corresponded several times since. I felt I would like him to let her know, in an unofficial capacity, of the opinion I had formed of Yuri Andropov during those years when I was meeting him two or three times a week. I wanted her to know that I felt at last there was a Soviet leader who might be open to meaningful talks with the West. As noted earlier, I knew that he had a particularly high regard for the bravery of the British seamen in the convoys which brought supplies to his country. I added that, having served my country to the best of my ability throughout my RAF career of 30 years, if there was any further way in which I could be of help I would be only too glad.

I was appalled to have my letter returned to me with a hand-written reply from Mr Thatcher on the back. He said I was far too experienced not to know that unilateral disarmament is one-sided (I had never mentioned unilateral disarmament), and altogether I felt it was a Number One brush-off.

A short while later, Andropov died. I had incidentally been shocked to see how ill he looked when I first saw pictures of him on TV as he came to ultimate power. Gorbachev took over and Mrs Thatcher was soon meeting him, saying that here was a man she felt she could do business with!

My time in Hungary was drawing to a close. I was filled with vivid memories that I was going to cherish forever. I was also going to take away with me a collection of bullets, which I had prised from the walls inside my house. Above all, I knew I could never be sufficiently grateful for having had a minister like Leslie Fry at that desperate time. He was certainly the right man in the right place at the right time, and not only that but with a wonderful wife like Penelope to support him. How well-deserved was his knighthood, and I was equally delighted to read that HM consul Miss Joan Fish was awarded the OBE. She had been magnificent through that most difficult of times, and like Leslie had worked ceaselessly to save the lives of many ordinary Hungarian people. Jimmy Green, our W/T operator, was rewarded too, with an MBE. We will none of us forget how tirelessly he kept Hungary in touch with the world, day and night.

There had been a particularly odious woman, the wife of a highly-placed AVH official, who had constantly passed loud snide comments in Hungarian about me and the British in general to her fellow conspirators at the functions we attended. I took great pains to learn how to say, in perfect Hungarian, how much I had enjoyed her comments over the years. I saved this up for the final occasion on which I was to see her. As I left I turned to her, and said my piece. The effect was instantaneous. Her jaw literally dropped, and I left feeling well pleased.

Eventually I awoke on 25 August 1958 to realise that this was my last day in Hungary. I filled my car with the housemistress's children and their friends. There was great excitement, because few of them had ever been inside a car. We drove round Budapest taking ciné film of all my much-loved favourite places. I even filmed the AVH trying to hide behind trees, and even lamp-posts. I experienced a glorious feeling of abandon as, for the first time since I had been there, I no longer needed to look over my shoulder to see who was watching and listening. I even waved to the AVH, but they did not wave back! The children loved every minute of it, and knew exactly what was going on. I knew there would be great stories to tell their families that night.

To my amazement, when I came to leave, the entire staff of my household lined up to say goodbye. It was a very emotional moment, for I knew by the nature of what I had been doing, that I was unlikely ever to see them or dear Hungary again. I shall always wish that I could have done more. So far as I know, I managed to help about 400 to freedom. Leslie and I said at the time that the Uprising was the first chink in the seemingly impenetrable Communist armour. I have repeated this through the years, and tried to make the Freedom Fighters feel that their great sacrifices were not in vain. Indeed, subsequent events have proved that it really was the first small step towards the end of Communism. Hard though it was at the time, and for years after, time and again the Hungarians have said to me, 'Dennis, you gave us hope.' Throughout my career, given the opportunity, it has always been my aim to save lives.

There is a postscript. In 1976, long before the collapse of Communist rule and the Warsaw Pact, Hungarian Freedom Fighters in Britain prepared to commemorate the 20th anniversary of their great Uprising. Their leader came to see me to ask if he might borrow some photographs he had heard that I had taken, for their exhibition of scenes of 1956. After we had talked for a while he said, 'Ah, you are the man who gave us hope.' and added he would like to put my name forward for a big honour. Later in 1976 I went to Munich where the Hungarian ruler in exile, Arpad Habsburg, invested me as an honorary member of the Knightly Order of Vitez.

Later still I learned that to the Freedom Fighters I had become known as 'The Light Blue Pimpernel'. This had come about because Baroness Orczy, the famous author of novels about the Scarlet Pimpernel, was herself Hungarian. Her stories concerned an Englishman who rescued aristocrats from the guillotine during the French Revolution, and who disguised his true identity by the *nom de plume* 'The Scarlet Pimpernel'. This is a ubiquitous little flower which turns up growing in unlikely places. After achieving his rescues the Englishman would always leave a small piece of paper behind with a drawing of the tiny scarlet flower. Thus, because of the colour of my uniform, and my exploits in trying to help these courageous people, I became known to the Hungarian Freedom Fighters as the 'Light Blue Pimpernel'. It means a great deal to me that this is how they thought of me. The manner in which they have stood true to their belief in freedom for Hungary over all these years has earned my undying admiration.

CHAPTER EIGHTEEN

TANGMERE AND NATO

Hungary, apart from being a complete change in my line of career, had – not surprisingly in the circumstances – made a deep and lasting impression on me, and this has had an impact on the rest of my life. I was wondering what my next posting would be, when I was told that I was to be given command of RAF Tangmere. I could not have been more delighted, and looked forward to it with eager anticipation. Although it had recently changed from Fighter to Signals Command it was still Tangmere, and I will always love it. I never dreamed when I first went there that one day I would command this wonderful station. I was there from September 1958 to May 1961. After two and a half years behind the Iron Curtain it was not easy at first to return to the 'normality' of England, where one did not have to be constantly looking over one's shoulder.

In 1958 Tangmere was still playing a vital part in RAF communications. This was carried out by many methods. There was also the need to calibrate UK early-warning radars up to 50,000 ft (15,240 m). This was achieved by flying a Canberra jet bomber along a precise predetermined course. We also calibrated landing aids at all-weather stations. It was a great delight to take up my old trade again and get in more flying, and in general bring myself up to date after nearly four years of limited opportunity in this regard.

An extra pleasure was to host the Joint Services Language School. Of course, the Polish, Ukrainian, and all the other foreign nationalities added interest and colour. Amongst the more unusual of the instructors was Father Hubarzevsky, who was head of the Russian Orthodox Church in the Ukraine. This Church was severely oppressed by both the Soviets and the Germans, but when religion is oppressed it always gathers strength. His was a most interesting personality. He was a brilliant linguist, and I found his ideas stimulating.

Another language instructor whom I remember well was a Polish diplomat who between the wars had been part of their Ministry of Agriculture. He told me of the disastrous agricultural policy brought in by Khrushchev, by which thousands of kilometres of hedgerows were dug up to make enormous fields. These hedgerows had been carefully nurtured over the centuries to shield the fields from winds howling over the open steppes, and without their protection all the topsoil was rapidly blown away. As a result the crops failed and thousands starved. The Communists dealt with this problem by executing the farmers, blaming them for the stupidity of the government's own policies.

The social scene played an increasingly important part in my life at Tangmere. We had two distinguished dukes whose estates were nearby. The Duke of Norfolk, the Earl Marshal of England and head of the leading Catholic family in the country, lived only six miles away at Arundel Castle. It is one of the most beautiful castles in England, situated on a mound where the green lawns set off the grey stonework to perfection. Below it is the River Arun, and it is hard to imagine that in bygone days this was a major port for large vessels.

Close by there had been a port in Roman times, and a few miles to the west was what is today called Fishbourne, the site of one of the greatest Roman palaces in what was then *Britannia*. Recent work there has revealed mosaic floors of most elaborate design, which are now on public view.

Tangmere was even-handed, for an eminent Protestant duke, the Duke of Richmond, lived even closer, at Goodwood. The Goodwood estate is famed for just that, namely estate trees which are centuries old. In addition, the Goodwood racetrack is world-renowned, and the annual racing week there in the summer is aptly known as 'Glorious Goodwood'. Indeed, to horse-racing has been added motor-racing, though not on the same circuit.

A few months after I had settled into the Tangmere CO's house Betya's time in quarantine was up. I had dispatched him before I left Hungary, knowing he had to comply with the six-month anti-rabies quarantine regulations. He had flown from Budapest in a regulation kennel, and from all accounts had barked nearly all the way to London.

My mother went to see him after his arrival, so that I could have a first-hand report that all was well. Although he had never previously met her, he seemed to know by instinct she was something to do with me. At last the happy day came when I could bring him back to his new home in Tangmere, where he became my constant companion.

One of the sidelines of the station was the pig farm. I was fortunate to have an excellent pig farmer, and this farm was very profitable, the proceeds from which helped to keep the station in sports, providing the cash to buy the strip for some 30 teams of soccer, rugger, cricket and other sports. It was a great saving, and meant that there was little waste from the messes, as any suitable food was able to go straight to the pig farm for swill.

The farm had many breeding sows, but its pride was a magnificent boar. None of the animals were confined, other than within the limits of the farm by wire and posts. Too late, I realised I should never have taken Betya anywhere near the pig farm, for a wire fence is no deterrent to a Vizsla. Far from being a boar-hunting dog, as is normal for the breed, however, he quickly formed the most unlikely friendship with the old boar, and the chief enjoyment for them both was to wallow in the smelly mud by the pond in the corner of the field. More than once, on particularly important official occasions, having seen as I thought to all the necessary last-minute details and arrangements, and dressed in my best uniform, Betya would appear, delighted with himself, covered from nose to tail in pig muck, and smelling unbelievably awful. There was nothing for it but to remove him instantly to a far corner of the garden and hose him down to make him respectable again.

One night I was suddenly told a Puss Moth had landed at the airfield, and with obvious pleasure my informant added, 'And the pilot is a very glamorous blonde lady, Sir!' This required instant investigation.

She was indeed: she was the famous aviatrix, Sheila Scott. This, however, was in her early flying days, and she had not yet achieved her world renown. She had lost her way and, finding Tangmere, had made an emergency landing. Right away, I was impressed by her dedication to flying, and her professional approach. It seemed she lacked knowledge of instrument flying, however, and I subsequently flew quite a lot with her, giving her instruction in this, and it was satisfying to see how quickly she became proficient in these skills. Our friendship lasted many years, and I do not think I have ever known anyone more dedicated to flying. Any money she earned was immediately channelled into it, and as she became famous she attracted sponsorship for her undertakings. She richly deserved all her success, for which she had worked very hard. She definitely had 'star' quality.

Because of the proximity of Tangmere to Goodwood, certain members of the Royal Family would use the airfield on private occasions. On one such, when the Queen and Duke of Edinburgh were due to arrive to visit the Duke of Norfolk, I ascertained from the Captain of the Queen's Flight, who was an old friend of mine, that there would be no objection if I arranged for the local schoolchildren to line the route at a prearranged place, so that they could see Her

Majesty and the Duke as they drove by. They graciously agreed to this, and it was all a great success. Obviously a royal visit entails a lot of work and planning, but we were always delighted to see the Queen, not only because of our feeling of affection for the monarchy, but also because we could get jobs done at the station which we had been requesting for years. Treasury officials had only to be told that she might visit a certain building for us to be given *carte blanche* to carry out any repairs or painting deemed necessary!

On her first visit, prior to Her Majesty's arrival, whilst making all the arrangements, I telephoned the Duke of Norfolk to ascertain what would be required in the way of escort for the royal car on its drive to his castle. I had RAF outriders ready with their motorbikes, and I had warned the police they might be needed. Imagine my surprise when the Duke assured me there was no need for any of this, adding, 'Just bung them along.' Writing these words today, it seems strange to be bunging along the monarch. How times have changed, and how different security has to be today.

To my great surprise, one day I got a letter informing me that I had been awarded the CBE (Commander of the Order of the British Empire), Military Division, for my work in Hungary and for Tangmere. As the British Empire is no more, I understand the honour is to be discontinued, as part of the general updating of a lot of things pertaining to the monarchy.

In due course I attended the investiture, which was held inside Buckingham Palace, unlike the one held in the courtyard during the war. This meant that my mother was at last to see inside the palace, something neither of us ever thought we would do. We were especially delighted that HM the Queen Mother was holding the investiture. One is given detailed instructions how to receive the honour, and the members of the Household seem to know all the questions before they are asked. For instance I had to bow my head at a certain angle to enable the Queen Mother to hang the order over it. For this occasion the order is threaded on a long ribbon, so this is easily accomplished. This ribbon is never used again, and the order is subsequently worn on a very short ribbon round the neck.

In the state apartment, usually the Ballroom, where the investiture is to take place, an orchestra is playing softly as guests take their seats. All too soon the recipients are lined up, and I found myself in front of the Queen Mother. I was completely taken aback when she asked, with that lovely smile which she always makes so personal, 'And how is my dear Tangmere?' We exchanged a few words about the station, and then she hung the order round my neck, saying it gave her great pleasure to present it to me, and once again she made it seem a personal gift. One moved across and in front of the monarch, and one is then guided away by a member of the Household, who hands over the case for the order. One then takes a seat in the audience. At the end of the whole ceremony the orchestra plays the National Anthem, and it is all over.

I became friendly with the then mayor of Chichester, Bill Pope. He had been an airman in the MT (Motor Transport) section during the war, and was stationed at Tangmere. One day we were reminiscing about the special relationship that had always existed between the city and RAF Tangmere, and I suggested that it would be a wonderful idea to cement the friendship by awarding the Freedom of the City of Chichester to Tangmere. Bill was at once enthusiastic, and said he would like to push this through while he was still mayor. He discussed the matter with his councillors, and he also broached the subject with the bishop of Chichester, as the blessing of the cathedral for the whole idea was of paramount importance. We agreed a timescale, and started planning. We were fortunate in that Roger Plumpton-Wilson, the Lord Bishop, was an exceptional man, whose great goodness and humanity made him popular and respected by everyone. We enjoyed many a good laugh together, particularly over the bishop and the Pope, not to mention the two dukes, and felt we were moving in very elevated society. The choir of Chichester Cathedral is renowned, and the dean and chapter took over the arrangements for the important role the cathedral was going to play.

The Central Band of the RAF took care of the military music side, working in conjunction with the dean and chapter, when they had given permission for the band to play in the cathedral. Great attention was paid to the choice of hymns and music for the occasion, and to planning the march through the city. The city chose the route, and the venue for the handing over of the Freedom Scroll and the signing of the Freedom Book.

Then there was the marching! By the late 1960s most of the RAF was highly technical. The majority of our airmen were technicians, and had had the minimum of drill and rifle training. However, they were a most intelligent bunch of men, and keen to do the ceremony justice. A lot of practice ensued, with bayonets fixed, a parade-ground circuit being a far cry from electronic circuits, but the British sense of humour rose to the challenge, and on the day they put on an impressive show. We were able to obtain the support of the Queen's Escort Squadron (today called her Colour Squadron), to swell our ranks and handle the intricate moments associated with the actual presentation of the scroll. A fly-past was arranged, led by a Hurricane and a Spitfire, followed by the station's own aircraft. The guest list was long and glorious, with all available past Tangmere station commanders invited, and with as many Battle of Britain pilots attending as could get there.

Fortunately, the day was fine. The parade assembled at Prior's Field, where the presentation of the beautiful illuminated Freedom Scroll took place. On behalf of the station, I presented the city with a silver statue of a young pilot of the 1940 era in full flying kit, to add to their historical collection of silver in the Town Hall. It was subscribed to by the station, and our parent command, who were most supportive throughout. It is typical on such occasions that something gets overlooked. At the crucial moment when the mayor and I were to inspect the troops I realised that I had forgotten my white gloves. Bill immediately gave me one of his, saying, 'We will have to have one each, Dennis, that will do if we carry it.' So we managed to get through the rest of the day, each of us carrying one white glove.

After the presentation of the scroll I had to sign the Freedom Book on behalf of Tangmere, and I was most interested to see how old it was. Some of its entries went back hundreds of years, and I was amazed to see how few freemen there were. The signing concluded the official ceremony, and bayonets were then fixed in preparation for the march through the town. This symbolic gesture represents a very ancient custom, signifying that the city has given the right to those granted the freedom to parade through the city with naked steel. This act also demonstrates that the bearer of the arms has a special affiliation with the city, is trusted to bear them loyally, and has a responsibility for its defence.

The mayoral party then proceeded to the Town Hall, where we took the salute as the troops marched past on their way to the cathedral. Though not large, Chichester is one of our most beautiful cathedrals, and we must have had a unique gathering of clergy there, resplendent in their robes. I was happy to see Father Hubarzevsky in his 'Golden Bowler' shining in all its glory! It all seemed a fitting climax to the occasion, and truly celebrated the unity of the people gathered there. The sound of the trumpets and the bugles of the military side of the music merged with the organ and the ethereal soaring voices of the choir to produce a quality beyond the human spirit. At the time I was deeply conscious of all the wonderful men and women who had died at or from Tangmere in the selfless service of their country. The day ended with a banquet at the officers' mess, with all the distinguished guests attending.

When I first had the idea of the Freedom of the City, I had a premonition that the shadows were gathering around Tangmere, and that its life would be limited. The threat appeared to have been removed from southern England to the north of Scotland, where probing Soviet aircraft penetrated our airspace and had to be watched and escorted by our interceptors operating from Scottish bases. I felt I wanted a lasting memorial to those who had served and given their lives at Tangmere. Now they had it.

There is a Saxon church at Tangmere, dating from AD 836, which was much in need of a new organ, and I decided it would be nice if I could run an appeal to raise funds to buy one. The Duchess of Richmond had always taken a great interest in all the activities of Tangmere, and she graciously agreed to be the patron of the organ appeal which, to my delight, proved a great success. Not only did we raise the money for the organ, but we were able to furnish the church with new hymn books, inscribed as a gift from the station.

In the church's little graveyard there are a number of graves of airmen, mostly dating from World War II, and also some German graves, from the same conflict. I had a long talk with the local vicar, who had been a Service padre during the war, and we felt that all these young men, even though our enemies at the time, had loved ones back in their homeland. I had the idea that it would be a fine gesture of reconciliation, and perhaps would build some bridges between our nations, if we could send a small handful of earth from these graves to each of their respective families. I made a tentative approach to the German air attaché to see if he agreed with this. He was very taken with the idea, and said he would deal with the need to contact the families in question. Of course he obtained the permission of the German ambassador, whom fortunately I had previously met, Felix von Horworth. He was delighted, and said he would in fact tell Chancellor Konrad Adenauer about it, as he felt it should be handled at this level.

The Duchess of Richmond was also very sympathetic to the project, and, thanks to her generosity, we were able to have small urns made from beautiful wood from the Goodwood Estate, to hold the earth from each German grave. The German authorities arranged the delivery of each of these urns, and Chancellor Adenauer was so touched by it that he gave £100 of his own money towards the organ appeal.

Throughout my time at Tangmere I had a superb batman, who by chance shared my surname, and he and his wife became my firm friends. When my next posting proved to be southern Europe I had to make the sad decision that I could not take my beloved Betya out of England again. My friends had always been very fond of him, and he of them, and they said they would love to have him. It was a particularly hard decision, but I knew Betya could not have a better home.

My premonition about Tangmere proved to be right, and the station closed not many years later. It was an especially sad day for me, and for many local inhabitants who had loved the station and all it stood for. I attended the closing ceremony, and watched the Freedom Scroll handed back to the city for safe-keeping. Tangmere was our last fighter station in southern England. Today we have no fighters south of Coningsby, 150 miles (240 km) north of London.

In 1961 Naples was the headquarters for NATO's Allied Forces Southern Europe. This comprised Italy, Greece and Turkey, as well as the US Navy's Sixth Fleet, which policed the whole Mediterranean. Relations between Greeks and Turks were always strained, and some careful diplomacy was required. I was transferred there as Chief of Air Plans and it was an interesting and challenging post, working with such diverse nationalities, and each country had its own holidays to celebrate. They invariably celebrated throwing off the tyranny of the British yoke, yet they still wanted to have us serving alongside them.

Naples is famously beautiful, and from the sixth-floor balcony of my flat I enjoyed a wonderful view of Vesuvius. Although quiescent, this volcano is not entirely dormant, and the farmers on its slopes have to leave their homes from time to time, but return as rapidly as possible, because the soil is so fertile. I could also see the islands of Ischia and Capri. However, this magnificent panoramic view had its disadvantages, in that the area was still subject to earth tremors. I remember one occasion when the whole building shook about 4 ft (1.2 m) from side to side, and things fell off shelves. I looked out of the window and watched people leaving the buildings and rushing towards the sea. They look upon the sea as their true refuge, because at least it won't fall on top of them.

This may have carried down through the centuries. In this posting I did a lot of swimming. It was fascinating to swim off the town of Gaeta at a depth of only 30 or 40 ft (10-12 m) and be able to swim up the ancient street along which Roman chariots had driven. It was possible to see a one-way traffic system which had been in existence some 2,000 years earlier, and what had been the local wine shop where there were still remains of many amphorae (large pottery wine containers). There was a baker's shop where parts of the old ovens were still in evidence. The whole breathtaking exercise was brought back to contemporary times by the sight of ropes, heavily encrusted with mussels, hanging down from 60-gallon (273-litre) drums floating on the surface, kept in place by the weight on the other end of the rope. This was one of the biggest mussel farms in the area. They allowed only very few people to swim there. From time to time they would haul up a rope, and harvest the mussels attached to it.

Another picturesque memory is the citrus groves, so attractive with their rich glossy green leaves contrasting with the bright colours of oranges and lemons. Some trees had an orange grafted on to a lemon, or vice versa, thus producing both fruits from a single rootstock.

As Naples was the principal base for the US Sixth Fleet, I was able to visit the USS *Saratoga*. It is impossible to describe the colossal size of these aircraft carriers, but some 5,200 men were accommodated in relative luxury on board. I understood that there were over 30 mess decks in use at any one meal. I was even told there were 20 different cinema shows run every evening. The efficiency of the organisation required in such an undertaking has to be seen to be believed. As part of my job I had to fly out to various ships, and this entailed carrier landings and take-offs in a Grumman C-1A communications aircraft. So vast was the *Saratoga*'s landing deck that this seemed no different from an airfield.

The security of all NATO work had to be of a high order. The 'need to know' rule was strictly applied. We had a separate 'Hot War' headquarters, carved out of a mountain north of Naples. This was top secret, and was used only by those who would occupy it in a war. In 1961 the Cold War blew hot and cold, with many alarms, and NATO forces were kept at constant readiness.

Imagine my dismay when one of my RAF officers came and told me his new refrigerator had been delivered to him at the entrance to this highly secret location, instead of to his residence in Naples. Its arrival had caused no little excitement, as it was delivered in an ordinary truck, driven by a highly voluble Italian, whose only anxiety had been whether his truck could make the steep gradient. It was like being in a Monsieur Hulot film. The officer for whom the refrigerator was destined was Derek Stevenson, a descendant of Robert Louis Stevenson. He was a brilliant linguist, and asked the Neapolitan how he had found out about this secret location. The question quenched the volubility for a moment, as the driver stared in blank amazement. He then said, 'EVERYBODY in Naples knows about the place, we built it!' This caused great consternation, but in the end nothing could be done, and most of us could not help but see the funny side of it.

The Americans were sometimes in a difficult position, particularly as they supplied most of the surface-to-air missiles. The US Navy admiral in charge of us all was deeply conscious of this, and asked me to undertake a delicate mission in Turkey. I knew and liked the Turkish people, which is why I was selected. I was accompanied by a US Navy captain, who could co-ordinate and countersign all signals.

Two coincidences helped to bring the visit to a satisfactory conclusion. The first was that I met a friend in the Turkish Air Force who had flown Spitfires, and his help was invaluable. The second concerned the Turkish Army colonel, who was a tough negotiator. We both saw one of the delegates at the conference apparently sound asleep, but were fascinated to see that he was still doodling on his notepad! The colonel and I caught each other's eye, and could scarcely refrain from laughing out loud. It lightened the whole tone of the conference.

This mission accomplished, it was necessary to convince the Greeks that no negotiations were going on without their knowledge. Accordingly I made a call on a Greek Army colonel friend, whose office was down the corridor from mine, and ascertained that there was no misconception about these events. This was terribly important, to avoid accusations from either side of conspiracy with the other.

Thanks to the first-class facilities provided by the Americans, I continued my sporting interests, and even took up a new one. In 1961 there appeared to be no squash courts in Italy, so the Americans introduced me to badminton. The bygone game of battledore and shuttlecock in Tudor England had developed into a furiously fast and exciting game. I was also delighted to be able to keep up my sabre practice, after having been first taught in Budapest by the Hungarian world champion. He was a great psychologist when it came to assessing his opponent in a big match. He explained to me that in the warm-up, if your opponent is German you go forward forcefully right from the start. If Italian, you 'accidentally' whip him across the wrist with the tip of your sabre, and apologise profusely for hurting him. If he is a Frenchman, you pick out the prettiest girl in the audience, and give her a knowing smile, and your opponent's attention is never wholly on the fight from that moment. Apart from all this, however, he was a brilliant tutor, for I still managed to beat opponents over 20 years younger than myself.

The Aeronautica Militare (Italian air force) was superbly hospitable at all times. One of their more senior members was Duilio Fanali, who had been one of their fighter aces in the war, and was well-liked and respected. It was the first time I had made contact with any combatants from the other side, and it was fortunate that it should be with someone of Duilio's calibre. We became close friends, and remained so until his death. He loved his country, and especially Rome, showing me that magical city with love and pride, and pointing out the giant stone lion he had ridden as a boy. I saw Rome by day and its matchless lighting at night through his eyes, and it was a rare privilege.

At an official dinner one night my attention was caught by a strong

American voice talking about dogs. I soon found my way to his side, and discovered he was MacKinlay Kantor, the renowned American author. He had won the Pulitzer Prize for his historical novel *Andersonville*, a compelling account of the American Civil War, in which he describes what was in fact the first wartime concentration camp. He also wrote the script for the famous film *The Best Years of Our Lives*. One of his later works was the authorised biography of the famed USAF General Curtis LeMay. His mother had been the first woman magazine editor in America, and his wife Irene was a talented artist in several media. In particular, she did the drawings for his book *Lobo*, which was a story dear to both their hearts about a wolf-like mongrel dog they took back to America with them, after having befriended it in Spain. She illustrated the book with as much love as Mack wrote it, and I enjoyed their friendship until their deaths many years later.

On one of his visits to London I met him at a famous Mayfair hotel. The lift attendant was Irish, and he and Mack enjoyed singing Irish songs together. We had to go up an extra couple of floors and return to the right one in order to complete the verses. He took me out to dinner at a top London restaurant, but the steaks were more than we could manage. Mack called the waiter over and said that he knew the American custom of doggy bags was not usual here, but I had a famous dog who was a Hungarian Freedom Fighter! He had not been able to join us that evening but he would certainly appreciate receiving something of the meal at home. The waiter looked a little dazed, but said he understood perfectly. Sure enough, at the end of the meal the head waiter appeared carrying a silver salver on high with a magnificent foil-wrapped parcel for the famous Hungarian dog. What a feast for dear old Betya. Peter Ustinov was sitting at the next table, and listening intently, and I felt sure that this cameo event would go into his notebook.

Suddenly the whole headquarters was agog with the news that President Kennedy was to visit, accompanied by Vice-President Johnson and their entourage, in several helicopters. JFK was a magnificent figure, over six feet in height, of commanding presence with his film-star charisma and youthful looks. My encounter with him was all too brief, but he made a great impression on me. I noticed how professional Vice-President Johnson was in his own role, but it was President Kennedy we all wanted to see.

Little did we know that he would so soon be assassinated. It is said that everyone remembers where they were when the news of his assassination reached them. For my part, I remember that on that November day in 1963 I was holding an official RAF cocktail party. I had just greeted the USN Admiral, and had to tell him there was an official telephone call waiting for him. His expression as he came back into the room was grave, but nothing could have prepared us for the sad tidings. It fell to me to tell the guests of the tragic event. There was a stunned silence, followed by everyone leaving quickly in a state of shock.

CHAPTER NINETEEN

A SORT OF RETIREMENT

When my next posting came through I did not realise it was to be the last in my air force career. I was to be in charge of postings, initially junior and latterly senior officers, back at the Air Secretary's Office. It proved to be a most interesting job, and it has subsequently been rewarding to see the way some of those I was able to recommend unreservedly for accelerated promotion have gone ahead in the fast lane.

Returning to England meant that I could be reunited with my faithful Betya for the rest of his life. My friends who had cared for him so lovingly while I was in Naples were totally unselfish and said he was always my dog, and must return to me. It was an unbelievable joy to go and collect him, and he seemed very pleased to see me. Suddenly, as we drove home, the full realisation of who it was dawned on him, and he nearly caused an accident as he tried to leap on to my lap, and generally expressed his happiness that it really was his long-lost master. My final move with him was when I retired as a civilian to Brighton. When he saw the suitcases coming out again, he looked at them with horror, and then lay stretched out as far as he could across some clothes that I was packing, looking up at me reproachfully.

It took a long time to reassure him, but of course he never left my side again. He never forgot my namesakes, who had looked after him so well, and there was always great excitement whenever I visited them and the car got near the familiar approach to their house.

The 1960s were not easy days for the services, despite the constant threat from the Cold War. Extensive cuts were being made in both manpower and equipment. I realised that I was helping to plan the format of a smaller RAF for future years.

In 1964 a Labour government came in and decided to buy American aircraft and cancel our own TSR.2. 'Bee' Beamont, a great friend since 1940, was the chief test pilot of this magnificent aircraft, and was nearly in tears about it. He felt that it was far in advance of anything that any other country had, including the USA, which indeed it was.

However, the manufacturing jigs and tooling were all smashed up, and the completed aircraft were used for target practice.

I could see that there were going to be a lot of redundancies in and around my rank. I realised that it was unlikely I would have much if any further promotion, and I investigated the possibility of a 'golden handshake' to 'jump before I was pushed'. I was in the ideal job to do this at the time. With mixed feelings I came to the conclusion that it was time to call it a day and bid the RAF farewell. I found out exactly what I would be entitled to claim for my redundancy. Even so, it was initially refused, and I have to thank Air Marshal Sir David Lee and James Callaghan (now Lord Callaghan) for my full entitlement. Sir David was Air Member for Personnel at the time, and an old friend. I told him what had happened, and he said I was entitled to the amount for which I had originally applied. He said he would take it personally to Callaghan, who was then Chancellor of the Exchequer. He too agreed at once, and signed the authorisation. I shall always be grateful to both of them.

On my last day, Friday 26 May 1967, we just had a drink in the office, and I walked out. That was the end of nearly 30 years of not merely a job, but a whole way of life. I was 48. It is a strange feeling finding oneself out in the wilderness at such a time. I had been putting out feelers for a worthwhile job 'outside', and had one or two possibilities to explore.

Then I was suddenly hit from an unexpected quarter. Three weeks after my retirement I went to bed feeling rotten, with a heavy cold. About two o'clock in the morning I awoke feeling that my head was going to burst. I had had odd buzzing noises going on from time to time during the previous week, which I put down to my cold. Now, however, I could not believe the constant awful noise like hissing steam going on inside my head. I then found that I could hear nothing at all on the left side. I stood next to my old Welsh 'Grandpa' clock, hoping against hope that I could hear his comforting 'tick', but my left ear produced nothing but the deafening hiss.

Little did I realise that I would never hear anything but that hissing on that side of my head again. I had tinnitus, and was totally deaf in my left ear. The nerves of the middle ear had been irreparably damaged. For some days I was sick if I even tried to sit up in bed, for the room just went round in circles, because the middle-ear balance system no longer functioned. It was weeks before I could stand properly and walk safely down the road. I then discovered an unexpected hazard: to this day I have absolutely no sense of direction for sound. My right ear still has acute hearing, and every sound seems to come from that side. Initially I had several narrow escapes with traffic, as I stepped in front of something which had approached on my deaf side.

When I was able to get around again I went to a specialist to see if anything could be done. He confirmed the 'catastrophe', and said that, as I had not died, they could not carry out a post-mortem on me, and therefore could not establish what had caused it, nor the extent of the damage. He was right when he said it was unlikely to get any better. Patting me on the shoulder, he said 'Just learn to live with it, old boy!'

He was right about that, too, but any sufferer from tinnitus will know just what it means. Jack Ashley MP is a magnificent example of someone who has risen above this invisible disaster. Background music, or a lot of people talking at a party, will beat me completely. I have probably nodded or smiled, or looked deeply concerned, at totally inappropriate moments. When my general health improved I tried one of the excellent jobs I had been offered, but found I was missing too much in discussions, and felt that in all fairness I could not continue.

I naturally explored every possible hope for a cure or relief. When visiting Hong Kong some 20 years later, I was introduced to a wonderful old Chinese doctor, who was a doctor of western medicine, and also a great authority on acupuncture. He was a fund of wisdom, and someone I will always be glad I met, though he could not help my tinnitus. He told me he had had success with it, but mine had been left just too long, and there was no vestige of life left in the nerve-ends.

In China during the war he joined the guerrillas fighting the Japanese invaders, and was thankful for his knowledge of acupuncture, for there were almost no medical supplies for the western medicine he had learnt. He was able to compare the results of both, and said it was amazing what wounds they could treat without anaesthetic. Of course recovery was quicker, with far less post-operative stress. They always tried to kill the Japanese officers, who were easily identified because they always wore their swords. He chuckled as he reminisced, 'Then they threw away their swords, and it was not so easy to find them.'

He had qualified as a doctor in Paris, just before the war. After a dinner at Maxim's to celebrate passing their final exams his fellow students ran off and left him to pay the enormous bill! Of course he could not, and so had to wash up for the restaurant for two weeks! It is an ill wind, for there he met a very pretty girl. They fell in love and married, and returned to China. When she was expecting their child, she returned to Paris to be near her mother. He was to follow her, but the war intervened. He later discovered she had worked for the Resistance, and had been caught and killed by the Gestapo. His baby too had died. From a bottom drawer of his desk he brought out some faded little snaps. They showed two young people very much in love, with eyes for no one else. It was clear how much these photographs meant to the old man. We looked at them together in poignant silence.

I have dwelt at length on all this because I want to emphasise that with great effort one CAN learn to live with tinnitus. I am rewarded when someone says that they never knew I had a hearing problem. It is my most formidable enemy to date, but I will continue to wear out the left side of my shirt collars as I turn my head to try and catch with my good ear what someone is saying. So, if you are standing beside me and say something which I ignore, please do not think I am being rude. Just go round to my other side!

Retirement is more often than not a frightening prospect, as it suddenly becomes a reality. I have already mentioned how keenly I miss flying, yet found this difficult to explain. It is said that if you visit a general's office you see maps of terrain, an admiral's has charts of seas and oceans, but with the RAF you find both. Our horizons stretch into space.

Despite inevitable sadness at closing the door on my flying days, I had been looking forward with interest to a new role in civilian life. I reckoned I would probably have close on 20 years in my new job. When my tinnitus put paid to my hopes of joining a big firm, I had to think again. I looked for a small enterprise which I could handle more on my own. I got involved with two old folks' homes, which did not work out. I helped an old friend from my early RAF days with a clever mechanical invention of his, but we could not get financial backing for it.

I bought a small precision-engineering firm, which I found more to my liking, and which specialised in precision work for one-off designs. Too late I discovered that my partner was tearing up the bills, and supplying optimistic figures to the bank by the simple ruse of moving the decimal point. The arrival of a writ for the non-payment of an account was my first intimation of this. After following up every account and explaining the sad situation to every creditor, I can only say I received the utmost kindness and sympathy from all of them, including cancellation of the writ. I was able to clear every outstanding debt, but there was no alternative but to close the business. I was pleased that I was able to give some help to my splendid employees in finding other jobs.

Another non-starter, which was close to my heart, was to set up a housing association for retired RAF personnel at Tangmere. As a result of the closure of the station, all these first-class buildings were empty. I got together a small team, and we were all very enthusiastic about the idea. Because of a change in political policy, and for other reasons, we had, with great regret, to abandon the project.

Towards the end of my last job at the MoD, I met a charismatic Polish film producer, S. Benjamin Fisz, as he liked to be known. He had been a fighter pilot with the RAF, and was a dedicated Anglophile. He was introduced to me by my great friend Tom Gleave, who had been a Hurricane pilot and been badly burned. He was one of Sir Archibald McIndoe's first plastic-surgery 'guinea-pigs'. Tom later worked as an RAF historian, and was asked by Ben to be technical adviser for a film he wanted to make to be called *The Battle of Britain*. Tom asked me to help.

Ben told me how the idea had come to him in the first place. He was in Hyde Park, and saw a Spitfire fly over rehearsing for the fly-past over London on the Battle of Britain anniversary. Some kids saw it too, and, as it looked different from the usual planes, they asked him what it was. Ben suddenly realised that, although it was, relatively speaking, only a few years since the war, there were countless children who had never heard of the Battle of Britain. He resolved then and there to make the film. He told me it was to be his tribute to his dead comrades.

I was able to help him with a few contacts and open a few doors, and watched the making of the film with interest. At the time, I was still in the RAF, so could only offer background support to his endeavours. The film premiered in 1969, and it is well worth a trip to the cinema if it comes round. Ben can be justly proud of his efforts, and he was able to count the film a very successful venture. Sadly, he died of a heart attack a few years ago.

He was a student here in the 1930s, returning to Poland for his vacations. When he was in Warsaw in the summer of 1939 his father could see that there was a war coming, and insisted that Ben leave at once. His mother was taking the waters at Baden Baden, as she did regularly every year, and Ben wanted to go and see her before he left. His father, however, insisted that he should leave immediately. Ben told me he passed his mother's train returning to Warsaw as his own train was on its way out of the station. He never saw either of his parents again.

When war was declared, Ben joined the RAF and became a fighter pilot. When he pinned up his wings, he visited his bank manager feeling like a man of some substance. He decided to open a bank account and get a cheque book. He asked for credit to start his account, and the manager asked him what collateral he had. In his delightful heavy accent, and with pride and complete confidence, he replied, 'I have my wings and my youth.' Unfortunately, the manager did not think this was substantial enough. Ben told me this story many years later, and he said, 'Isn't it funny, Dennis? Now, I ring up the bank manager and say I want to make a film, and will need to borrow several million, and he says, 'Fine, let's meet and have lunch to discuss it'.'

The Battle of Britain film was carefully cast. Sir Laurence Olivier played Lord Dowding, and Trevor Howard played Sir Keith Park. The latter wrote to Trevor some revealing letters, telling him exactly how he hoped he would portray the character, and his reaction to certain events at the time. Trevor took these letters to heart. By this time Lord Dowding was very frail and in a wheelchair, but he took a keen interest in the film, and would visit the set whenever he could. On those occasions Sir Laurence Olivier sat beside him studying his every mannerism and inflection of voice. All those who knew Lord Dowding are unanimous in their admiration of his portrayal, and were amazed how he even managed to look like him.

The premiere was a grand occasion, in aid of the RAF Benevolent Fund. All those who had been in the battle and could get to London did. One paper described us as arriving at the cinema 'wrapped in smiling modesty, and out-of-date dinner jackets', which I felt captured the tone exactly. We were all asked to be in our seats at a certain time, and then Lord Dowding arrived in his wheelchair. Looking round the packed cinema he asked in his firm clear voice, 'Are they all here?' The warmth of the rousing cheer that greeted this query must have touched his heart, and he said, 'Then let it begin!'

I think we all relived the special moments of our wartime days that evening. Afterwards, as we waited to go to the Guildhall, a group of Poles came running across the street and hugged Johnny Kent, to whom I was talking at the time. 'Oh Johnny, it was just like that, wasn't it?' Their faces beamed with enthusiasm as they embraced the beloved Englishman who had been posted in 1941 to command the Polish Wing. They were a great crowd. In September 1939 they had witnessed their country's elite cavalry regiments charging with swords and lances against the tanks of the invading *Panzer* divisions – probably making the last cavalry charges in history. As a result, they had only one thought: to fight the enemy, both Russian and German. Most of them had little or no English, and Johnny Kent got down to learning Polish, no easy language.

His daunting task was to weld them into a fighting force fully integrated with Fighter Command. The addition of such experienced and aggressive pilots was a godsend. Johnny was adamant with his eager charges that they must at all times keep R/T silence, except in cases of dire emergency. They were also told that it was important not to leave their formation. As portrayed in the film, on meeting German aircraft, to Johnny's horror he saw Polish pilots flying off in all directions in hot pursuit of the enemy, whilst the radio waves were alive with Polish exclamations. Their leader awaited a rocket from headquarters. Instead, he had personal congratulations from Dowding, who told him that his Polish Wing was now fully operational, and had just the right spirit.

Johnny loved his Polish Wing, and always said this command meant more to him than anything else in his career. He had a long and cruel last illness (Parkinson's Disease) which he bore with his usual courage and fortitude. He was tended to the end with devoted care by Monica Head, a wonderful nurse whom all the Poles love and respect to this day. At his funeral the little church was packed with his surviving Polish friends, and Monica had a place of honour amongst them. I shall never forget seeing 'Gandhi' Drobinski, one of their leading aces, gently touch the coffin and say, 'Rest in peace, dear friend.'

After the war, 'Gandhi' applied for British citizenship, having grown to love this country, and having married an English girl. Despite his many decorations, gained in the service of Britain, he was told that his wartime years here did not count for his domiciliary qualification! He was curtly told he would have to wait another five years. After living and working in America, he finally did become a British citizen in 1960.

After the premiere, the Lord Mayor put on a magnificent celebration for us but, for all the pomp and glitter of the Guildhall, the highlight of the occasion was the attendance of Lord Dowding. I will always remember seeing him in a corner in his wheelchair, with his Battle of Britain 'boys' queuing up three or four at a time just to sit at his feet and exchange a few words with him. It seemed he had lived for that evening, for he died only a few weeks later.

I got to know Ben well, and in 1974 he told me he wanted to make a film about the Royal Flying Corps in the First World War. He thought it would be a good idea to adapt the theme from *Journey's End*, the classic book and play about life in the trenches. It was not to be another blockbuster, but a telling and accurate account of those times. He said he wanted it to be his tribute to the English public school. Perhaps only a foreigner would think of that.

He asked me if I would be technical adviser, and I said I would be delighted. The last time I had had a job offered me that was anything to do with aircraft was when the Battle of Britain Museum was being started, and I was asked if I would like to be in charge of it. Regretfully I had to refuse, as I was still having problems with my health. Now I looked forward with enthusiasm to my first film, and a return to work associated with flying.

Ben had selected four young actors: Malcolm McDowell, who was a big star; Simon Ward, who had made his name as *Young Winston* in the big Churchill film; David Wood, a talented actor who also wrote children's plays; and a newcomer, Peter Firth, who played the eager young officer just arrived at the front. Christopher Plummer, a lead in *The Battle of Britain* film, also played a major part. When I attended the first reading of the script for *Aces High*, I was impressed by the way the youngsters had researched their roles.

Jack Gold was a first-class director who quietly got exactly what he wanted from everybody. A lot of the technicians had worked with him previously, and they made a talented and happy team. Everyone wanted it 'right', and it was my job to see that it was. I had to teach actors how to enter a room, how to salute, and how to stand to attention in the presence of senior officers. Anachronisms had to be eliminated: modern cigarette lighters were out, but cigarette cases were in. Then there was the question of what the young officer arriving at the front would carry his kit in? I rang up my old ex-RFC friend Air Marshal Sir Reginald Lydford, and without hesitation he said, 'Oh, a leather suitcase.'

We had the hottest days just when we wanted Flanders mud, so the hoses came into action, and the guns were duly bogged down. When a tent was moved, the dried-up grass was sprayed with green paint. The man in charge of special effects was Derek Meddings, who had just returned back from 'blowing up Malta Harbour' for a James Bond film. I watched him meticulously preparing 'hits' on a mock-up fuselage, using little patches of canvas with a tiny explosive charge under each one. These were carefully stuck on the fuselage, wired up and detonated in rapid sequence. Clouds produced by the smoke machine drifted by the mock-up cockpit as it was rocked manually on its gimbals to simulate turbulence or banking in flight.

We had two top aerobatics pilots for the combat sequences, and I suggested that if they could weave round and between trees, and show their height from the ground from time to time, it would give a great sense of drama and speed. They produced some great flying for us, using Stampe biplane trainers with wingtips squared off to resemble SE5a fighters.

Christopher Plummer and I soon became good friends. He was said to be difficult, but I felt it was more that he was a perfectionist. He had a problem with his puttees, which are like narrow bandages, wrapped from ankle to knee. I wore them in my Burma days, where they were washed frequently by the 'dhobi' and were beaten thin with stones. Christopher's were new and thick, however, and made his legs look like tree trunks. I rang up Reggie Lydford again, and asked if it would be correct for Christopher to wear riding boots, as he had joined from a cavalry regiment. Reggie said it would, and all was well.

I noticed how Christopher would improvise on the piano as he accompanied two days of filming a sing-song in the mess scene. He would also play a little between shots, with obvious enjoyment. He told me he had originally trained as a concert pianist, which told me a lot about his success in *The Sound of Music*.

Malcolm had played a somewhat sinister part in *The Clockwork Orange*, and I wondered how he would bridge our generation gap, but we liked each other immediately. One day he was having difficulty with a scene in which he had to send his pilots out on a mission in which it was almost certain that some of them would be killed. Knowing I had probably been faced with the same dilemma in the war, he asked me how one could send one's friends to almost certain death? I agreed I had had to do it, but explained that I would always lead the mission myself if I could. He understood this, and went ahead and played the scene beautifully.

Something else I learned about filming was that they have terrific food! Ours came in a double-decker bus. Actors and technicians work hard and long hours, and food is important. Food reminds me of Flash Harry, the greyhound I had bought as a puppy from a friend who had just bred her first litter. He stayed with her and raced with two of his brothers, and I had the *Greyhound News* and his racing papers with his name on them sent to me at MoD. The defence of the realm halted, as my staff studied form – especially Flash's!

He was an inconsistent racer, winning only if he saw a gap where he could nip through, otherwise he did not bother. Consequently his odds were good. He went lame a week after unexpectedly beating a much-fancied bitch. I knew nothing about greyhounds, but soon discovered that they have prodigious appetites. I began to worry when I saw his reproachful looks after he had emptied his plate in record time. I lived in Brighton then, so I took him to the railway station and asked a porter if I could weigh him on their scales, as he had just finished racing, and I wanted to be sure I was feeding him enough.

Flash was a silver brindle, 83 lb (38 kg) of grace and elegance, and the porter said, 'That's a nice dog you have there. What's his name? Ah, I thought I recognised him. Won a few bob on him! Here, George, here's Flash Harry!' So it went on. Staff converged from all over the station, and Flash had a royal escort to the scales, where his supporters busily made sure a toe was under the scales so they could advise me they were sure he should have extra rations! Flash took it all regally, and surveyed his public with gracious indulgence. I subsequently found out that everyone from the tramps to the crossing sweeper and deckchair attendant had all 'made a few bob' on Flash. After Betya died I got a rescued Vizsla, Istvan; he and Flash made a marvellous couple and lived into old age.

To return to film-making: the dogs, of course, came with me, and were very happy in the back of the hatchback. Needless to say Flash's name soon got around, and I can only say that he highly approved of the leftovers from the converted bus. We had visits from such people as Douglas Bader and, of course, my 'Guru' Reggie Lydford, to whom everyone enjoyed talking. We also had visits from other veterans of the RFC. One came with a page from a school atlas which had been torn out, stuck on a piece of card, and hung round his neck with a piece of string . . . his only navigation aid!

I decided it would be a nice idea, and good publicity, to give a special daytime viewing for the RFC veterans, each with a guest. I got together with our publicity man and his glamorous secretary, who did the old boys a power of good. We laid on a little party which was a great success. They were greeted with coffee, wine and madeira cake. After the show there was a fine selection of drinks and canapés. Flash could not have done better! At the end of it all we just brushed the crumbs off the empty trays and turned the empty glasses and bottles upside down!

Ben reserved his big guns for the cameo roles; he cast Sir John Gielgud, Trevor Howard, Richard Johnson and Ray Milland. Watching such masters, and talking with them, was a great privilege. For the public-school shots Ben wanted, I managed to get Eton to allow us to film there for two days. Who else to play the headmaster but Sir John Gielgud? I can still hear his lovely voice telling the boys, 'Play the game for the game's sake!' Ben watched this scene and just said, 'Pay him the money.' At that time it was the fashion for young boys to wear their hair long, and the young Etonians were faced with the stark choice of being paid £2.50 a day to be in the film, or of keeping their locks long.

The film had a royal premiere in 1976, with the Queen and Prince Philip, in aid of the Soldiers', Sailors' and Airmen's Families Association. It was followed by a superb dinner at Claridges. It was good to meet up with so many of those connected with the film, with whom I had so much enjoyed working.

I have a lot to thank Ben for, not least that at a dinner party at his house I met a boyhood hero of mine, Cecil Lewis. I was able to tell him how his book *Sagittarius Rising*, about his flying experiences in World War I, had inspired me, and been a great influence on my decision to join the RAF. Not long after, in his late eighties, he floored

Sue Lawley on the radio programme *Desert Island Discs* when he asked her if she had ever tried making love in a hammock. He assured her it was very difficult, but he would like a certain romantic record to remind him of it.

In 1982 the Battle of Britain Fighter Association was asked if they had someone who would be willing to go to the London borough of Newham for a ceremony the mayor wanted to perform. In September 1940 many women and children were due to be evacuated to a safer area, and had gathered at Canning Town to be picked up by two coaches. By mistake the drivers went to the quite different borough of Camden Town, and the women and children had to stay overnight in a school, ready to be picked up first thing in the morning. That night the school received a direct hit from a land mine, and there were no survivors. Councillor Julie Garfield thought in her mayoral year that it would be nice to plant a tree in their memory. No one knows how many were killed, for it was not possible to trace everyone who had taken advantage of the evacuation plan.

It was a touching and simple ceremony of remembrance and dedication, for I felt it meant something personally to all who attended. Back in 1940 it was a tragedy shared by the whole community. I met the man who had been deputy mayor at the time, Bill Chapman. I was deeply touched when he came up to me and said, 'We can't always put into words or write just how much we appreciate all you and your friends did for us in the war, but when we meet someone like you we can at least shake your hand, and say, 'Thank you'.'

I have maintained my interest in Newham ever since, and got to know Julie and Bill well. She was a wonderful lady, with a great sense of humour. One of her delights was to stop the mayoral car on her way home from one of her duties, and pick up her fish and chips! She gave a special party for personal guests in her mayoral year, and invited me.

There are few occasions in one's life when one meets someone who can change one's whole outlook, but I met such a man that night: Lord Elwyn Jones. For many years he had been Newham's MP, and when Harold Wilson came to power he said he wanted him to be Lord Chancellor. He and his wife were obviously delighted to be back in Newham, and it was amazing how he remembered the names of so many, and without hesitation enquired after various members of their families. I knew I was in the presence of a great man. There was much laughter and light-hearted conversation, however, as he regaled us with stories of his famous Welsh rugger-playing brother, Idris, whom I had admired over the years. He agreed Idris had been one of the greatest Welsh international players ever.

Lord Elwyn Jones, as a young man early in his legal career, had been sent with the prosecuting team to the Nuremberg trials of the Nazi leaders after the war. It was not difficult to see what a lasting impression the experience had had on him, and I was sorry that time did not permit us to talk longer about such an historic occasion.

I always hoped our paths would cross again, but it was not to be. His alert mind, his ability instantly to grasp the salient point of any matter, and above all his humanity and compassion, gave me a very different view of the political arena, though politics as such were never mentioned during the evening. I could well understand the warmth of his welcome by one and all at the party. I have no recollection of the dinner, only of being at the table with Julie and him and his wife. Of the few serious moments every one counted, and that one meeting is one I shall never forget.

Julie sadly died of cancer a few years ago, and I went to her funeral with her family. There was a large attendance, and I felt sincere affection for her from one and all. I still keep in touch with Bill Chapman.

CHAPTER TWENTY

GATHERING OF THE 'EAGLES'

In 1984 my friend Tom Gleave called me to say he had been asked to take part in a seminar at the USAF Air Command and Staff College at Maxwell Air Force Base, at Montgomery, Alabama. The seminar was to take the form of a discussion between an RAF pilot and a Luftwaffe pilot on the differences and similarities of how each fought the Battle of Britain. Tom said he was not able to accept the invitation, and could he put my name forward? I felt rather uneasy at coming face to face with a Luftwaffe pilot under these conditions, but I was anxious to help Tom out, and I felt that it would be an interesting experience. I had always got on well with Americans, and found them delightful hosts. I told Tom I would do my best.

Colonel David McFarland, USAF, gave me further details from Montgomery. He made the arrangements to fly me there and back, and accommodate me at the Air University. He met me at Atlanta, and drove me to Maxwell, which is a vast and magnificent establishment, catering mainly for US Air Force officers, but also for students from all over the world. It is actually on the site where the Wright brothers established the first flying school.

In due course I was introduced to Dr Heinz Lange, who was to be my opposite number. Like me, he had joined his air force before the war. He had fought in many theatres, and later studied law at Kiel University, and became a doctor of jurisprudence. He proved to be a most interesting man, and we hit it off at once.

David McFarland had gone to endless trouble in planning the occasion, and both Heinz and I felt the seminar went well. It was attended by several hundred students, and they seemed to find it very interesting. It was the first of its kind that had taken place there, and we were told they hoped for similar seminars every year. I had been apprehensive on account of my hearing problem, and David arranged that I should sit with my good ear towards the audience. We were also 'miked up', and to my great relief it all worked perfectly. I felt I had taken a big step forward, especially as it was a completely new venture.

I was astonished at the apparent lack of knowledge of the Battle of Britain: a handful present had heard of the Spitfire, but apparently nobody of the Hurricane. At dinner I sat next to Mary Goodie, the young lady from TWA who had so competently organised the veterans with tickets. She had sat in on the seminar, and found it interesting, but like others in the audience initially was confused by 'Hurricane', because she was familiar only with the other type. I have been friends with her ever since.

To my delight I was asked to return the following year. Heinz was sadly unable to attend, so I shared the platform with a famous ace, Johannes Steinhoff. I came to like him, too, very much, and I admired his courage. Only days from the end of the war he had crashed and been terribly burned. He had spent nearly two years in hospital, and came to England where McIndoe had worked miracles in restoring his tear ducts. 'Macky', as Johannes said I was to call him, had made the mistake of arguing with Goering, and had never been promoted beyond colonel. After the war, he became Chief of Staff of the reborn Luftwaffe, and attained the rank of general. It bore out what I had heard from other Luftwaffe pilots, that Goering was always quick to pour scorn on them for any lack of success.

It was a delight to meet up with Heinz again on a third seminar in November 1986, and we are both glad to put the wartime behind us. I told him about the urns of earth that I had sent to the German families, and as he is active in the German Fighter Pilot Association, he wanted to tell them about it. He appreciated it when I said that I hoped it would 'build bridges between our countries'.

I admire the Luftwaffe pilots who come to these seminars. They have a double disadvantage, for they have to use a difficult foreign language, and also were on the losing side. They always hold their own, however, and come through as men of strong character. On one occasion, when there were several Luftwaffe and RAF pilots participating in a discussion, a slide went up, and one of them said, 'Ah! That is Galland.' It was followed by another, and the tone of voice was very different, 'And that is *Mr* Mölders.' I had always looked upon Mölders as the Rommel of the Luftwaffe. He was much respected on both sides. I once had a long-drawn-out engagement with him. After much circling and manoeuvring we both ran out of ammunition, so we saluted each other and went our ways.

In June 1987, I was invited to attend the Gathering of 'Eagles', which was an assembly of pilots who were judged to have contributed to aviation in some special manner. Their ages ranged from a 92-year-old veteran of World War I, to astronauts of the space age. This too was an idea of David McFarland which has become an annual event, and it formed the conclusion of the university year. With unique talent he brings together 18 or 20 aviators, together with their spouses. Each is hosted by two young USAF majors, officer students who especially apply for this duty, and one of these was Major Trudy Clark. I have watched with great pleasure the promotion of these young officers, and Trudy has just made general. Quite the most glamorous and charming general I could ever hope to meet.

My personal host officer was Major Dave Stringer. Now a colonel, he and his wife Diane and their children have become close friends. Indeed, they tell me their son owes his second name to me. Their company has always been most enjoyable, and I have found it stimulating and rewarding to know such an intelligent and young-hearted family.

A programme of events and seminars is carried out over three or four days. All transport to get the participants to and from Montgomery is taken care of. Montgomery had banners out to say 'Welcome to the Eagles', and the traffic was always stopped for our coach. It was as good as a ticker-tape welcome. Various contributions help to make the event self-funding, and chief among these is a lithographed print of an artwork depicting an aircraft flown by each aviator attending, together with a small portrait of him at that time. There are several hundred of these, and we are all asked to sign each one. Each of us is given two as a gift, and the others are sold to contribute to the funds.

I was fortunate in that, the year I attended, the artist was a talented young American, Jay Ashurst. He has now become very well known as an aviation artist, but he still regularly paints the lithos for the annual gathering of Eagles. He and his family have become personal friends, as have many I have been fortunate to meet there, including the young officer hosts.

For Eagles themselves the highlight is that each has a 'This is Your Life' experience. Thus, when the musicians struck up 'Rule Britannia' a powerful spotlight was aimed at me as I stood up. Then, to the accompaniment of a running commentary by Dave Stringer, slide after slide appeared on a gigantic screen. The first showed my mother in her cloche hat beside the Avro 504, from whose cockpit a small boy looked out. Was this really happening, in front of several hundred US officers, wives and guests in the vast Montgomery Civic Centre?

Another friend from that occasion was Ken Walsh, who died not so long ago. He was awarded the Congressional Medal of Honor, America's top military decoration, for exceptional heroism in the Pacific War, in particular at the Battle of Midway, a strategically-placed island in the Pacific. Representing postwar aviation was one of the world's most famous pilots, USAF General Charles E. 'Chuck' Yeager, who on 14 October 1947 became the first human to fly faster than sound.

Another Medal of Honor winner I met was Leo Thorsness. He had a distinguished battle record in Vietnam, but was shot down only eight missions short of completing his combat tour. He endured six brutal years as a prisoner in some of the most notorious Viet Cong camps. His wife was unceasing in her efforts to obtain his release, and she was there with him. Both got a resounding cheer from the students at the final ceremony. Especially fascinating was Joe Engle, who flew the space shuttle *Columbia* manually back from the moon after all the computers had failed, making a perfect touchdown. He was modest about his achievements, and said, 'You are a pilot yourself, you know you just have to push all the right knobs!'

I must mention one other couple, the Australians Nicky and Dot Barr. Nicky and I instantly established a rapport, as he had been a leading member of Australia's 1939 rugby team. Their world tour was cancelled because of the outbreak of war, so Nicky enlisted immediately in the RAF, and requested a flying course. He was told there was little prospect of that but, because of his educational qualifications, he would probably be granted a commission. On enquiring 'What as?', he was informed that the RAF desperately needed paymasters.

Too late for Nicky, the team were told by their High Commissioner that they would lose their identity if they enlisted in Britain, so they had better return to Australia. Fortunately Nicky had friends in high places, and asked Lord Somers, who had been governor of Victoria, for help. He took him to see his friend, who was none other than Lord Trenchard. 'Boom' read the very brief file on his RAF career, which he dismissed with the two words, 'Shred it.' Nicky then joined the RAAF, and had a hectic war in North Africa and Italy. He was shot down three times, and wounded three times, and also badly burned, and was captured by the Italians. After being recaptured once, he escaped a second time, and got involved in clandestine operations behind enemy lines. For this he was awarded the Military Cross, most unusual for anyone in any air force in World War II. He added this to his OBE, DFC and Bar and many other 'gongs'.

The seminars continued, and I met up with two more Luftwaffe pilots. Hans Ekkehard Bob, known as 'Bob', told how he got too close to a B-17 during a raid over Germany, and crashed into it. He and the crew of the B-17 bailed out successfully, but then his troubles began. The German equivalent of the British Dad's Army turned up as they landed, and it took a long time to convince them he was not a German-speaking American spy who had bailed out with the rest of the B-17 crew.

Ulrich Steinhilper I still meet, as he comes over to Biggin Hill for the airshow. He was shot down early in the war, and was sent to Canada, where the PoW camp consisted of Luftwaffe and U-boat prisoners, all eager to escape. Ulrich escaped five times, although he was recaptured each time. After the war he became a typewriter salesman. In due course he saw how advantageous it would be to be able to transpose bits of text, and make alterations, without having to retype everything. He worked out an idea, and took it to his bosses at IBM. They thought it was too advanced and would never be commercially viable, but they thanked him and gave him 20 Deutschmarks for it! So the idea for word processors was born. Uli nevertheless stayed with IBM, and rose into the higher echelons.

On my first visit to Maxwell, after the seminar I was asked to stay with a couple called Floyd and Rosa McGowin, who had always been great supporters of the Air University. Their home is the epitome of the beautiful Southern homestead, and could have come straight out of *Gone with the Wind*. It is in a tranquil setting of towering pine trees. Floyd has his own little airstrip, and the most immaculate collection of private aircraft I have ever seen. One would think they never came out of the hangar, but he uses them all regularly. Since that first visit I have been back many times, and they have been most generous with their hospitality, not only personally but also in arranging functions to coincide with events at Maxwell.

In November 1990 David McFarland put the emphasis on the Battle of Britain for his gathering of Eagles, having four British pilots and four German. I was delighted to be invited yet again, and once more it was an unforgettable event. I met my first lady Eagle, who was to become yet another friend. Dora Strother was one of two WASPs (Women's Airforce Service Pilots) chosen in 1944 by Colonel Paul W. Tibbetts (who had flown *Enola Gay* to drop the first atomic bomb) to demonstrate the safety of the new B-29 Superfortress. She also became a proficient helicopter pilot, only the 27th woman to accomplish this. Another Vietnam Medal of Honor hero, who withstood seven and a half years of imprisonment and torture, including nearly four years in solitary confinement, was Admiral James Stockdale, USN. His wife had campaigned tirelessly for his release, and went on to help other wives in similar tragic circumstances. Together they wrote the best-selling book *In Love and War*. I was proud to meet them both.

I never thought that I would shake the hand of a man who had walked in space, and untethered at that. Such a man was Robert Stewart, who had walked in space with a 'James Bond' style of backpack and said, 'It was quite simple. You had one lot of puffers for one hand which made you go up and down, and another lot on the other side which puffed you sideways.' He said there is a sense of movement only when lined up with the space capsule. His one 'scary' moment was when he thought he would turn round and see what it looked like to look into infinity, and he could only take about ten seconds of it before he had to turn round to make quite sure the capsule was still there.

The 1990 gathering of four Luftwaffe pilots and four RAF pilots began at the National Air and Space Museum in Washington, DC. The NASM usually had only a single lecturer, but David and Air Vice-Marshal Ron Dick, our air attaché, persuaded them that it was a once-in-a-lifetime chance, in view of our ages. Ron presided as our question master. Donald Lopez, who had been Assistant Director of Aeronautics at NASM, was an Eagle in 1990 and so knew David, and so it was agreed.

Not only did all the seats go, but they also filled their planetarium, where the seminar was shown on a screen to a full audience plus many standing.

Our team was: Desmond Hughes, Defiant; John Cunningham, Blenheim; Brian Kingcome, Spitfire; and of course I had the Hurricane. The German team was: Dietrich Peltz, Junkers Ju 87; Hajo Herrmann, Junkers Ju 88; Wolfgang Schenck, Messerschmitt Bf 110; and Ulrich Steinhilper, Messerschmitt Bf 109. The discussion between the eight of us went well, and we were most impressed by the knowledgeable audience. Desmond, as he usually did, asked the audience if anyone had heard of Defiants, and was surprised at the number of hands that went up. He explained to the rest that it was a fighter with a crew of two, the pilot and a gunner who manned the machine-gun turret. He said that having passed out his training with top marks for his firing prowess, he was immediately posted to fly Defiants, the one fighter in which the pilot never fires a shot. Thus, his greatest skill was never used. This ensured a sympathetic chuckle from the audience.

John Cunningham, one of our most famous pilots both during and after the war, was nicknamed 'Cats' Eyes Cunningham' because of his success with night fighters. In reality the night fighter was guided by a navigator using radar, which was secret, so it was put about that he had remarkable night vision. He told the story of how he was asked to test the first 'seeing eye' bomb. The idea was that a Blenheim would be armed with the bomb, and then fly above the German raiders. The bomb would then be released, and would then 'seek' the nearest bomber, with deadly effect. Unfortunately, the first aircraft it saw was Johnny's. It locked on, and he had a very anxious time putting his Blenheim through every possible manoeuvre trying to shake off the relentless seeking mechanism. With an enormous sigh of relief he eventually succeeded, but it was definitely going to be 'back to the drawing board'.

We had a lively session of questions from the floor, after which we signed prints and books. We were amazed at the length of the queue. I looked up after about an hour and a half to greet the next in line, and saw a girl on elbow crutches. I asked her what had happened? She said nonchalantly, 'Oh, the wings came off my hang glider. Will you please sign this book for me?' I promptly signed, with admiration for her cool courage.

My prestige with my fellow signatories went up considerably when a glamorous friend of mine, Christine De Lisle, from New York, suddenly appeared in front of our tables. We embraced warmly and I was very touched that she had come all the way for the occasion. As she was in show business I was delighted to have her professional approval of the evening. We eventually cleared the queue shortly before midnight. The museum staff and guards were marvellous, and made no problem about the doors staying open so late. To crown it all, one of the United States Capitol Police gave me a police badge, a great memento of the occasion.

The following day we flew down to Randolph Air Force Base at San Antonio, Texas. To my delight, one of the officer hosts from my first visit to Maxwell, Keith Fennell, by this time a colonel, was to fly one of the two aircraft assigned to us. It was a happy reunion, and a memorable flight as we went low enough to see a lot of the countryside, and down along the Mississippi. How vast America is! We had a stop for lunch at Scott AFB, Illinois, where it was a delight to meet up with Keith's wife Linda again, and also General Willis and his wife, all of whom I had met previously at Maxwell.

Randolph, a famed prewar training field, gave us a marvellous welcome. It is a beautiful place. My outstanding memory of it is the memorial known as 'The Missing Man'. This depicts four aircraft in formation, with a gap for 'The Missing Man', haunting in its simplicity. The great moment for us, however, was when we were taken to see the Alamo. The only original part left has become a tiny chapel, which has niches in which are displayed banners of the countries of every defender of the Alamo during the Mexican wars. None of us had any idea there had been international defenders.

Desmond found a banner commemorating two Irishmen, and I found one for the single Welshman there. Somehow all four of us felt we could relate personally to those 'Few' who made a great individual sacrifice in the defence of that historic site.

CHAPTER TWENTY-ONE

GOLDEN ANNIVERSARIES

Fifty years on from the Battle of Britain, we all knew that 1990 was going to be a busy year for us, and a last big reunion. Apart from the great pleasure of the get-togethers with so many old friends, we were all determined to use the publicity the year afforded to full advantage in order to raise money for the RAF Benevolent Fund. We signed everything that was saleable, from certificates for plates, mugs and ashtrays, to prints, philatelic envelopes and books. It was amazing how much interest there was, and how keen the collectors were. The Battle of Britain was just beginning to creep into British school history lessons, and we all suddenly became aware that we had indeed passed into 'living history'. We had sometimes been called that in the past, and had laughed about it, but here it was now staring us in the face.

I am always impressed by the work and research youngsters put into their school projects. Their search for knowledge, their attention to detail and their desire to get it right, show great dedication and hard work. I have always found it a pleasurable and rewarding task to help any who want to come and see me, and bring along their tape recorders and notebooks. It has been gratifying to hear what good grades they have obtained in the end. Some first-hand accounts of the true history of those stirring times will thus live on when we are no longer around.

The functions in that year were many and varied. There was another memorable gathering at the Guildhall, graced by our beloved patron the Queen Mother, who celebrated her 90th birthday that year as well. I was nominated to be installed as a Freeman of the City of London, and I felt greatly honoured when I attended the short private ceremony the following year. The City of London has always been dear to my heart, and it has many traditions whose origins are shrouded in the mists of time. One privilege to which my Freedom entitles me is that I may drive a flock of sheep over London Bridge. I would dearly love to do this . . . Welsh sheep, of course!

Rolls-Royce gave us a wonderful day out at what was then their aero-engine factory at Leavesden, north of London. Some of us managed to get airborne in two-seat Spitfires, and each of us also received a specially commissioned framed silhouette painting of himself, by artist Michael Pierce. Similar silhouettes are a feature of the limited-edition fine-art book *So Few*, telling the stories of 25 survivors of the Battle of Britain. At the insistence of all 25, this great volume led to a sequel featuring 25 men of Bomber Command, *So Many*. Some copies of the limited-edition of *So Many* are still unsold. When they have found buyers the two books will have raised over three-quarters of a million pounds for the RAF Benevolent Fund, far more than any other product in the fund's history.

There was an evening of great nostalgia at the Savoy. This hotel has an atmosphere of its own, never more so than in those wartime days when Service men and women were made to feel particularly welcome. The dinner was superb, and we danced to the tunes of 50 years ago. As we reminisced, the years just seemed to roll back.

Then came the climax of all the events during those memorable few days in September. We were invited into the forecourt of Buckingham Palace, on one side of which grandstand seating had been put up for us. Her Majesty and Prince Philip were to come out and walk among us, chatting informally. After this there was to be our March Past outside the palace railings, from one gate to another, with Her Majesty taking the salute. As many of us as could manage that short 'March' were quite determined to do so!

It was a glorious day, and the Mall was already packed, people having come from far and wide to share in the occasion. How many had lost dear ones and homes 50 years before? There were many families bringing younger generations born since the war to join them on this most special of days.

A young RAF officer clicked smartly to attention, and the policeman smiled indulgently, as I showed my treasured pass entitling a Battle of Britain veteran to enter the forecourt. I stepped through the archway at the security check, which was so necessary, as this was the era of IRA bombs in London. Then on into the forecourt. As I looked around there were so many familiar faces. Our limbs were stiffer, and our faces showed the lines which the years had etched upon them. The shape of our silhouettes had certainly changed for most of us, but there was the same sparkle in the eyes and the same distant look to the far horizon, and above all I could hear the ever-cherished laughter.

My abiding memory of any reunion with my comrades of that time, and throughout the years since, is laughter. No matter what the hazards or problems of those days, and the different ones of today, there is always laughter when we get together.

What varied lives many of my friends have led. There is the

successful sheep farmer from Australia. My Free French friend Henri Lafont became Mr Paris Airshow. Norman Hancock is a successful architect. Of course, there were our Polish friends, some of whom have been very successful in business after staying on in this country, while others like the Czechs had managed to get here from behind what was still the 'Iron Curtain'. We had two tickets each, and so were accompanied by wives or relatives, and it was as much a reunion for them, and a very emotional one.

We had plenty of time to chat and take photographs before going to our allotted seats in the grandstand. The seats were arranged in blocks, and the Queen and Prince Philip walked up and down taking separate blocks. She looked charming in a summery green outfit, and the Duke, still tall, slim and upright, was in the full dress uniform of a marshal of the RAF. They talked to many of us. Most of us were wearing our prized Battle of Britain ties, which are dark blue with a very small gold British Isles and a gold Tudor Rose, a royal emblem that we were given permission to use. Seeing one veteran wearing a different tie, the Duke asked him, 'Where is your Battle of Britain tie?' The reply caused a chuckle from all who heard it: 'Rolled up all ready on my dressing table . . . in Australia!'

After they had passed down each line, those of us who had said they thought they could manage the March Past were asked to slip away and forgather ready for the big moment. We had the Central Band of the RAF, which had already been playing, and superbly executed movements by the current RAF drill team had been going on. At last we were all in position, and the brisk martial music ceased. The Queen stood on the saluting dais, a small lone figure, with the Chief of Defence Forces and the Duke slightly behind her. Everything seemed silent for a moment, and then suddenly a slow measured drum beat started. The wives and all those in the forecourt told us afterwards that the slow measured beat brought home to everyone that that was the briskest pace we could manage. For our part it was 100 per cent concentration, making sure we could manage a march even at that slow tempo. I had a blind man next to me, and a man with tin legs in front of me. My deaf side was towards the band and the crowd, but even so I could not miss the huge cheer of warmth and affection that suddenly swelled out of the crowd as we set off.

The waiting wives told us afterwards that all thought of decorum in the forecourt was forgotten, as we took our first steps in what is probably the shortest March Past in Service history! They all rushed to the inside of the palace railings and the gate by which we were to re-enter the forecourt, to await our return, hopefully without mishap.

I met the Chief of the Defence Staff later on, and he said he had found it a very moving moment himself. When it came to the salute as we approached the dais, out of the corner of his eye he saw the Duke of Edinburgh at the salute as well. It was an unforgettable moment for everyone concerned. I certainly breathed a sigh of relief that it had all gone so well.

We then settled down in our seats to watch a unique fly-past covering many years of aviation. It had taken a lot of rehearsal and split-second timing to work out the times for take-off for all the various types of aircraft with vastly different flying speeds, and from many airfields. They all converged on the Mall to form an accurately-spaced procession and fly over Buckingham Palace where all the royal family were gathered.

Special cheers were reserved for the single Lancaster bomber, and the two whose day it was, the Hurricane and the Spitfire. Then the grand finale: the jets of the current RAF fresh back from the Gulf War. But it was the deep throb of the Merlin engines of what we will always consider 'our' aircraft that lifted the heart, certainly mine. All of us many a time had felt we owed our lives to their tough reliability, which had often got us home against all odds. This is what we had tried to express to our hosts at Rolls-Royce on the memorable day out they gave us. Deaf many of us may be these days, but we can always hear a Merlin engine, if only in our memory. Certainly their sound brought a lump to more than one throat that day at the Palace.

Just as we all thought the fly-past immaculately completed, a murmur accompanied by a slightly uncertain ripple of laughter went through our grandstand. Looking up once more, we saw four Canada geese from St James's Park, which runs alongside the Mall next to the Palace, flying in perfect formation in a tight circuit round our seats. Having completed their manoeuvre, they turned and flew off. This left us all very quiet for a few moments, and with an uncanny sensation of the spirits of the pilots of the past.

The never-to-be-forgotten year ended with a banquet in the Battle of Britain Hall at the RAF Museum, Hendon. We were the guests of the RAF Benevolent Fund, in appreciation of the famous fund-raising book *So Few* already mentioned. The occasion was generously sponsored by Pol Roger and Sichel of champagne renown. To our immense satisfaction we were able to see we had achieved our target of collecting £20 million in 1990 for the Benevolent Fund.

We were the first of the 50th anniversaries that were to follow over the next five years. There were, of course, many splendid occasions, and the most heart-warming of all was the Burma campaign. Here at last the 'Forgotten Army' in 1995 was properly remembered, and the survivors honoured. The Gurkhas drew specially warm cheers from the crowds whenever they appeared. I think the British are very sad to see the famous Gurkha regiments being disbanded, and to realise what deprivation this is going to mean for so many families in Nepal. It is the end of a 150-year era of army history.

The final night of the VJ celebrations was a reception at the Tower of London. It was a perfect summer evening, and the refreshments were served on the surrounding lawns. The royal yacht *Britannia* was moored nearby, and the Queen arrived by royal barge, with Tower Bridge providing a perfect backdrop. I felt very humble as I walked round the lawns, for it was an evening shared with the truly great and heroic. I counted seven VCs, most of whom were Gurkhas, and three George Crosses.

One fellow-guest I got talking to was a highly-decorated artilleryman who had seen much bitter fighting, including that for the monastery on Monte Cassino, Italy. He said how much his wife was enjoying it. They had watched the elegant little gold chairs being brought out, and wondered who they were for. His wife said, 'I think they are for us.' He reckoned they could not be, but was amazed when she was proved right. 'I never thought they would be providing chairs like that for people like us', he said. He had only been willing to die for his country! Despite an impressive fireworks display which followed, I couldn't help thinking that the money which went up in smoke could have provided months of luxury for most of the Gurkha families in Nepal.

The evening finally came to an end, and we left along a passage through crowds who had waited after the fireworks to watch the guests leave. As we walked through them a woman's voice called out 'Thank you for fighting for us', and it was taken up by others in the crowd. Somehow, it made all those long wartime years seem worthwhile.

List of Aircraft Flown

Airspeed Oxford
Avro Anson, Lincoln, Tutor
Beechcraft 18 Expeditor
Blackburn B.2, B.2 Major, Shark
Boulton Paul Defiant
Bristol Beaufighter I, II, VI, X, Blenheim I, Blenheim IV, Blenheim V
British Aircraft Swallow
Chrislea Ace
Consolidated Liberator III, IV, V
De Havilland Chipmunk, Devon, Dragon Rapide, Moth, Moth Minor, Puss Moth, Mosquito VI, XIX, Vampire FB.5
Douglas Dakota
English Electric Canberra B.2, B.6
Fairchild Argus
Fairey Barracuda III, Battle, Fulmar, Junior, Swordfish
Fiat G.50
General Aircraft Cygnet, Monospar
Gloster Gladiator, Meteor III, F.4, T.7, F.8, NF.10, NF.12
Hawker Audax, Demon, Fury, Hart, Hind, Hurricane I, IA, IIB, IIC, IID
Lockheed 12
Martin Baltimore
Miles Gemini, Magister, Master I, II, III, Mentor, Messenger
North American Harvard, Mustang
Percival Pembroke, Proctor
Republic Thunderbolt
Stinson L-5 Sentinel, Reliant
Supermarine Spitfire I, II, VA, VB, VC, VI, VIII, IX, XI, XIV, XVI, F.21, Walrus
Vickers-Armstrongs Valetta, Valiant (co-pilot) Varsity, Wellington II, X
Vought Corsair
Westland Lysander I, II, Whirlwind

Service Career Details

Dennis David was born in London on 25th July, 1918. He left school at the age of 14 to work as an apprentice in a family friend's business in the City of London. He joined the RAFVR in 1937 and obtained a short service commission in February 1938. He completed training as a fighter pilot at Royal Air Force Station Sealand near Chester. He was then posted to Royal Navy Air School at Ford, Sussex to help with flying tasks, while waiting for a vacancy in a fighter squadron in the RAF. This came through and he joined 87 Squadron in early 1939.

He accompanied this unit to France shortly after the outbreak of war in September, as part of the Air Component of the British Expeditionary Force. During the heavy fighting of May 1940 he was credited with at least 11 victories over France according to the citations for his DFC and Bar, awarded on 31 May and 4 June respectively. He continued to see action with the unit over the South-West of England during August and September, whilst on the 16th of the latter month he was posted to 213 Squadron, as a flight commander, claiming one further victory here. On 23 November he was posted to 152 Squadron to fly Spitfires, but on 24 March 1941 was rested, joining 55 OTU as a Flt Lt instructor. He moved to 59 OTU on 19 June as Assistant CFI. He returned to 55 OTU on 23 November 1941 to become Acting Wg Cdr, being promoted Sqn Ldr in February 1942, and moving with the OTU to Annan in April. He was awarded an AFC on 1 January 1943. In February he was sent out to the Middle East, initially as SASO, 209 Group, but on 19 July he took command of 89 Squadron as a Wg Cdr, leading this unit to Ceylon in October. In March 1944 he became Senior Controller at Trincomalee, and then in May, base commander at Minneriya, followed by Kankesanturai in August. He was promoted Grp Capt during the year and became Air Adviser to the Commander of 15th India Corps in the Arakan until January 1945, when he became SASO, 224 Group.With the end of the war, he became SASO, Air HQ, Dutch East Indies in Batavia, during Allied operations against Javanese insurgents. He returned to the UK in April 1946, remaining in the RAF but reverting to his substantive rank of Sqn Ldr. Initially he served with HQ, Reserve Command, from July 1946-September 1948, then being sent out to Libya as station commander, RAF El Adem, from September-November 1949. From then until March 1951 he was i/c Flying, 324 Wing, in the Mediterranean area, then returning to the UK to HQ, 18 Group, Coastal Command, until April 1953. Promoted Wg Cdr, he then attended RAF Flying College, Manby. After graduation he had a tour at the Air Ministry London 1954 to 1956. During this time he became Honorary Aide to Viscount Trenchard, until his death. David's next posting was as Air Attache Budapest. From September 1958 to May 1961 he commanded RAF Tangmere, his acting rank of Group Captain being formalised during 1960 when he was also made a CBE. From Tangmere he went as Chief of Air Plans to Allied Forces Southern Europe, a NATO post in Naples. David's last posting before retiring on May 1967 was at the Air Ministry in the Air Secretary's Department. He then became chairman of a board of directors in an engineering firm. He participated in seminars in America with Luftwaffe Aces on the Battle of Britain at the Air Command and Staff College at Maxwell, Montgomery and also one at the Smithsonian. Since then he has remained involved in work for a number of service charities.

Claims:

(Taken from *Aces High* by Christopher Shores)

WITH 87 SQUADRON

1939

2 Nov		He 111 Damaged	Hurricane I	L1777	Poperinghe
		(This was an aircraft of 2(F)/122 which suffered 30% damage; David's own Hurricane was damaged by return fire and he was obliged to force-land)			

1940

10 May		He 111	Hurricane I	L1630	Senon & Thionville
		(This was an a He 111H of II/KG 53, one of four attacked by four Hurricanes; two of the Heinkels crash-landed due to damage)			
		Do 17	(six Do 17s of III/KG 2 were attacked by David and Sgt G.L.Nowell, who claimed two or three between them. One crash-landed near Trier and a second was damaged, but reached its airfield)		
	1/2	Do 17			
11 May		Ju 87	Hurricane I	L1630	
		(Six claims made against Stab and I/StG 2, which suffered six losses, three crashed and three crash-landed)			
		Do 17 (This was one of three Do 17Ms of StabSt/StG 2, flying with the Ju 87s, all of which were lost)			
12 May	1/2	He 111	Hurricane I	L1870	
14 May	1/2	He 111	Hurricane I	L1630	N.E.Brussels
		He 111 (He 111Ps of I and III/KG 27, initially attacked by 85 Squadron; six and one probable claimed – three actually shot down and one damaged)			
16 May	1/2	Bf 109E	Hurricane I	L1630	
	2	Bf 109Es Unconfirmed			
18 May	2	Bf 109Es Damaged	„	„	
19 May	1/3	He 111	„	„	
		Bf 110	„	„	
		Bf 110 Unconfirmed	„	„	
		Bf 109E Unconfirmed	„	„	

11 Aug		Ju 88	,,	P3404	10m SW Portland Bill
		Bf 109E	,,	,,	10m SE Portland Bill
15 Aug		Ju 87	,,	V7207	1m E Portland Bill
		Bf 110 Probable	,,	,,	
25 Aug		Ju 88	,,	P3404	1m W Portland Harbour
		Bf 109E	,,	,,	3m NW Portland
4 Sep	2	e/a Damaged at night	,,		
15 Sep		He 111	,,	,,	3-5m SW Bolt Head

WITH 213 SQUADRON

19 Oct		Ju 88	,,	'J'	4m N Manston

TOTAL: 13 and 5 shared confirmed destroyed, 4 unconfirmed destroyed, 1 probable, 5 damaged.

Bibliography

This Bibliography will, it is hoped, assist readers in following up some of the topics, times, places and people which occur in the book.

Where there is only a line but no title in italics, then no further reference was found in a County Library search, and the reader might like to pursue the matter further in other ways. If the title is known, but no publisher can be found, there is a double ** in the left margin, and a ? in the publisher position (before date; after author).

Aces High Vols 1 & 2 – Christopher Shores – Grub Street – 1994 and 1999

Aces High – S Benjamin Fisz – Director Jack Gold – available on video

Aerospace Dictionary, Jane's, editor Bill Gunston – Jane's (around 1990, new edition expected in 2000)

Aircraft Cutaways, Classic World War II – Bill Gunston – Osprey – 1995

Aircraft of World War II – Bill Gunston – Chancellor Press – 1997

Aircraft of the National Air and Space Museum, Famous – Walter Boyne – Smithsonian Institution – 1984

Airports Then and Now, Britain's – Leo Marriott – Ian Allan – 1993

Allied Fighters of World War II, New Illustrated Guide – B. Gunston – Salamander – 1992

Anytime, Anyplace, 50 years of the USAF – Phil Chinnery – Airlife – 1994

A Study in Infamy – The Operations of the Hungarian Secret Police (AVH– G Mikes – Deutsch – 1959

Battle of Britain, The – S Benjamin Fisz – film, 1969 – also available on video

Battle of Britain, The – Basil Collier – Fontana/Collins (paperback)

Battle of Britain, The Jubilee History – Richard Hough and Denis Richards – Hodder & Stoughton – 1990

Beaufighter – Chaz Bowyer – W. Kimber – 1987

Beaufighter, Bristol – Victor Bingham – Airlife – 1994

Bedouin, The Nomadic Tribes of the Desert – M Alotaibi – Wayland – 1986 – for children

Bedouin – (This Changing World Series) – S Kay – Crane – 1978

Blenheim, Bristol – Chaz Bowyer – Ian Allan – 1984

Born Free – the story of Elsa the Lioness – Joy and George Adamson – Collins – 1960

Budapest, With Raoul Wallenberg in, Memories of the War Years in Hungary – Raoul Wallenberg – Holocaust – 1981

Budapest, a Cultural Guide – Michael Jacobs – Oxford University Press – 1998

Budapest – Bob Dent – Blue Guides – 1996
Burma 1944, The Chindit War: the Campaign in – S Bidwell – Hodder Headline – 1979
Burma, the Longest War 1941-1945 – L Allen – Dent – 1984
***Camels – Ships of the Desert* – J. F. Wates – ? – 1975
The Aircraft Cockpit: from Stick-and-String to Fly-by-Wire – L.F.E. Coombs – Patrick Stephens – 1990
Concentration Camp Survivors, Journey back from Hell: Conversations with – Anton Gill – Grafton – 1989
Crime and Compromise: Janos Kadar and the politburo . . . – William Shawcross – Weidenfeld – 1974
John "Cat's Eyes" Cunningham, the Aviation Legend – John Golley – Airlife – 1999
Dowding and the Battle of Britain – R Wright – Macdonald – 1969
Entertainment in the Second World War, a Light-hearted look at – Bill Pertwee – Hodder & Stoughton – 1992
Eyewitness in Hungary, the Soviet Invasion of 1956 – Bill Lomax – Spokesman – 1981
Fighter Airfields in World War 2, RAF – John Falconer – Ian Allan – 1993
Fight for the Sky, the Story of the Spitfire and the Hurricane – Douglas Bader – Sidgwick (Sidgwick & Jackson) – 1973
***Fighters of the Fifties* – Bill Gunston – ? – 1981
Fighter Test Pilot – from Hurricane to Tornado – R Beamont – P Stephens – 1973 & 1986
Fighter, the True Story of the Battle of Britain – Len Deighton – Michael Joseph – 1990
Forgotten Army, The – Far East and Burma campaigns
***The Forgotten Ones of South East Asia Command and Force 136* (paperback) – Arthur H. Stockwell – ? – 1989
Frommer's Budapest and the Best of Hungary – Joseph Lieber – Macmillan – 1996
Glubb Pasha, a Biography – J Lunt – Harvill Press – 1984
Greatest Generation, The – Tom Brokaw – Random House – 1998
Ground Crew since . . . , Through the Hangar Doors – RAF – F. J. Adkin – Airlife – 1986
The Gurkhas: the Inside Story of the World's Most Feared Soldiers – John Parker – Headline – 1999
In Gurkha Company: the British Army Gurkhas 1948 to the Present – J. P. Cross – Arms & Armour – 1986
Valour: a History of the Gurkhas – E. D. Smith – Spellmount – 1997
Gurkhas – Sandro Tocci – Book Club Associates by arrangement with Hamish Hamilton – 1985
Habsburg Monarchy 1809-1918, A History of the Austro-Hungarian

Empire – A.J.P. Taylor – Pelican – 1981
Hawker Aircraft Ltd – Derek James – comp. by D. N. James – Chalford – 1996
Hawker Hurricane – Francis K Mason – Aston – 1990
Hungarian Revolution – George Mikes – Deutsch – 1957
Hungary 1867-1994, History of Modern – Jorg K. Hoensch – Longman – 1996
Hurricane at War – Chaz Bowyer – Ian Allan – 1974
Hurricane Combat, the Nine Lives of a Fighter Pilot – K W MacKenzie – W Kimber – 1987
Hurricane Squadron, No 87 at War 1939–1941 – Perry Adams – Air Research – 1988
Hurricanes over Burma – M. C. Cotton – Grub Street – 1995
***In Love and War* – joint book by Admiral James Stockdale and his wife on his time as POW – ? – Date ?
King Abdullah, the Zionists and Palestine 1921-1951, The Politics of Partition: – Avi Shlaim – Oxford University Press – 1990
Little Ships of Dunkirk 1940-1990 – Christian Brann – Collectors' Books – 1989 (** see also a book by Paul Gallico)
Maginot Line, The Great Wall of France: the Triumph of the – Vivian Rowe – Putnam – 1959
Pasha, General Glubb – Commander of the Arab Legion – Trevor Royle – Little, Brown and Company – 1992 – (paperback edition 1993 by Abacus)
** *Pilots of Fighter Command* – portraits by Cuthbert Orde
POW, the Uncivil Face of War – R. Garrett – David and Charles – 1981
Roman North Africa – E. L. Manton – Seaby – 1988
Sealion (Seelöwe) The Invasion of England 1940: the Planning of Operation – Peter Schenk – Conway Maritime Press – 1990
Seven Days of Freedom – Noel Barber – Macmillan – 1974
So Few – commemorating 25 surviving Battle of Britain fighter pilots – sponsored by RAF Benevolent Fund – popular edition published by W. H. Smith Exclusive Books
So Many – commemorating 25 surviving Bomber Command pilots – sponsored by RAF Benevolent Fund – popular edition published by W H Smith Exclusive Books
Trenchard, Man of Vision – Andrew Boyle – Collins – 1962
Twelve Days in May – Brian Cull *et al* – Grub Street – 1995
Vampire – The Complete History, de Havilland – David Watkins – Sutton – 1996
V-Bombers: Vulcan Victor and Valiant: Britain's Airborne Nuclear Deterrent – Tim Laming – Patrick Stephens – 1997
** *Vizsla, The Complete Hungarian* – G. Gottlieb – ? – 1992 (Nimrod did a 1985 edition)

Index

Abdullah, HM King 93
Aces High 185 et seq
Adenauer, K 173
Air combat 1
Akyab 65
Alex (dog) 57, 63, 72, 73
Andropov, Yu 114, 163
Annan 51
Arens, H 77
AVH 118, 127, 153 et seq

Bader, D 91, 188
Badminton 176
Bandidt, A F 53
Bandon, Lord 63, 100
Barr, N 194
Battle of Britain 38 et seq
  (film) 184
Betya (dog) 122, 145, 161, 168, 169, 173, 179, 188
Biggin Hill 116
Black Buffaloes 75
Bobby (dog) 84
Borêt, J 38, 45
Bowman, G 52
Browning, Gen F A M 68
Budapest 119 et seq
Burma 63 et seq

Camels 88, 90
Castel Benito 55
Chamberlain, N 17
Christison, Gen P 63, 97, 99
'Chuck' (Gurkha) 69
Church Fenton 30
Churchill, Sir W 39, 43
Cobham, Sir A 15

Cock, J 41
Collins, W 104
Colmore, C 20
Cope, K 115, 116, 140
Cornwall Aviation Co 11
Coward, N 62
Crosby on Eden 48

David, W Dennis, joins RAF 13,Qualifies as pilot 15, Investiture 36, Air Liaison Officer 63, SASO 74, Reserve Command 82, El Adem 86, Deversoir 92, Northern Coastal Group 97, MoD 100, Air Attaché 107, Convoy to Vienna 136, Order of Vitez 166, Tangmere 167, Naples 174, Retires 180, Tinnitus 180, Civilian jobs 182, Films 183, Maxwell AFB 191, Freeman of City 199
David, W Dennis, RAF Units: 5 E&RFTS 11; 5 FTS 13; 87 Sqn 15, 30; 213 Sqn 45; 152 Sqn 46; 55 OTU 48, 51; 59 OTU 48; 89 Sqn 54; Deversoir Wing 92
David, Mrs R 3
Davies, R 46
Debden 15
Deere, A C 31
de Gaulle, Gen C 48
Desert lily 56
Desert sores 59
Deversoir 92
Dewar, J 28, 36, 45
Dickson, Lord 102
Dowding, Lord 35, 184
Drobinski, B H 185
Dunkerque 30

Edwards, H I 74
El Adem 87
Exeter 38

Farouk, HM King 93
Fisz, S B 183
Flash Harry (dog) 187
Flying instruction 12
Ford 15
Fry, Sir L 110, 164

Galland, A 34, 192
George VI, HM King 20
Gero, E 125
Gibbon, F/Lt 12
Gielgud, Sir John 188
Gleave, T P 183, 191
Glubb Pasha 94
Göering 35, 43
Golden Crest (horse) 85
Gomulka, W 160
Gremlins 52
Griffith, D W 82

Hanworth 11
Hawker Aircraft 16
Herbert, A P 6
Hough, R 54
Howard, Trevor 184, 188
Hubarzevsky, Fr 167, 172
Hungary 109 et seq
  Revolution 187

Intelligence operations 122
Java 75
Jenny (horse) 84
Jeff, V 20
Jones, Lord E 189
Jordan 93

Kadar, J 133, 149
Kantor, MacK 177
Kennedy, President 177
Kent, J 184
Khrushchev, N 134, 151, 159
Kinloss 99
Kirkbride, Sir A 94
Ksapenko, Col 112

Lafont, H 49
Lange, Dr H 191, 192
Lille 2, 19
Locker–Lampson, O 6

Lovey's 9
Luftwaffe pilots 25
Lydford, Sir R 186, 188

MacLean, A 76, 97
MacRobert, Lady 99
Malan, A G 51
Malaya 71
Maleter, Gen P 131, 134, 143, 160
Manby 100
McFarland, D 191
McGhie, F 55, 61
McGowin, F and R 195
Menuhin, Y 162
Merville 19
Mindszenty, Cardinal 162
Minneriya 61
Mould, N 85
Mountbatten, Lord 62
  Lady 64
Mowat, G 32
Mumford, D 44
Mutiny (RAF) 80

Nador, Col F 123
Nagy, I 133, 140, 160
Naples 174
Norfolk, Duke of 168, 169, 170

Old–Meadow, R 12
Olivier, Lord 184
Orde, C 47

Paris 49
Park, Sir K 36
Pecket, F 33
Perry, F 8

Elizabeth II, HM Queen 169, 201, 203
Elizabeth, HM the Queen Mother 21, 170, 199

RAFVR 11, 13
Rakosi, M 115

Rangoon 70
Refugees 26
Richmond, Duke of 168
Duchess of 173
Rothenstein, Sir W 47

Sabre 176
Scott, S 169
Sealand 14
Sherras, F 38
Shoreham Aircraft Museum 32
Singapore 72, 79
Smith, I 56
Squash 9
Steinhoff, J 192
Storrer, J A S 53
Sukarno, A 77
Suleiman, Sheik 87
Surbiton County School 7
Szabo, Mrs 119, 145 et seq

Tangmere 45, 167
Freedom of Chichester 171

Tennis 8
Thatcher, D 164
Tigers 73
Tongwynlais 3
Toul 22
'Touring' 122
Trenchard, Lord 102
Lady 162

United States Legion in Hungary 163
Visits to 192 et seq
Uxbridge 13

V–bombers 100
Vavuniya 58

Warmwell 46
Waters, E and D 79

Aircraft mentioned in text

Avro 504 11
Avro Anson 87
Blackburn B.2 11
Shark 15
Bristol Beaufighter 39, 56
Blenheim 18, 22
Consolidated Liberator 63
de Havilland Mosquito 77
Vampire 92, 95
Dornier Do 17 1, 23
Douglas Dakota 68, 76, 91
Fairey Barracuda 61
Battle 15, 18, 22
Gloster Meteor 92
Grumman C-1A Trader 175
Handley Page H.P.42 28
Hawker biplanes 14
Hurricane 15 et seq
door from L1630 32
Heinkel He 111 1, 24
Junkers Ju 87 1, 24
Ju 88 46
Kawanishi H6K ''Mavis' 60
Martin Baltimore 55
Messerschmitt Bf 109 2
Percival Proctor 91
Republic Thunderbolt 77
Stinson L-5 Sentinel 64, 65
Supermarine Spitfire 16, 46
Walrus 15
Westland Lysander 23